Talking Painting

Talking Painting: Writings on Art and Artists, 1977–2025

Ian McKeever

Royal Academy of Arts

Royal Academy Publications
Florence Dassonville,
Production and Distribution Co-ordinator
Carola Krueger,
Production and Distribution Manager
Peter Sawbridge,
Head of Publishing and Editorial Director

Copy-editing and proofreading: Linda Schofield
Design: Patrick Morrissey/Unlimited

Colour origination and printing:
Gomer Press, Wales
Printed on 100 gsm Arena Natural Rough

Royal Academy of Arts
Burlington House
Piccadilly
London W1J 0BD
www.royalacademy.org.uk

EU Authorised Representative
EAS Europe, Mustamäe tee 50,
10621 Tallinn, Estonia
gpsr.requests@easproject.com

British Library Cataloguing-in-Publication Data
A catalogue record for this book is available from the British Library

ISBN 978-1-915815-23-1

Distributed outside the United States and Canada by ACC Art Books Ltd, Riverside House, Dock Lane, Melton, Woodbridge IP12 1PE

Distributed in the United States and Canada by ACC Art Books, 6 West 18th Street, Suite 4B, New York NY 10011

Contents

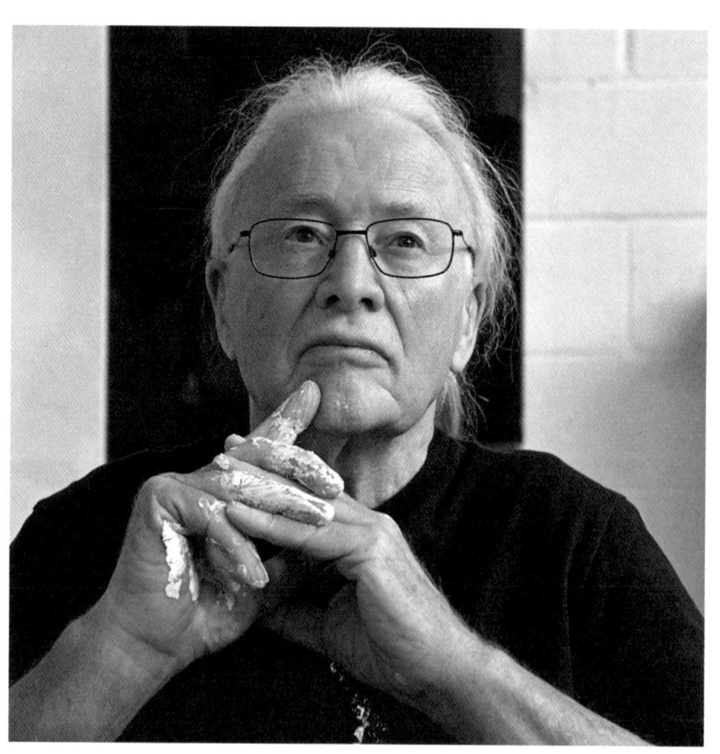

Early Days
(1977)

London sometime in the mid-1970s. I am in my late twenties. I have somehow managed to inveigle my way into the offices of *Studio International*, the then pre-eminent British art magazine. The American art critic Clement Greenberg, godfather to the Abstract Expressionist painters, is giving a talk.[1] Greenberg, his authority worn with style, is imposing; he is to be taken seriously. At one point in his presentation, which moves between Abstract Expressionism and Primitivism, he solemnly declares something to the effect: 'Mark Rothko painted three great paintings, Barnett Newman painted two and Willem de Kooning one.' I am perplexed, which ones? If anyone should know, Greenberg should, after all, he is 'the man'. Frustratingly, of course he does not say. Leaving as soon as the lecture is over, I go back to the studio to thumb through catalogues, hoping to identify the three, the two, the one. Needless to say, I did not and never could. Only later did I come to understand Greenberg's statement as perhaps a reference to the seminal shifts in an artist's work that could conceivably be said to be held within – even identified by – specific paintings, the three, the two and the one.

During the mid-1970s, the formative years of my own work, the art scene in Britain was on a cusp. On the one hand, the late throes of abstract painting and the influence of the American Abstract Expressionists were on the wane, having lapsed into a kind of gestural formalism, while on the other, the relatively new but by now over-arching influence of Conceptualism had moved increasingly to the fore. These two approaches to art could not have been more distinct, as different as chalk and cheese. The painters were wet and messy, emoting; the Conceptualists were bone dry and cerebral. Each camp carried its ethos as a badge of honour: one had to be either wet or dry, gut or brain, no half measures. I found myself drawn to aspects of both, yet fitting comfortably into neither, hovering somewhere between. Although I worked within the messy processes of mark-making, of painting, photography held an equal interest for me.

Its cool, detached mechanism, its more clinical way of bringing images into the world, had a rigour that the painting of that time seemed to lack. The works I made then could broadly be said to be a dialectic between these disparate modes of making, and hence understanding, art. I banged them up against each other. Yet, for me, it was always somehow about the *nature* of painting.

Field and Flow, the Drawing and the Photograph
(1979)

Drawing is a noisy process. The noises of mark-making somehow resonate back through a drawing. The marks hold their noise. It is a kind of residue that operates between action and representation, a debris that edges in between the marks and gaps revealed, echoing the frictions and fictions of things drawn across a surface, in pursuit of an object. Noise is information lost in the process of translation: a residue that will not change state and cannot be reorganised. In the case of drawing, residue occurs as the process moves through action, towards mark and representation. The order inherent in the drawing always edges towards chaos.

Photography does not have this residue. There is always a real sense of silence. Perhaps this is why I find photographs so hard to look at: they are so overtly visual. The quiet click of the shutter and the subsequent processes hardly amount to noise; they are a tightly formulated set of procedures with little room for extraneous activity. Nothing is casual, nothing is improvised. Even on the level of representation, the information provided is densely packed with few pauses in it. There is no room for hearsay, no gossip; everything is in its place. What is there is really represented, and nothing is extra.

Drawing is rooted not in what is perceived, but in the act of mark-making, which patterns, arrests and fixes. What is registered is primarily activity: the marks and traces that constitute this activity are a series of stops and starts, of interacting gestures, punctuated by gaps – which all precede any notion of objective representation. Only after this activity has been exposed through doing may we ask what else the marks might go on to represent. Photography does not have this foundation, for what it initially presents is a world, like Paul Cézanne's 'without gaps',[1] a surface textured with a basic grain, and modulated within a tonal framework. The parts all serve the same function, that is, to be receptive to whatever light falls on them. This is a democratic procedure in which each part has the potential to receive more or less light, and in which a change to one part is a change to the whole.

In this sense, the first ground of the photograph, the film, is a sophisticated surface already primed with reference. The basic difference between this loaded ground of the film and the blank ground of a drawing's support distinguishes the two processes: one is reductive, the other primarily accumulative. To begin with, the photograph is a decision to leave something out; the drawing is a decision to put something in. The photograph is potentially as complete as it will ever be the moment it is taken, and subsequent developing and printing processes are mere commentaries on that initial action. Light patterns the film (negative) and this in turn patterns the paper, effecting a transfer from negative to positive, which is as direct a translation as any used in a conventional printing process. The photograph is at its most random when it is first taken; subsequent processes order it, each tightening up on the preceding one. Drawing's method is continually self-evolving but with a potential to discontinue, since it emerges from an infinity of possible marks. Each mark is unique and can influence or disregard any preceding one, thereby determining its own contribution. Thus, the drawing arrives at its own destiny.

There is a sense of authenticity within a photograph because it locates the photographer as well as its subject. The camera's perspective pinpoints the photographer's position even as it describes the scene. Indeed, the one locates the other. To change perspective is to change the location of the photographer. A broader perspective, a multi-view, can only come out of changing frames of reference, that is, shifting locations. Place is fixed in time and time is held in place. Occasion becomes a very tight specific, and thus highly authentic. This verification of time and space, this ability to specify, makes the photograph a powerful means of documentation. A photograph contains extensive cross-references and clues that indicate its authenticity. Conversely, a drawing cannot document an occasion. It can comment on it, reveal a sense of it, but its inability to verify time in place and place in time prevents the emergence of anything even resembling a fact. The closest a drawing can get to locating the fact of place is in a map, which, through scale, conveys proportions and relationships outside time. Beyond this restricted use, drawing is always an approximation, always in a state of probability, for speculation and improvisation forever get in the way. Sense of place comes only from location of place. The tendency towards a multiperspective constantly relocates the drawing in the same way that time is distorted through anticipation and remembrance. The drawing cannot reproduce anything accurately (least of all itself).

Drawing and photography are like landscape in that they are able to expose and obscure, reveal and conceal. They can erode and produce an image, or reveal abstractions, or reduce further to expose new ground, new relationships. 'It rains, it snows, it paints', as Daniel Buren has remarked.[2] It draws and takes photographs too. These activities also pattern, arrest and fix, like rain into puddles of water or falling snow into drifts. Photography and drawing are like the agents of land erosion, breaking down and rebuilding surfaces. From drops of rain (individual moments of chaos), rainfall collects itself into an ordered whole, transforming surfaces and establishing a new grain that mirrors the overall oneness of falling rain. This is a precarious co-existence of order and chaos, in which singular drops splashing down onto a surface build up to flowing water that washes away sheets of soil and excavates gullies and grooves.

It has been estimated that the impact of a violent storm can blast into the air more than a hundred tons of soil per acre. Such displacement is never seen, but it can be sensed, and surface changes record it. Here in the rain prints, in the saturated soil, in the mudflow, are held the clues that graphically reflect the actions of past events. And through these, the grains and lines, the textures and tones, there emerges a patterning of representation. These patterns describe the profiles and horizons of evidence and the limits of actions. Substance grows out of the fields and aggregates that patterns describe, and out of the distance between action and consequence. David Smith alluded to the fact that the earth's surface depth does not seem important, since depth is visually inaccessible. What is important is pattern, the traces of interactions, the patterns of nature in relation to those of man.[3] They are always there, always discernible on the surface of the things that they help to constitute and describe, defining the areas of activity, the fields of drawing and projection. In colluvial deposits, the accumulations of talus, the scarring and sealing of etched surfaces, a landscape is codified: so, likewise, are drawings and photographs, in their marks, smudges, tones, grains and gaps.

Robert Smithson referred to pointless vanishing points, the far and always so elusive edge of the landscape.[4] As you move towards it, it recedes to reveal a new horizon. Never to be stood upon or finally located, it is continually relocated and redefined. To zoom in closer, in an attempt to find it, is only to change the problem. As fields disappear, furrows appear; as furrows are walked into, clods of earth are isolated. Moving in still closer, evidence of frost-shattering may show itself, or signs are revealed of sediment relocation from rain washing the soil from the surface. From one order to another chaos. The landscape moves continually from horizon to grain, from where it might end to what it might be. A transition, restless, and at times reckless. A ground that is inconsistent, that at any moment may shift its inclination, may swerve and tilt, bank and bend, in order to prevent the concrete, the irrefutable. Any kind of foothold is on shifting soil, whose gradient may have to be climbed over or slid down. In such uncertain terrain crevices may in turn expand into crevasses, or contract into hairline seams almost too fine to be seen. These seams may turn out to be flow lines, directional indicators of a more fluid state, describing the emergence of a new grain, as yet another change takes place.

Here is the constant conflict, Piet Mondrian's ideal of horizontal versus vertical, of unification versus isolation.[5] By far the largest proportion of the earth's land surface is on a slope of less than five degrees. Water, wind, temperature change and organic growth, activated by gravity, ceaselessly flatten the land. Marcel Duchamp sensed that our centre of gravity is somewhere in the region of the stomach, but to me it seems to be everywhere.[6] Permeating the whole body, it is in everything, eroding and redistributing matter in search of an ideal state, a state encouraged by the sedimentation of the earth. In this flow of things there is no cessation, no inertia, just endless movement, displacing, distributing and locating, yet again to displace. This sense of movement, this contradictory co-existence, this continuity and discontinuity, forever uniting and dividing, cementing and fracturing, rejects definition. Attempts to search for either sublime or irrefutable structures, for either metaphysical or possible systems – like the crazy perfections of Jorge Luis Borges's cartographers in *On Exactitude in Science*,[7] where all is mapped, and in the end, all is map – lead nowhere.

Published in *Field Series*, exh. cat., Nigel Greenwood Gallery, London, 1979.

Night Flak
(1981)

I am in Liverpool on a one-year Arts Council residency in collaboration with the Walker Art Gallery. My studio is on the top floor of a disused police station. Off to one side there is a roof terrace from which I can see across the city. At the time of the Toxteth riots the night sky is orange with flames and smoke. Over the winter months Liverpool is a tough place to be.

Having arrived here halfway through one body of work, now finished, I am about to start another. The previous groups of works such as *The Waterfalls* and the *Island Series* used a large photograph as a foundation to then paint onto it. Now I want to confront a traditional blank canvas. To paint from scratch, but where to begin? The pristine surface of a blank canvas has always somehow held me in awe, too beautiful in itself to allow me to feel I could make an intervention. It is as if within it there is already the whole history of painting's tradition, so what could I possibly add to it? I know painters have often circumvented the paradox of the void of a blank canvas by devious routes, doodling into it or just splodging paint on it, anything somehow to break its spell and make something to kick against. But I need another way. So I have decided to work only at night, in the dark, when I cannot see the canvas or the colours I am squeezing out of the paint tubes to put onto it. To paint blind, so to speak.

When I told a friend of my intention, she replied, 'If you don't want to see what you're doing why don't you paint with a bucket on your head?' And indeed I could. However, my thinking goes a little deeper. I have been reading the German Romantic poet Novalis. More specifically, his extended cycle of poems *Hymns to the Night*.[1] In these, Novalis weaves together images of womanhood, the subterranean landscape and the night, evoking for himself through these differing worlds an embracing shelter that shields him from the cruel realities of the full light of day. Having often worked well into the night myself, I am intrigued by the difference to working in the glare of the day. The quiet hours of the night somehow hold another sense of time, letting the mind wander off in different directions. One somehow finds oneself, goes deeper into oneself, in that dark, still veil between one day and the next.

The six works that became the *Night Flak* took me about six months to make. Each work is in a diptych format, one half a large drawing made during the day, the other a painting on canvas made at night. After six months of working nights I feel wrecked. It is not just the lack of sleep but also a peculiar sense of disorientation. Going into the studio each night, squeezing out from a tube a colour that I thought was cobalt blue, only to find in the morning that it was viridian green, does strange things to your perceptions. You paint differently with different colours: some like to sprawl across the surface, natural spreaders, while others like to gather themselves into a tight cluster, reticent to open up. It is as if some colours were extrovert and others introvert. Something unfamiliar happens when you mess with this. It is like eating a piece of meat that tastes like cheese, you cannot quite make sense of it. And the night, it takes over, becomes your day, and the daylight hours blur into an uncanny dreamscape.

At the end of my residency the six completed pieces, now entitled the *Night Flak Series*, are shown with some slightly earlier works of mine at the Walker Art Gallery. I cannot say they are good works. The colouring in the paintings looks arbitrary, which indeed it is. The paint surfaces are overworked, gnarled, quite ugly. I find them difficult to look at. As paintings, they are not successful; and yet on another level they did what they set out to do. After the exhibition closed, I destroyed four of the six and put the remaining two into storage.

Black and White ... or How to Paint with a Hammer
(1982)

About two years ago I said to a friend, 'I have some ideas for new works, and I think they would work best as paintings.' He replied, 'But you are not a painter!' I did not know what to say and asked 'What does that have to do with it?' At that point we looked guiltily at each other, sensing the other's culpability: I for having suggested that one could paint when one felt it to be appropriate, he for having intimated that painting was what 'painters' do, and it was best left that way. We had both said what we believed and felt to be true, but with it came the naggings of doubt. Either way, wrong or right, someone's feet were being trodden on.

Let us talk of love and hate, of all those prejudices that we push into the corners of our thoughts.

Let us fall into the abyss that separates our thoughts from what we do, and in that dark hole abandon ourselves to passion.

But foremost, let us think of painting, its incredulity.

Supposing truth to be in painting ... What then? I for one cannot think about painting without also thinking about Christianity. Both admit of no comparison, and both are riddled with the same preposterous idea that if one can pierce through the surface, peel away wondrous layers, there is a truth to be found and at the end salvation's holy sepulchre. It is as if all those layers of painting are but one store of one would-be great, common painting. A truly noble proposition, but at what price and with what guilt? Guilt must be endured to glimpse sacred domains. And what could be worse than to sense the truth yet feel its incumbent guilt? What can one do except protest, 'My guilt is real'? No, away with you, pious truth, and your beguiling sidekick guilt. Let me hide in my ignorance, sheltered by what I do not know, let me close the surface that is painting behind me.

I remember the recurring feeling of seeing Hamish Fulton's work, never black and white but grey, the grey of shrouded dreams.

I remember standing under a waterfall, framing it in the camera and thinking of a Barnett Newman painting. No matter which one, more the feeling.

I remember the Moroccan palm trees did not photograph in black and white.

I remember looking at an Anselm Kiefer painting and thinking of a Bruce Springsteen song: 'Hey kid! You think that's oil? Man, that ain't oil, that's blood, I wonder what he was thinking when he hit that storm, or was he just lost in the flood?'

Walking in the woods I used to think of Robert Smithson's entropy; now I think of the blue flower.

Helping a friend carry a recently finished, large and heavy oil painting of mine from the studio into the living room, the contrast was immediate and immense. The room ... clean walls, thick-piled carpet and the smell of cleansed living. The painting ... thick, rough wood, raw cotton-duck and heavy oil-crusted surface, like some kind of wild animal fashioned out of materiality.

I remember trying to say 'I love you' with a drawing. I could never have said it with a photograph.

I remember so many paintings are only photographs for me.

I remember sometimes hoping there was nothing on the film, so that I could start again, but never could.

But then can truth ever really be remembered?

It is in itself a matter of absolute indifference whether a thing be true, but a matter of the highest importance to what extent it is believed to be true. So take up your stance from there. The layers that are painting tell lies in more ways than one; it is just a question of how you choose to spread them. Accept that in lying you must lay yourself open to guilt or discovery. You have the option either to sleep the night away or to spread any layer you choose. However, you cannot lie out of ignorance. And anyway, all those reminiscences are mere protocol, arrested adolescent inhibition. Passion's generosity has for too long obscured your purpose and there is a time with all passions when they become squandered fatalities. The wood you fired in passion's name is that same wood you walked in – but mere rambling is no man's game. You have to be tempted by painting's desire. Painting is sexual. That mysterious 'other' is only the other that she allows.

You know that the demands of painting place one beyond good and evil, and that the struggle in art is against one of moralising.

Accept that belief is right.

The guiltiest are still the least ashamed.

But no! I want to be told something new. Yes, I dare to ask it. Stop telling me what I already know. Do not let me into your confidence but right under your skin, between the layers where desperation lurks. Show me the desires that make our differences clear. Truth's guilt belies a desperate man. For what I know I am guilty of, and on the surface of that painting in hard black and white boldly glares what I know to be truth, and its guilt. Guilt, concealed behind a landscape so pure even the most gentle tread will leave its mark. It is for good reason that the museum sign reads, 'Do not touch'. The most loving caress may expose the fake. So be silent, you are offered in hard black and white the crime of reason. Yet take care, for it is not the reasonable man of old, housed in his concepts, but a lodger, ready to sleep anywhere, and worse still to take what is not his. This house of the Lord is only sacred to he who worships there, to he who gets down on his knees.

Get off your knees, painter!

The altar is only good for eating off, even He was smart enough to know that.

Published in *Black and White ... or How to Paint with a Hammer*, exh. pamphlet, Matt's Gallery, London, 1982.

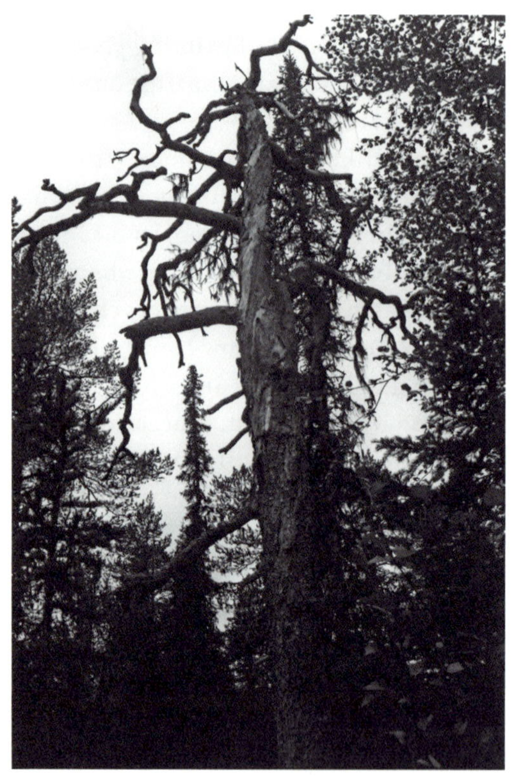

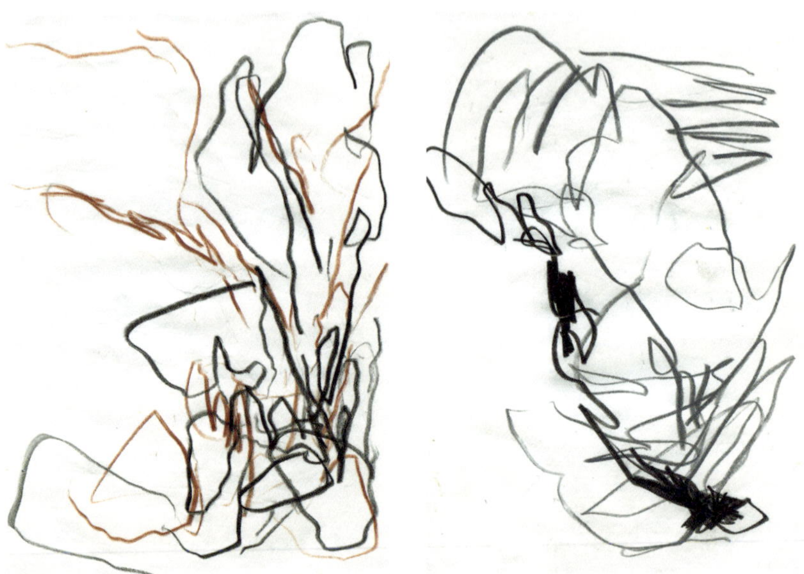

Swedish Lapland
(1986)

Above the Arctic Circle the mountains of Swedish Lapland comprise an elevated plateau crowned with peaks. One looks out over expansive valleys laced with the winding silver ribbons of rivers, glistening lakes at numerous levels, and to white summits with hanging glaciers, whose incessant streams ceaselessly pour in torrents down into the valleys below. It is a landscape awash with water.

On the low ground, around lakes and deltas, along valleys and winding streams, willow trees form almost impenetrable thickets. Fanning out further, graceful strands of silver birch, interspersed with rowan, alder and aspen, march up towards a low and erratic tree line. Above this, vast expanses of tundra, covered with willow, shrub, mosses and lichens, stretch out towards rolling heaths where mountain campion, lousewort, wavy hair grass and species of sedge break the monotony of the shrub.

At higher altitudes, lichen-covered stones lie scattered everywhere, providing shelter for pockets of hardy flowering plants. Here, below melting snowfields, the ground is damp and spongy, potted, marked with dark-brown earth ridges and raised tussocks of peat, caused by the repeated freezing and thawing of water in the surface layer of soil. Evidence of glaciation abounds, in the form of U-shaped canyons, hanging valleys, scarred rock faces, glacial cirques and lakes, large and small, cupped in sockets by ice from the obdurate rock. At such heights the snows frequently do not melt until late June, and on the higher summits the snow is perennial.

In the morning, as perspective rolls the landscape flat like a postcard, it takes on a size.

In the morning, as distance opens up the landscape like a map, it takes on a scale.

In the morning, as the mist lifts, and the silver birches discard the metal of night light, the landscape takes on a space.

In the morning, textures surface and describe.

Restless moods, like the day, do not wait for each other.

On ground high up, hard, boulders the size of pieces of furniture bash against each other. A huge and seemingly endless demolition site. To either side and ahead, rocks stagger and stack away in the distance. To scree, whose slopes, blurred, graded and grained, begin to articulate other profiles. Here, devoid of any immediate reference, I am reminded of the astronaut's problem of assessing distances on the moon, because of its unfamiliarity. Or of John Ruskin's observation, 'We never see anything clearly ... We suppose we see the ground under our feet clearly, but if we try to number its grains of dust we find that it is as full of confusion and doubtful form as anything else.'[1] The landscape becomes a dialectic of texture and structure, as gravity's aggregate teases it in and out of focus.

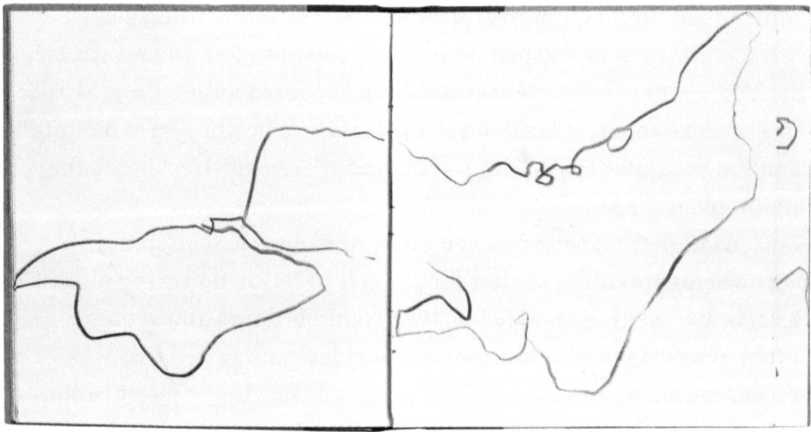

Under a jagged overhang, on the sheltered side of the river, slump two ice wedges. Each perhaps 15 feet high by 10 feet wide or so, tapering down at the bottom to low protruding points. Looking like they have just been placed there, they hover out from the rock, their indented surfaces in sharp contrast to the blocked stone around. As if made to fit badly, their erratic curved edges echo the angular rock above them.

Further downstream, as the ravine widens out and levels off, the river branches and thins, until eventually it is barely perceptible, running under a gently sloping stone field. Here, well-rounded stones sprawl out in all directions. Lines of larger stones form conspicuous ridges running parallel to the general contours of the ground. Sheltered on three sides we decide to camp. Facing to the open side where the ravine sweeps down into the valley below, leaving a wide horizon, we pitch the tent.

In the evening as the clouds descend, rolling over mountains and engulfing valleys, perspective is wedged in, then squeezed out. Slammed up hard against their shadows, silhouetted mountains, stacked up and backlit, fleetingly reshuffle. Above, pink clouds, extruded, swirl up and pucker in tight pockets. Intense colours stagger and shudder as the night begins to fall.

And the day rolled into mist and the mist folded into night, and the temperatures fell below. And thinking sank into that cold place where for a moment it freezes into clarity. Now, thinking back to then and other times, I remember, I no longer know where my nerve ends finish and something else begins. Brittle extremities seem to explode and flicker into generalities, as space pulsates out of stasis. Just hints of movement are able to evoke whole histories of antediluvian and cultural change, which collide and collude into a nervous vorticial space. Everything is precarious. One only has to think, to move, for it all to disintegrate or reconfigure itself. Out there, there are times when, even walking through the landscape, things move too fast.

Edited transcript of a tape and slide presentation commisioned by Whitechapel Art Gallery, London, 1986.

Grønland
(1988)

At the Geological Museum, under a display of five chunks of rock with a curved photographic image behind placed so as to resemble a diorama, the label reads: 'Amitsoq Bay – Western Greenland: ancient crystalline rock called Amitsoq Gneiss, originally a granite pushed up to the surface about 3,800 million years ago.'

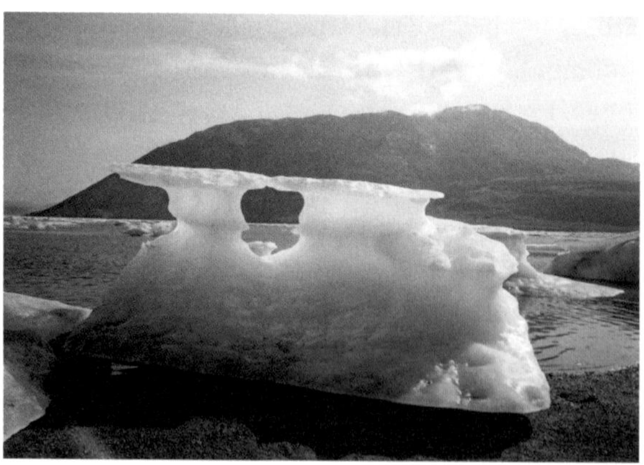

28 June
The blurb in the brochure told him that Qaqortoq had a population of about 4,500, Scandinavian-style houses, a fountain in the town square and a number of taxis. From the air he had seen that the roads through the town went nowhere, stopped sharp by the surrounding mountains and fjords. From up there he had also clearly seen the massive bulk of the ice cap bellying up against an intense blue sky.

1 July
Igaliku, the bay ringed by icebergs the size of houses. He moved from iceberg to iceberg with the scrutiny of a scientist. Searching out the key profiles he made the necessary photographs. Sometime in the future these numerous fragments, in an ever-expanding jigsaw, would be pieced back together again. He had read that scientists believed

Antarctica to be the central mass of Gondwana, the ancient mother continent from which all others separated. They had been torn apart, island continents, gigantic, their rupture too big to be perceived. Around the polar margins this rage still stirred, and even when still, the silence felt like a groan. In the retort of the carving ice and the 3,800 million years of sediments lying ribboned in the folds of Amitsoq Bay he sensed these murmurs, and all things were imaginable. He continued his work moving slowly and systematically until out of vision. Searching for Gondwanaland would in the end be the only way to spend time.

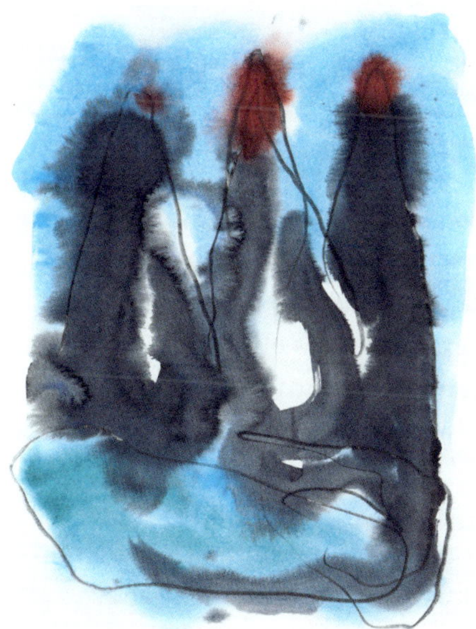

13 July

Talus seeped into the corners of the eyes. Its slow encroachment crept at the speed that was felt. It would take six or more hours to reach the hanging valley. Looking back to Eqalorutsit Kangigdlit, the glacier piled out from between the mountains like a huge gaping mouth, all teeth, animal. Under the lip of the glacier where the river ran into the fjord, he could still see the bright red geodesic dome secured by steel wires, its presence and scale all shot to hell by the size of the glacier. A toy, it looked unreal, creepy, as if from another world. The rain was

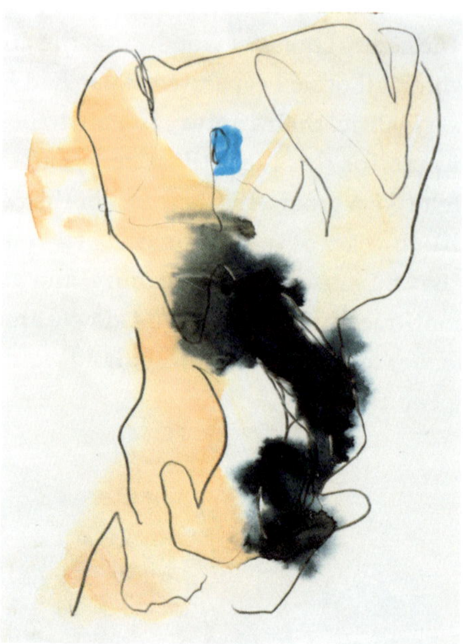

horizontal. As he scrambled up and away from the dome, he tried to remember which film he had just stepped out of.

It is said that the peoples of Thule, northwest Greenland, thought of themselves as the only people in the world until disturbed by Europeans in the nineteenth century.

19 July

Qorassauq, a field of crystalline stone chips with intermittent outcrops of boulders slowly picking themselves to pieces.

20 July

In the night the trilobites resurfaced. Deep sea shales and mudstones yielded a variety of the species with rudimentary eyes or blind. Camped among the boulders, freed from the blurring interference of the mosquito netting, their precise minutiae crept up until the size of mammoths. In Inuit the weather is spoken of as a person.

3 August

Motzfeldt Sø. For two days it had rained continuously, with heavy mist. During this time, he occasionally got out of the tent to stretch

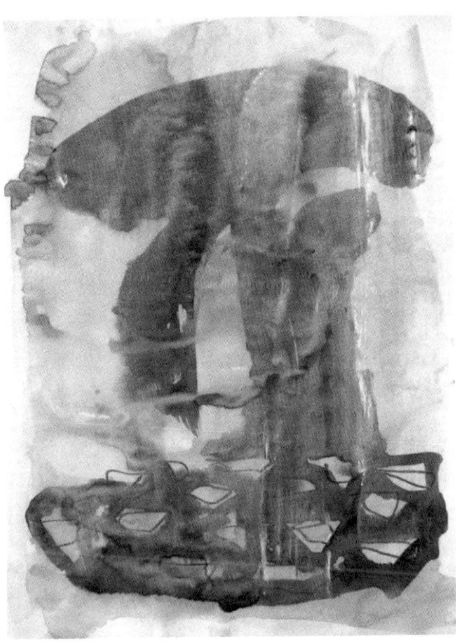

his legs and to photograph the mist. As had always previously been the case, this would be just another fogged film. On the morning the mist cleared he looked out across the valley. The regular mountains triangulated down into the flat sandy valley base. The river, a milky green, was impassable as it carried the previous day's downpour and meltwater away. He had a strange feeling of parchedness. The landscape had a symmetry of dryness.

9 August

Michel Foucault's *The Archaeology of Knowledge* he had rammed under a pile of rocks a few days before.[1] On a shelf in the general store in Narssaq, along with the video tapes and cassettes he found a book entitled *Qilakitsormiut*.[2] He took it off the shelf and began to scan the pages. There was something disconcertingly concrete about words that were as expansive and as incomprehensible as the land. Arlannaanniluunniit, it was enough to know such words existed.

Published in Ian McKeever, *Grønland*, Galerie Tanit Munich and Morat-Institut, Freiburg im Breisgau, 1989.

Papua New Guinea
(1991)

16 April
I am in Port Moresby, travelling with a friend, the Dutch sculptor Waldo Bien. Our plan, and it is a rough plan, is to cross Papua New Guinea south to north heading west through the highlands. Port Moresby has a palpable air of violence about it. The city is in curfew from 6 pm to 6 am and we are strongly advised not to go out at night. Our instinct is not to hang around. So, the next morning we negotiate a flight by light aircraft that will take us inland to Wau, and from there we hope to be able to start walking.

21 April
The landscape is dense vegetation and unnavigable on our own. Over the next days a loose rhythm establishes itself of going from village to village finding guides, usually young men, via the chief. This has the added benefit that when we do arrive somewhere, out of the blue, so to speak, with our guides, we do not look like we have dropped out of the sky.

23 April
The decorated front of the Haus Tambaran is a chequered sheet of linoleum. Coca-Cola cans perched on the end of thin poles march along the ridge of the roof. In the next village the Haus ridge is a riot of mud mounds and brightly coloured feathers.

29 April
I always carry teabags with me when travelling. We are sitting in a large circular hut, with the chief and several of the men. A fire burns in the middle with a cauldron of water suspended above it. The conversation turns to what do we drink in England? Tea, I explain, taking a teabag out of my rucksack and handing it to the chief. He inspects it, then passes it around for all to see. I tell them it is put in a mug of boiling water, left for a minute, then drunk. Retrieving the

teabag the chief lobs it into the caldron which must have a couple of gallons of warm water in it, then stirs it around with a stick. Handed a mug he then scoops out some of the brew, tries it and passes it around. The looks are somewhat quizzical, and I am left pondering how to explain the finer points of making a cup of tea.

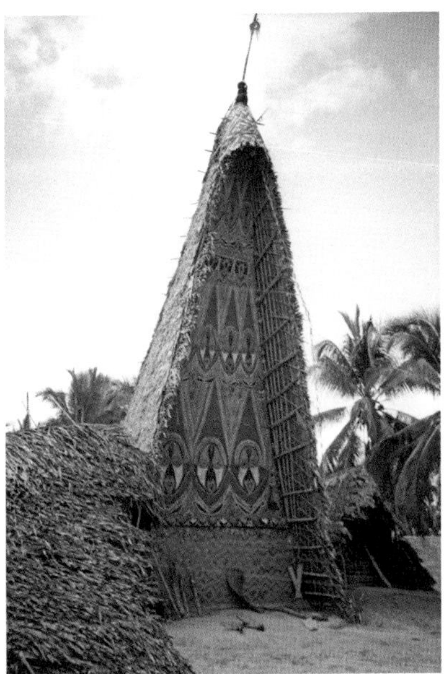

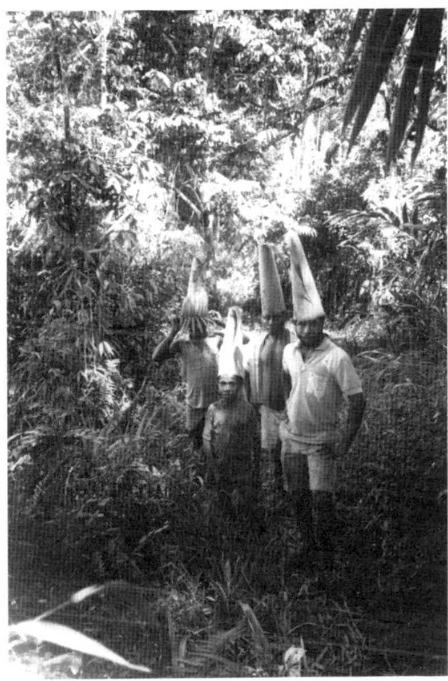

30 April

Yesterday a game of basketball was being played on rough ground as we arrived, against a team from a neighbouring village. It seemed everyone, except the infirm, was on the pitch. At some point the score was disputed and out of nowhere all hell broke loose with the game descending into a mass brawl. Stepping out of the hut this morning we were surrounded by men covered from head to toe with white ash powder overpainted with different markings, looking ghostly and scary. Carrying spears and bows and arrows they were going to war against the neighbouring village. Apparently, such inter-tribal battles are not unusual, and people can be seriously hurt. The battle is more analogous to hunting, as by stealth and wily cunning they stalk their opponents in the jungle. Fortunately, we are only bystanders, and the chief arranged for two men to guide us out of the danger area and back on our way.

6 May

At the local kiosk the men buy strips of old newspaper, torn into rectangles the way we used to do as children when toilet paper was in short supply. These they roll into cylinders with the dexterity of women rolling Cuban cigars. The tube is then secured with a paper collar, which as they smoke the 'cigarette' down, they move along to stop it uncurling. The taste, a mixture of damp paper (everything in PNG is damp) and printers' ink, is foul. In the evening the hut is pungent with the fumes, and in the morning one's lungs feel like someone has gone over them with sandpaper.

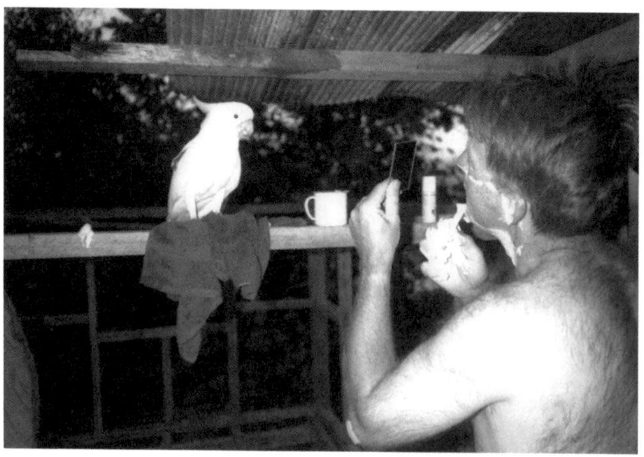

11 May

The situation is delicate. Approaching a village we have unknowingly walked over the burial grounds. A group of angry men have stopped us and clearly are not happy. It is tense. Eventually we persuade them to take us to the chief. Over the course of the evening a payment is agreed upon, and all seems to be forgiven. The Papuan have a complex payback system, which functions both as a judicial system and a means of barter. If you hurt or aggrieve someone, you pay them back; equally, if you help someone, you are paid back. Increasingly as we travel our rucksacks are getting lighter, as spare T-shirts, boxer shorts, Elastoplast, anything is traded. The small black plastic cannisters for 35 mm film rolls are popular with the men. The next morning, we are taken to a long, high escarpment about a mile from the village. As we start to climb up, we pass under an overhang. Set into the wall of this depression are wooden structures resembling crude scaffolding, and nestling into these are tied the crouching mummified remains of several bodies. We are being shown another burial ground.

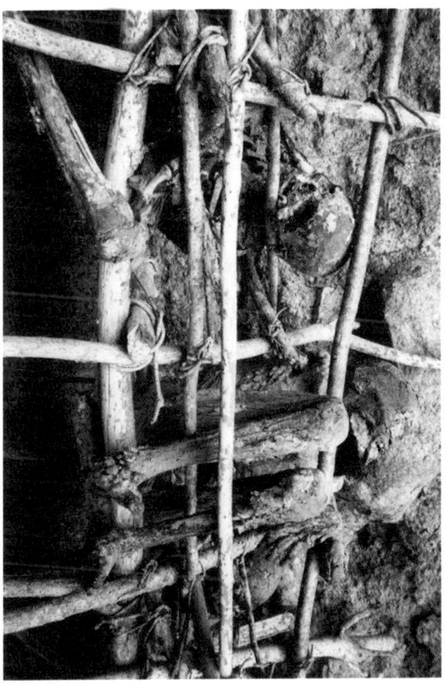

12 May

We walk down to the edge of the lake, having been told that the village on the island is celebrating a yam festival. We borrow one of the chiselled-out log canoes and very gingerly paddle over. The yam houses are extraordinary, made of an open latticework of bamboo poles tied together with grasses and thatched, then decorated with flowers and feathers. The yams sit on a network of cross poles acting as shelves and are enormous, some must be 6 feet long and over a foot in diameter. It is a wonderful sight. Again, we have to explain we are not working for one of the mining companies and are invited to sit by the fire and eat yams. The fire seems a sacred place in PNG, the ritual of sitting around it a sign of acceptance, if only temporarily.

15 May

There are more than 800 different languages spoken in Papua New Guinea. The most common language is Tok Pisin, a mixture of English, German and Dutch. We have been walking for over three weeks and are now high in the mountains. The vegetation has thinned out, and looking across the valley as the damp evening air begins to rise there is an incredible sense of stillness. We can hear in the distance the deep repetitive thud of a log drum. The drums are used as a messaging system similar to Morse code. The sound carries for miles. Asking as to its meaning we are told a young woman in a village on the other side of the mountain has disappeared and would the village look out for her. A woman's lot in Papua New Guinea is not an easy one. The men spend a good part of their time in their long houses and although they ostensibly go out hunting during the day, it is the women who do the work. Meat is scarce and when it is available at its best it is the meat from the blind pigs that forage around the villages.

21 May

The highlands, Mount Hagen. An elderly woman sits on the side of the road making loose net sacks from a roll of blue nylon string. Into their webbing she is weaving strips of foil from chewing-gum packets and bright bits of paper. The ingenuity is incredible. The town is a hub, rough and ready, with many people passing through. We join a motley group waiting for one of the flatbed open trucks that act as the local transport system. After a couple of hours hanging around, we all pile onto the back and the truck leaves. It will carry us across the valley, the journey taking several hours. Having left the town, Waldo and I are periodically asked to crouch down low so that we cannot be seen. Hijacking and robbery are not infrequent, and our presence only adds to the risk. From this hunched-down position, we get a good bird's-eye view of the globs of visceral-red spittle that often end up on the truck bed generated by our fellow travellers' incessant chewing of betel nuts and leaves. Occasionally stopping to let someone off, the passenger goes through an elaborate ritual of extracting a kina note that has been folded into a tiny square and secreted somewhere about his body. This is then ceremonially unfolded and handed to the driver.

22 May
It is incredible to think that up until the 1930s, when two Australians Mick Leahy and Mick Dwyer led an expedition into the highlands in search of gold, no white person had been to this central mountainous area of Papua New Guinea. It was thought to be uninhabited. Some people can still remember life before the white man arrived. Now, as a fertile high plateau it is the centre of coffee production, bringing with it armed truck drivers and crime.

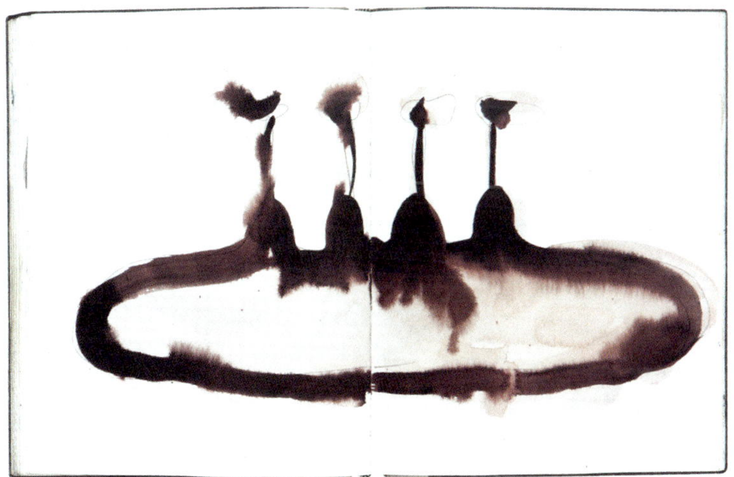

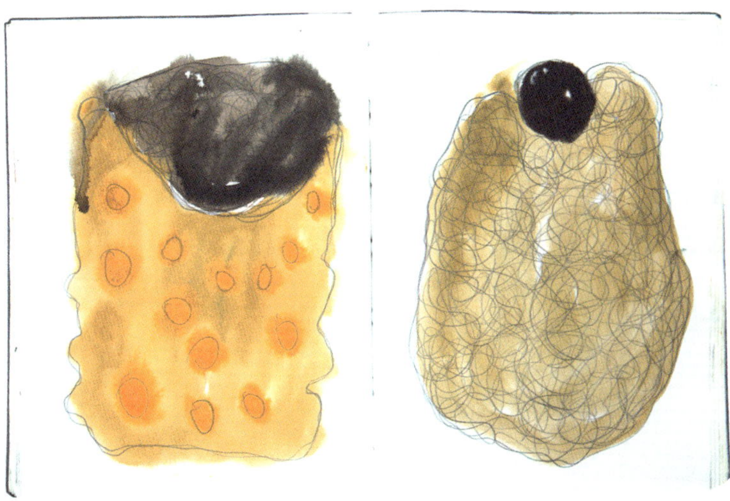

27 May

Colin and Wixie are our guides for the next few days. Before setting off we are all standing in an abandoned Haus Tambaram. Looking down, Waldo sees on the floor a short piece of hollow bamboo tube. He picks it up. It is about the length and diameter of a large finger and is incised on the outside with regular geometric patterns. We ask what it is. Colin and Wixie explain that it is part of a penis gourd and, after further prompting, go on to explain how it is secured to the body. As we try to figure out how this might work one of the elders of the village enters the Haus. Seeing the piece of bamboo, he takes it in his hand, rolls it deftly between his fingers and places it in the hole in his distended right earlobe. Smiling, he then leaves. We look across to Colin and Wixie, neither of whom have holes in their earlobes.

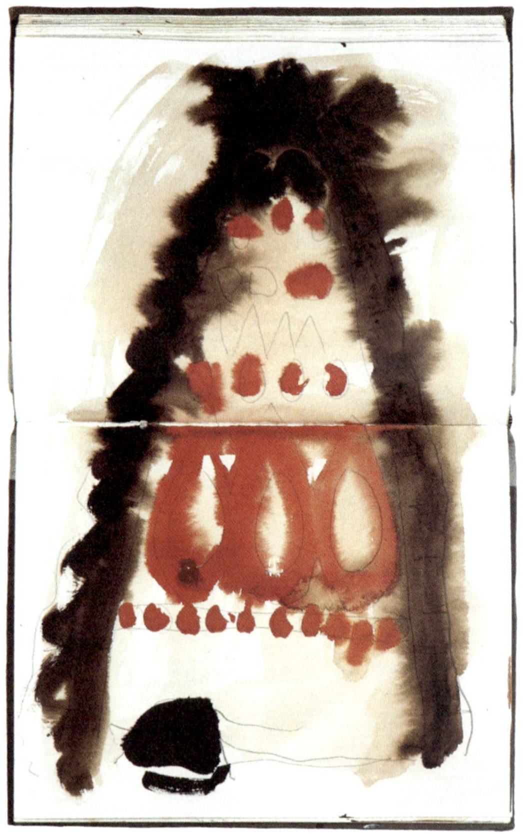

1 June
The days are long but leisurely as we walk from village to village. Our two companions, always ahead waiting for us, spend their time decorating their bodies with flowers and leaves. They are fun to be with. A plane is due in soon to pick up a passenger to take them to the hospital in Wewak. The airstrip is on a steep grassy slope dropping off sharply to the valley floor below. The next morning our guides come to say farewell as we prepare to board the plane. I have virtually nothing left to give them. My rucksack is empty except for a pair of trainers, so I hand these to them. As I look out of the window waving, they wave back, each wearing one trainer. The sight is comic and endearing.

2 June
Wewak, from the dense vegetation of the interior to the expanse of the ocean and sky. From a world of infinite form and shadows to a world of infinite light. We take a walk along the beach and stop to talk to a group of men chiselling out a long log to make a canoe. At about 6 o'clock the sun drops out of the sky as if it were a falling tennis ball. From one moment to the next it becomes night, the sky a pure deep blue.

9 June
I have returned to the UK. Waldo is in Amsterdam, in hospital, having been diagnosed with malaria. After a few hours with my family and a visit to the doctors, I find myself in the hospital for tropical diseases, as for the past few days I have had hot sweats. Tests confirm it is not malaria but they do not know what it is. After two days' observation and more tests the consultant asks if I would take an Aids test. I am not keen on the idea so discharge myself and go home.

Over the next weeks the sweats subside, and I am back working again in the studio. At the end of a couple of months the walls are covered with perhaps 100 gouaches, as I attempt, probably in vain, to visualise a world that already feels a lifetime away.

Black and White ... and Very Grey Areas
(1993)

Being a painter in Britain is a strange business. The English do not quite know what to think or do about painting. They prefer it offshore and do their best to keep it there. When they do let it drift inland, they like it clear-cut, either figurative or abstract, a story or a formal problem. Beyond that they get stuck and as the going gets rougher they give up, become lazy. The idea that they might open up their minds to another kind of visual space, let loose the subconscious or the animal in themselves, is sure to guarantee that they head straight back to the island.

Of course, there are painters like Roger Hilton and Alan Davie who have ventured against the stream into the rough ground, but then they are seen as oddballs, not quite fitting in or playing the game, and so are kept offshore. And we painters are the poorer for it. Our roots, our real roots, the Celts, old blood, the liquid and flow of our early history is lost, suffocated under the weight of the Academy. Joshua Reynolds, Thomas Lawrence, the list is long and continues. What an impoverished tradition of mediocrity we painters on this island have to fight our way clear of. Even J. M. W. Turner and John Constable are soothed into this land of pastoral. Ssshh! lest we wake the monster in this beautiful land!

Four sides of the box
The working wall,
The looking wall,
The unused wall,
The back wall.

There is always a good reason not to start the day's painting. The rain is beating down so hard on the roof that you cannot hear yourself think. The painting is looking back at you as deadened as a sheet of cardboard. There is always a good reason not to start a new painting. Sometimes, the two problems, starting the day's work and starting a new painting, become entwined and either flow or not, but more often the question specifically of how to start a painting is a particularly thorny one. It is a curious thing, that as a painter one is always asked how you know when a painting is finished, rather than how you start a painting. There is somehow the assumption that the ending is what matters, but, as a painter making the work, the opposite is true. After all, to start a painting is at the same time also to start to finish a painting. In simple terms, the first mark dictates the last mark. That sounds very calculated, but it is not. It is more an attitude of trying to paint a work cleanly, so that it grows clearly and inevitably, rather than being a series of false starts. How do you start and finish a painting of false starts unless it is itself a conscious strategy?

A few years ago, someone came to my studio and said that the works did not look like anyone's paintings. Further explanation led me to understand that what they were really saying was that the paintings, which were loose and gestural, did not look like they had been painted by anyone specific. The marks did not seem to have a signature. They were generic. I liked that.

I have never wanted to own the marks that I have made, and I have never wanted those marks, those gestures, to be a signature. With few exceptions I find the gesture in painting embarrassing. It is like a public secret we all know, but at the same time do not really know at all. I can cringe in front of a clever gesture. So, I would like a dumb gesture, and paintings which on that level are deadpan. All paintings on some level have to be dumb. Part of their fascination is between clear articulation and dumbness. A painting only has to give you so much, after which there should be a point where you are blocked off. Looking at a painting is about trying to get past the block, but a good painting never lets you through.

A Painting Is a Door

The painting is mute,
Not a word.

I wait

Image, before that,
Space, before that
Open, before that
Closed, before that
Full, before that
Empty, before that
Clear, before that
Veiled, before that
And, the back becomes the front.

I cannot paint today because it is raining.
I cannot paint today because the wind is blowing.
I cannot paint today because it is not yet night.
I cannot paint today because it is the looking wall.
I will not paint because the dog is barking.
I will not paint today because you are not here.

From now

I am painting in front of you.
I am painting behind you.
I am painting away from the light.
I am painting towards the night.
I am painting the figure out.
I am painting the abstract in.
I am painting to block off.
And, I am painting to open and close the black, the white and the grey.

> The black is thicker and shorter than the white.
> The white stays lean until it is interfered with.
> The black is fat.
> You can get close to black, never to white.
> Up against the black (you are always in proximity to it)
> It stays close and pushes against you.
> The white always backs off, even before you get near.
> There is a place in the black and maybe only a space in
> the white.
> The 'thing' in the black is not in the white.

It is possible that we painters are all attempting to paint the same painting. In which case things are not so bad, as we can always excuse ourselves and pass the buck if the pressure gets too much. However, it is also possible that we are only ever trying to paint our own individual single painting. In this case things are much harder, as there is no alternative but to get on with it and live with the consequences. But then, on the positive side there is also no need for gimmickry, for triviality and for naming.

Vast ideas of time and space intrigue me. I would like to have the speed of a mountain. Even to paint a painting at the speed of a mountain – that slow. At which point it is improbable that one would be perceived as painting landscape.

Published in *Black and White ... and Very Grey Areas*, exh. pamphlet, Cairn Gallery, Nailsworth, Gloucestershire, accompanying the exhibition 'Door Paintings', 1993.

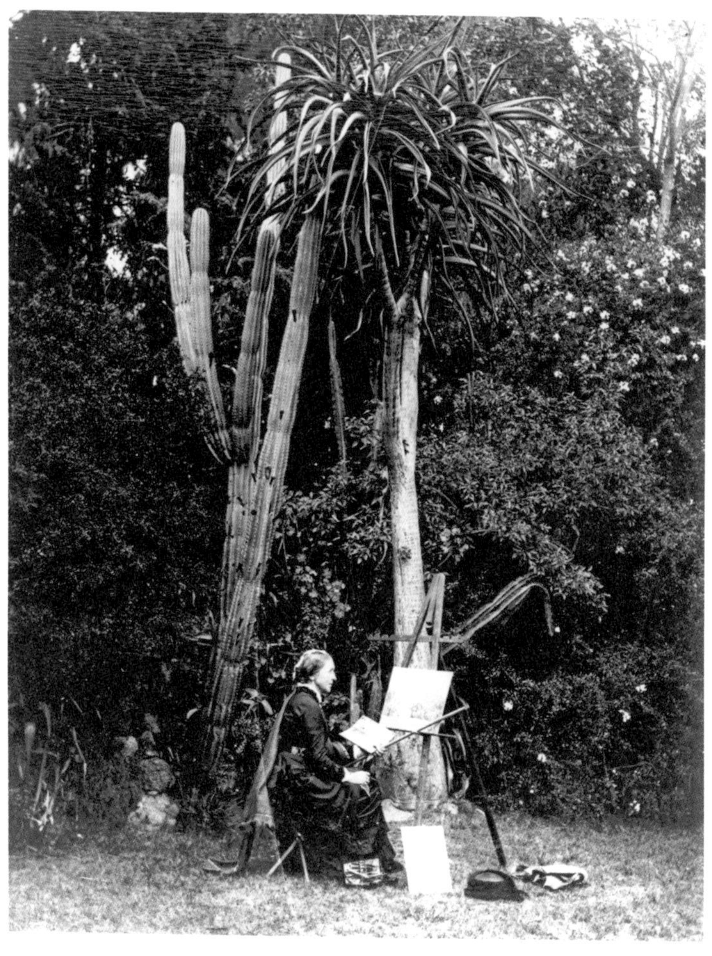

Marianne North, Olana, Hudson, New York
(1995)

1871

Marianne North is in America on a trip that takes her up along the northeast coast and into Canada. While in the Hudson Bay area she is invited to visit the artist Frederic Church at Olana. After missing the train and one or two other setbacks she arrives a day late, but the Churches are good hosts. Mr Church is particularly keen to show her the two white asses he has recently imported from Damascus. White and distinct like the icebergs he had cajoled in Labrador some years earlier, only this time with a different temperature – a warmth instead of bristling cold.

For Church, whiteness is a kind of luminosity, which is never pure white but rather the white of light or heat, whatever the case may be. But always it is luminous – a means of transmission that makes however precarious a substance out of space, through which things can move. Without it the air is full of holes and pockets of oblivion into which we fall. For Marianne North, white is more the texture and taste of vanilla. This is white from the other side, the inside, sweated out from within, where white is not to do with negotiation, but with the body and how its being is internally self-identified.

Through such self-individuation we own our bodies. Here, white can be held and stored as stillness. This was where silence lay. But where now does silence reside in colour?

American white is luminous
Dutch white is strait-laced
Italian white is of the ghost
Spanish white can be knife-edge sharp
and English white is like dew, a fleck of flake
that drops away
as soon as it is touched.

January 1877, Ceylon
Marianne North visits Julia Margaret Cameron:

> Her oddities were most refreshing, after the 'don't care' people I usually meet in tropical countries. She made up her mind at once she would photograph me, and for three days she kept herself in a fever of excitement about it, but the results have not been approved of at home since. She dressed me up in flowing draperies of cashmere wool, let down my hair, and made me stand with spiky cocoa-nut branches running into my head, the noonday's sun's rays dodging my eyes between the leaves as a slight breeze moved them, and told me to look perfectly natural (with a thermometer standing at 96°). Then she tried me with a background of breadfruit leaves and fruit, nailed flat against the window shutter, and told them to look natural, but both failed; and although she wasted twelve plates, and an enormous amount of trouble, it was all in vain, she could only get a perfectly uninteresting and commonplace person on her plate, which refused to flatter.[1]

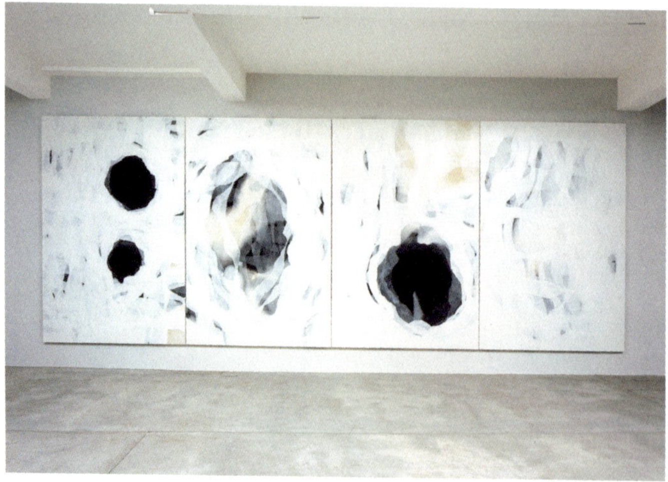

Mary Kingsley in Africa; Mary Gaunt in China and Siberia; Margaret Fountaine in the South Seas; Lilian Richmond Brown in America. There is a tradition of nineteenth-century women explorers.

Marianne North began travelling and painting in 1869 after the death of her father, the politician Frederick North.

Between 1871 and 1885 she visited and worked in the Americas, Jamaica, Japan, Borneo, Java, Ceylon, Australia and South Africa. Throughout this period, she made hundreds of small oil paintings *in situ*, mostly of botanical subjects but also, occasionally, of local scenes. In 1882 a special pavilion commissioned by Marianne North to house 832 of her paintings was opened at Kew Gardens, the installation of the works and all the decorative details within the building made by North herself. After her last trip to Chile in 1884–85 she settled at Alderley in the Cotswolds, debilitated by the years of travel. She died in 1890.

The devil and the deep blue sea

Concerning the meaning of grace in his book *On the Heights of Despair*, E. M. Cioran postulates that women have the capacity to be happier than men because they are in a state of grace.[2]

Simone Weil suggests that imagination is continually at work, filling up all the fissures through which grace might pass.

To paint is to be of him and her, to desire both and to sense the breach. 'Distance is the soul of the beautiful' continues Weil,[3] and so it would seem to be. Hollow or complete, the body strives for a place where it might not know itself.

Published in *Ian McKeever: The Marianne North Paintings*, exh. cat., Matt's Gallery, London, 1995.

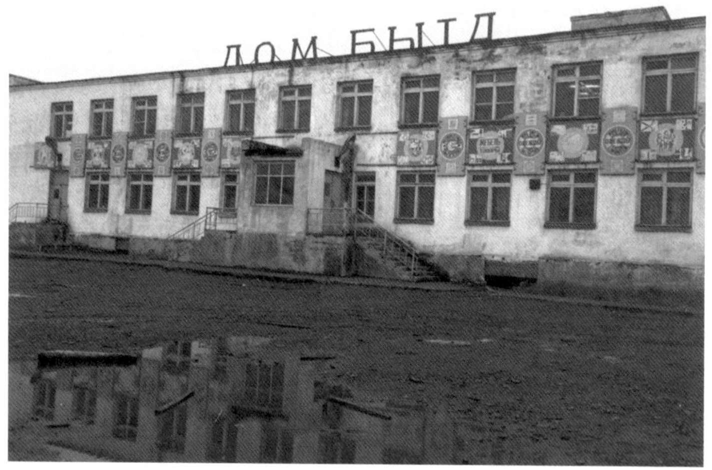
ДОМ БЫТА

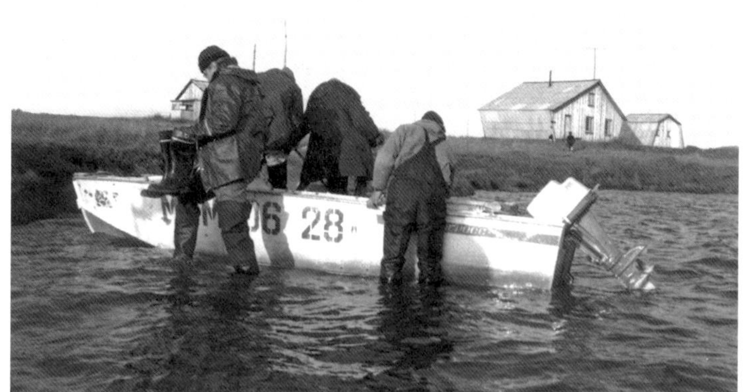
06 28

Northeast Siberia
(1995)

Chaun

The biological research station at Chaun is situated about 15 km in from the mouth of the River Chaun. The landscape is a wide meandering delta basin with waters flowing down from the distant encircling mountains. It is flat tundra, looks and feels ageless, and due to the prevalence of river water, lakes and pools gives the sense of being an island. The very volume of water evokes the threatening sensation that big and fast waters can have of being high up against the body, of nudging the body over.

Founded by the late director of the Magadan Institute of the Biological Problems of the North, Professor V. L. Kontrimavičius, the station is a cluster of simple wooden buildings connected by duckboards. When viewed from way out in mid-river it appears bleak and desolate, and in the winter must be desperately so, but standing on the duckboards feels good and almost homely. The buildings are all slightly different, with peculiar, pitched roofs and sloping walls. Each gives a sense of being an experiment, which as they were built by the scientists themselves, they probably were.

The scientists are all based at the Institute in Magadan and come to the station during the brief summers to do fieldwork. There are seven scientists present, one or two with their families. The atmosphere is relaxed and easy. Scientists, like artists, seem to spend a lot of time just looking and thinking around things, engaged in refreshingly simple observation. There are other parallels too. Both scientists and artists seem to divide their time between doing fieldwork and going back to base to do the actual donkey work itself. On the surface it looks like both are moving in the same direction, only on different trains, so to speak. But when one actually looks at what is happening inside the trains as they go along, then things get trickier. Art is trying to be just what it is and not much more, while science is trying as hard as possible to add up to something else. In a way, the scientist accumulates knowledge to define, while the artist offloads as much as possible in order to defy. It is as if one buys and the other spends.

The men and women at Chaun are all good anglers. They seem to fit a spot of fishing in whenever the opportunity arises. They travel on their research sorties by lightweight aluminium outboard motorboats, usually in convoys of two or three. There are two reasons for this: each boat is too small to accommodate everyone, but perhaps more importantly, in case of a breakdown the others can assist. Being out on the open river is more like being out at sea: it is big, exposed and deceptively cold, even in midsummer. When the scientists do pull over to the riverbank, fishing seems inevitable. The fish, salmon, are easily lured out of the water. The only fishing I did as a child was coarse fishing at sea, where the line is thrown out as far as possible and then reeled in. This is a very abstract way of fishing, while here at Chaun one could sense the fish being teased literally off the riverbed.

From one of the buildings I can hear Jethro Tull music playing. Outside on the nearby tundra, driftwood has been arranged into a garden, looking like a cross between a Japanese formal garden and a backyard. The need to somehow shape the land, lay a human structure over it, must at times here be overwhelming. Making sense of place as opposed to simply ‘out there’. How far will the music drift, beyond the garden, then what?

We had arrived at Chaun by helicopter; we leave in small outboard motorboats. The two could not provide a more different view of the tundra. From the air it is a vascular system of waterways and permafrost structures. A geometry one can intelligibly travel through. On the ground, of course, one is lost in texture and the details of yellowish-pink cloudberries and their uncanny likeness to salmon flesh. The space is all detail; it is too big to comprehend in any other way. Only out on the water can one sense the tenuous line back to one’s own body. We had jokingly set ourselves the challenge of how to hold permafrost. Of course, it is everywhere here, and like something that is everywhere, you know that it is there, but you cannot put your finger on it.

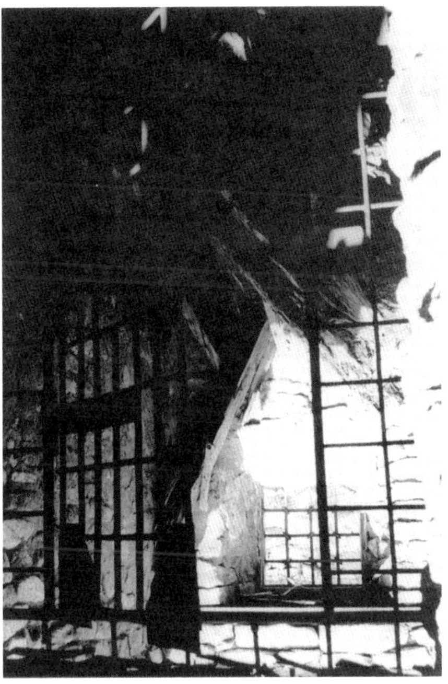

Pevek

We have travelled on from Magadan though the northern wastes of Joseph Stalin's Gulags to Pevek. Towns and villages that on our Russian colleagues' maps were no more than numbers, but identified by Aleksandr Solzhenitsyn as such regions as Kolyma, stood stark in the otherwise empty tundra.[1] Now abandoned, they were no more than shanty towns, housing the dispossessed descendants of the mass slave labour force that fuelled Stalin's empire. What remains of the particular site we visited are a few ruins of small buildings, their crumbling stone walls waist to shoulder high. The odd wrought-iron barred window sticks up and out against the sky. One of the ruins is piled high with old leather shoes and boots, the soles and uppers peeling away from each other, distressed as if still scars of the past. It is a bleak hard landscape, which in the winter with freezing temperatures and in the summer plagued by mosquitoes must have been a harsh environment in which to simply survive. Yet, strangely, being here on a warm summer's day, there is something comforting about it, as if amid all the history of pain and horror a healing is taking place as the landscape slowly takes it back into itself. Driving a

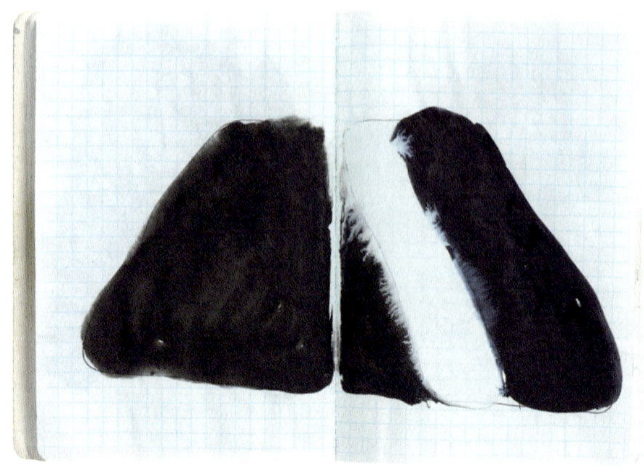

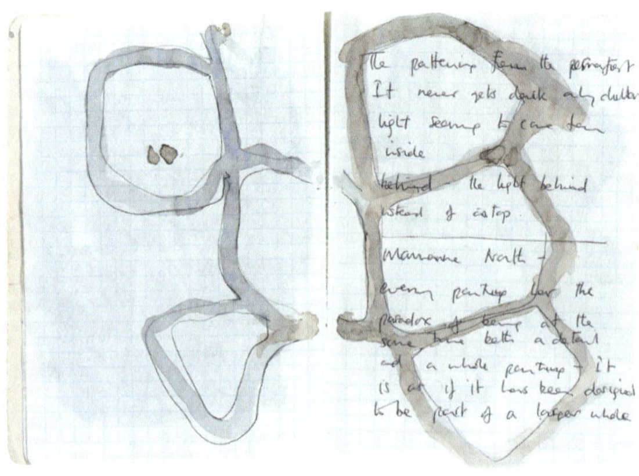
The patterning from the permafrost
It never gets dark only duller
light seeming to come from
inside
behind – the light behind
instead of on top
Marianne North –
every painting has the
paradox of being at the
same time both a detail
and a whole painting – it
is as if it has been designed
to be part of a larger whole

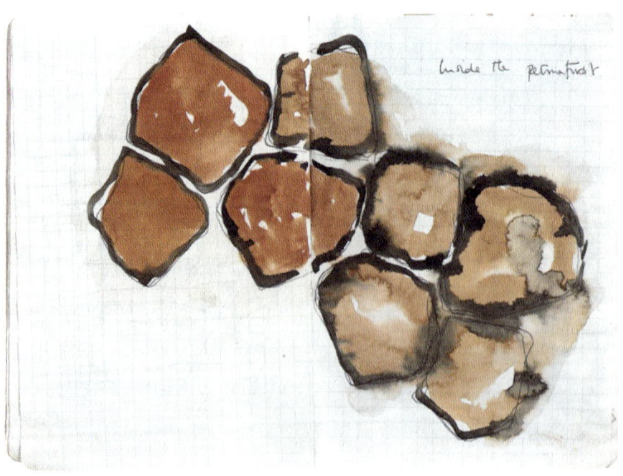
Inside the permafrost

few kilometres further on we stop at what looks like the scarred remains of a quarry. Advised to stay in the truck, Berman and a colleague with whom I am travelling get out with their Geiger counters, take readings, then quickly return to the vehicle. I am told it is the remains of a uranium mine. The labourers forced to work there expected to live no more than a year or two.

Pevek is a cluster of low-rise concrete apartment blocks, sitting on permafrost. Rudimentary footpaths and roads going nowhere beyond, give the place an added sense of desolation. Due to the extreme cold of the winter months, the sides of the concrete apartment blocks often develop huge cracks, sometimes from top to bottom. To hold the walls together and to increase insulation the authorities spray the outside of the whole building with thick, yellow, polystyrene foam, windows, the lot. The building looking like a large pillow. While still wet, children throw objects, old gramophone records, shoes, crockery and knives and forks, anything they can find, into this dirty, yellow, sticky ooze. Once dry, they are fixed for good.

Some occupants meticulously cut out the polystyrene areas covering their apartment windows, which open inwards, carefully removing the offending foam to let in the light. Others simply punch out a random hole to let light in. While others still, do nothing, perhaps out of indifference or a desire to maximise insulation. Viewed from inside, such apartments have a strange sense of the unreal, as if one has walked into a dystopian movie set.

Published in *Ikijää, Permafrost*, exh. cat., Porin Taidemuseo, Pori, Finland, 1995, pp. 17–20, 88.

Painting Is Not Flat Art
(1995)

Painting is not flat art,
Nor is it a model,
Nor is it a picture,
Nor is it a representation,
Nor is it an idea,
Nor is it a fact,
Nor is it a concept,
Nor is it a proposition,
Nor is it an object,
Nor is it a one-off,
Nor is it all of those things
which hide behind painting
but are not.

Bethany, Connecticut

Published in *Ian McKeever: The Marianne North Paintings*, exh. cat., Matt's Gallery, London, 1995.

Thoughts on Emil Nolde
(1995)

I went for the first time to Seebüll with Harald Behm. We drove there in Harald's old Cadillac the morning after the opening of my exhibition at his gallery in Hamburg. Cruising at a steady 110 km/h, we drifted along dead-straight flat roads, the horizon clean, the sky big, super-big and dense as a plate of steel – we could almost have been on a ship.

We were going to the Nolde Stiftung, to look at the works but more specifically to see the *Ungemalte Bilder* – the 'unpainted pictures'. The name alone fascinated me, casting doubt over their existence in the first place. As if out of a story by Jorge Luis Borges, it suggested works full of deep intrigue. Emil Nolde created them during the years 1938–45, even though he was forbidden to paint by the Nazi regime. He painted more than 1,300 small-format watercolours, mostly on salvaged scraps of paper. Their titles reveal something of their enormous range of subject matter: *Summer Breeze*, *Alone*, *The Strange Lady*, *Twilight Creatures*.

The unpainted pictures are breathtakingly beautiful and for watercolours extremely densely wrought. They have more the feeling of gouaches in the build-up of paint, but still retain the luminosity and transparency of watercolour. They glow. During the few hours we were at Seebüll, in that bleak landscape under those vast skies, I was struck by a strong sense of vulnerability. Demons the size of atmospheres could be conjured out of them. Big enough to eat you. Perhaps in such a place there was only the choice either to be engulfed or to picture everything that was outside of oneself.

• • •

There are painters whose work is open and generous, in that it provides protein for other painters, and there are painters whose work, for want of a better expression, never leaves the plate. Nolde, like that other great force of northern painting Edvard Munch, is open and generous. Both are steeped in that particularly northern tradition of contradiction, the introspective versus the wildly excessive – of long nights and sometimes clear days, out of which a very different sense of the self emerges to that of southern warmth and glow.

As much as anything, this is a difference of the idea of inside and outside – of what is public and what is private and how the boundary between the two is described. One could say it is the difference of where the window is that separates the self from what lies beyond. In the southern tradition, the window is constructed with a clear view beyond and the self is composed against it. In the northern tradition, the window itself may be malevolent, may even try to take the self from the inside out. This is a quality, as much the difference between the Classical and Romantic traditions, that also gives the northern tradition its particular sense of intensity and claustrophobia.

The paintings of Nolde are intense and there is within them often an acute sense of foreboding and pressure. The heavy skies across the flat water lands that border Germany and Denmark must have done much to instil this quality within his work, just as the endless vanishing horizon probably allowed Nolde to range over the incredibly broad subject matter that he pursued. For it was very broad, a range we are no longer used to seeing, nor expect from living painters. From seascapes to whirling dancers, portraits, flower motifs, religious themes, ghouls and spooks, anything could and was conjured out of those northern skies.

Placed in this no man's land, Nolde seems to have drawn on influences as much from the margins as from the centres. One can see in his paintings echoes of the Swedish eccentric Carl Fredrik Hill, whose work roams a world of fantastic landscapes and beings. Hill spent many years of his adult life in mental institutions, having crossed over the line of self-awareness towards a compulsive inner migration. Nolde, more so than the other German Expressionists, also at times walks in his paintings that thin existential line where the self could be lost in a frenzy of work. Equally, within the play of the mask and the macabre one can sense the presence of the underworld of James Ensor. As a disguise, the mask often peoples Nolde's portraits, and even more apparently innocent subjects such as a flower painting or a seascape can be a clear deception, imbued as they frequently are with an air of unexpected threat, or a restless heat that throws us off our guard.

Nolde, along with a painter such as Max Beckmann, is perhaps the last artist who could take on board the great tradition of religious painting, and work with it literally and authentically. Nolde visited that true masterpiece of religious painting, Matthias Grünewald's Isenheim Altarpiece at Colmar, in 1927. For an artist today to paint such epic religious themes would almost certainly appear a cliché. When Barnett Newman came to use the subject for his majestic *Stations of the Cross* cycle of paintings in the 1950s, it was already only possible as a pure abstraction. Later, when Francesco Clemente in the rush of the 1980s figurative painting revival made such a cycle, the subject could only be a pale pastiche. Yet there is still the question of how a painter can bring dignity back to such big themes. Within our own painting tradition in Britain, where the kitchen sink school of a more urban imagery holds sway, perhaps the question is even more acute.

...

A recent arrival in the post – the last four songs of Richard Strauss on a cassette. They make the hair on the back of your neck stand up. That magnificent fragility of age wells out of the music. There is a wonderful excess in the songs that is fully owned up to and not shied away from, just as there is in the work of Nolde. The fourth song, set to a poem by Joseph von Eichendorff, 'At Sunset', emanates warmth and by association a redness. The pure quality of colour.

To give a red its redness is to use it well so that the colour is not pictured or owned by an image but is primarily itself. Colour needs to be at a distance in order to sing true – to do its job so that it stands apart as first and foremost colour. In that sense Nolde is a real Colourist. His images are held off balance by colour. A blue sky is splitting into green and yellow before it can be rolled into the sky. The green and red of dancing gypsies makes the dance, and the yellow of sunflowers is firstly yellowness. The colour is always real colour, more powerful and distant from the diffusion of impure colour that is the world of everyday life.

So much of what colour is, is about light. The letting out or the holding back of light; luminosity and darkness. Nolde's images as such do not 'shine', but rather the colour 'shines' for them. In that sense one could say Nolde's images are at the luminous end of colour, not the colour end of that which is being illuminated.

Nolde's use of colour appears always charged and emotive. But at the same time, it also feels perfectly natural, as if it could not be any other way. Novalis, in his fragmentary novel *Heinrich von Ofterdingen*, refers to the blue flower, a symbol of paradise lost, of yearning for the unattainable.[1] Nolde worked a lot with intensely coloured flower imagery – crazy imagery, such as a knight on horseback silhouetted against overpowering giant chrysanthemums. In the flower paintings by Georgia O'Keeffe, the sexual connotations of such imagery have been usurped as being somehow negatively feminine, not of a man's world. But Nolde staked his claim also to the petal and the stamen and dared to talk about that which is also of men.

• • •

In 1913–14 Nolde and his wife Ada travelled with the German New Guinea Scientific Expedition to New Guinea via Siberia. Two places I have visited, so I feel an affinity. To travel is to find time, another time, just as much as it is to arrive at a place. And each place has its own place, or as Eduardo Galeano so eloquently put it, 'The days set out from the east and started walking'.[2] I also travelled to Siberia with scientists, Russian and Finnish, and the difference between how a scientist might work out in the field and how an artist does has probably not changed since the time of Nolde. Like an artist, the scientist seems to spend a lot of time just looking and thinking around things. Engaged in the refreshingly simple activity of observation. Walking the line between passivity and reception where, if one is lucky, insight may occur. Nolde spent more than a year on the road during his expedition. A travel timescale we have little sense of. In this period he produced numerous watercolours and drawings which subsequently fed back into his work. As did the material he made on his periodic trips to ethnographical collections.

In talking about painting, we tend to shy away from the more difficult areas of the human condition. But they are there and certainly in Nolde they are there in abundance. The paintings are often fiendishly charged with sexuality or a sense of abandon and isolation, with an overbearing malevolent vacuity or alternatively the glow of being alive. All of which pushes us back up against our own psyche. Other paintings by Nolde are imbued with an incredible wisdom. There is an expression common among painters that painting is an old man's game, meaning that it takes years to be able to paint well, almost effortlessly. Then the work takes on a silvery touch and the artist as maker appears to be absent. At this point absence can have more weight to it than what we might construe as being present.

Published in *Emil Nolde*, exh. cat., Whitechapel Art Gallery, London, 1995, pp. 18–19.

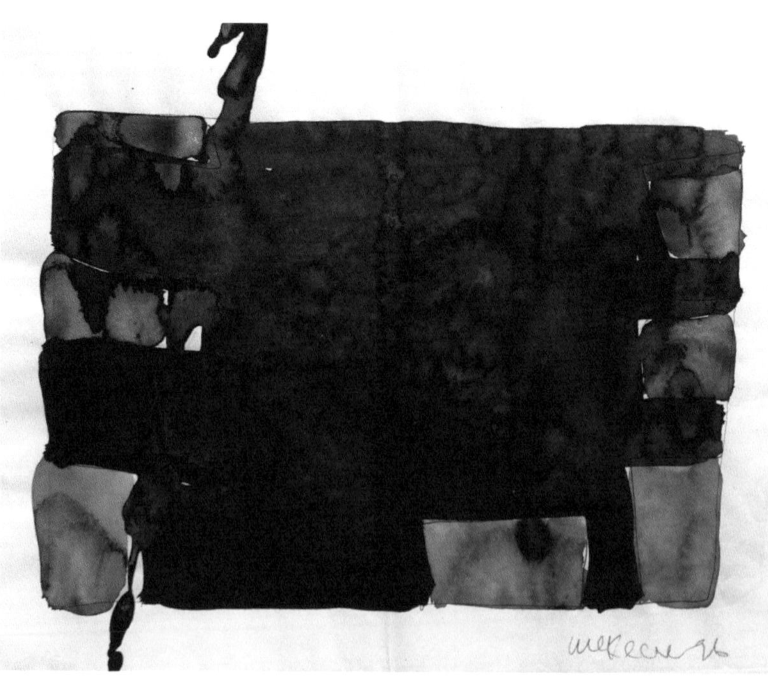

Siberia
(1996)

I am back in Magadan. Again, sitting in the kitchen of Berman's apartment. The television is placed on top of the refrigerator; the same system of stacking hot and cold found in hotel rooms in Cairns. Berman is a scientist working at the Institute for Northern Ecological Research in Magadan. The last time I was here in the summer of 1995 we travelled with a group to the tundra of the northern coastal plains: Pevek and the Chaun Estuary.

This time I am stuck in Magadan. Plans to travel on to the Kamchatka peninsula are stalled by the heavy snow. There are no flights and no one seems to have any idea when there might be one. Magadan under the snow is a different place to when I last saw it. Somehow its crude concrete apartment blocks become a kind of architecture, as they sit up square out of their footings of snow. No doubt a different place to the city Ronald Reagan referred to as the 'arsehole of the world', the hub that serviced Joseph Stalin's labour camps. On Soviet maps, even the ones the scientists had used on my visit the previous year, the locations of the camps are simply identified by anonymous numbers, No. 23, 29 or 37. Those in the slave labour force living in these camps, manually working the neighbouring mines, the raw materials of which were then often shipped out of Magadan, were themselves no more than a number with a life expectancy of perhaps two years to then be replaced by another number.

Yet here I am with time on my hands, a lot of hanging around, but that is a part, and often a good part, of travelling. For one travels to be disarmed, and sometimes in those hours, which either have their own time or no time at all, there is the opportunity to just gaze and be open. To register those small details that make up differences. For there is an edge where cultures meet and a second edge where the edges of cultures meet. This second edge – of often more fleeting and disconnected details – is sometimes more poignant and disarming. Moments can then appear to sneak around outside of time.

It is early one evening and we are going to visit a local artist. Walking there with that special shuffle of keeping in contact with the icy ground, in order to stay on one's feet. And the dull, dark, early evening light against the snow. Everything rounded and vaguely silhouetted as in a painting by Edvard Munch. A few months earlier I had seen two or three rooms of his paintings in the museum in Oslo, and in the next room a group of early icons, and was struck by their connection. Thinking then as now of how his figures with their closed, rounded half silhouettes become forms as the dark snow freezes them into ghostly icons.

Valera, the artist we are visiting, is a landscape painter. The smallish naturalistic paintings are hung on his studio walls against a background of faded floral wallpaper. Valera has made many expeditions into the mountains of eastern Siberia and he paints outdoors what he sees there. He also makes videos of the expeditions, straightforward records, no frills and without art. We spend the evening watching videos of expeditions to Kamchatka, Jack London Lake and the area around Yakutsk. It is a strange sensation to be watching videos in Magadan, and I wonder what difference it makes to watch them here as opposed to back home. Then I realise, as the night goes on, that here, things are gradually going Magadan ...

At the weekend, with Berman driving his small Lada, we head out of the city towards the surrounding foothills, where he, his colleagues and friends meet to ski. Afterwards, in what looks like a cross between a dacha and a village hall, we gather and sit down to a lavish spread of sausages, salami, salted fish and an assortment of jams and preserves with black bread and copious quantities of vodka. The atmosphere is festive except for one gentleman, perhaps about 50 years of age, who had not been out skiing, but who now sits at the table speaking to no one and only occasionally taking a slice of salami or a pickled gherkin. Later that evening, driving back into the city, I ask Berman about this silent guest. He tells me he has never seen him before and will most likely never see him again and that he is in all probability a KGB agent, checking up on what they and I are up to. Even though the Soviet Union is ostensibly now open, one cannot but feel the oppression of the past lingers on.

My flight back to Moscow is delayed at least three days because of the severe weather. During this time Berman makes regular phone calls to try to ascertain what is going on. These calls are never to the airport, if indeed such a service exists, but through a network of contacts, who then make a further call and so it goes on. As if it is a secret whispering society, which eventually comes back round to Berman's phone with news or with none. When eventually through this grapevine the news comes that the flight is on, it is a mad scramble to get out to the airport, only to then sit there for several hours until the departure is announced. At this point there is another scramble as people jockey and push to get on the plane first, as if there are more passengers than seats available. When I do eventually get to my seat, it is two thirds down the aisle in a row behind which a curtain is drawn across the aisle and seats. The plane is freezing cold with everyone still dressed in their heavy coats, hats and gloves. Halfway into the flight I get up to use the toilet and pull back the curtain behind me thinking there will also be a toilet at the rear, which is nearer. My path is blocked, the whole of the aisle and the remaining rows of seats are stacked high with frozen turkey legs piled up, without packaging or anything around them. We are literally travelling in an airborne freezer. After using the toilet at the fore of the plane I return to my seat to ponder where, in a land in which to see anything more than a forlorn seagull is to imagine the exotic, these bird legs have come from.

When during the flight the possibility of a little warmth does rear its head, it is in the form of the inflight meal service. This is not distributed via the aisle but by being passed from the front row over their heads to the next and so on. Whenever a good portion moving slowly via this overhead system appears, chicken leg on a bed of rice, it is seized upon and retained for consumption while a more miserly specimen is passed on. By the time my plate arrives in the final row, it is a modest bone wrapped in skin sitting on a bed of soggy cold rice.

Russia is vast, it is approximately an eight-hour flight from Magadan to Moscow. From Magadan to Anchorage in Alaska the flight takes half this time. Because of the time-zone difference, people in Magadan are watching on the TV, while they have breakfast, Moscow's evening soaps and vice versa in the early evening, Moscow's breakfast shows. There is something unnerving, one could say almost surreal, about this dislocation of time in which one people appear to be living part of their lives in other peoples' time. In a moment which in reality has hours ago long gone by. It is as if an uncanny time lapse occurs which suspends things, one's presence becoming an afterthought, the delayed shadowing ghost of a moment gone, unable to touch the hard stuff of reality. A voice disenfranchised unable to be heard in the present.

Revised version of 'Gradually Going Magadan', published in *Strangers in the Arctic: 'Ultima Thule' and Modernity*, Marketta Seppälä (ed.), exh. cat., FRAME, Helsinki, and Pori Art Museum, Pori, Finland, 1996, p. 190.

Thinking about Georgia O'Keeffe
(2002)

Most artists desire more exposure for their work than they get; however, a very few suffer the opposite: overexposure. Georgia O'Keeffe is one of them. She has suffered the same fate as Vincent van Gogh, of not enough actual paintings being seen, at least in Europe, overcompensated for by an excess of picture postcards, glossy coffee-table books and a popularised biography, drawing attention to certain events in the artist's life, colouring our understanding of the work.

This excessive merchandising can stop us from seeing the work; after all, we think we already know it. We become lazy, treat the words *picture* and *painting* as being synonymous and stop looking. So, it becomes easy to dismiss O'Keeffe as being kitschy and sentimental Americana. Or else, historically, just a part of early, awkward American Modernism, which of necessity had to be gone through in order to get to some real painting. Mention O'Keeffe's paintings to many people and the shutters will come down. One can almost sense the embarrassment.

Yet, in this current time of all-knowing art, when just about everything made as art is a critique of something or other, there is an urgent need for the unadorned painting, which can embarrass us. Perhaps it is important to experience a direct statement that is not afraid to address our visually underused more delicate emotions, not afraid to sense the embarrassment involved in such an encounter and which dares to ask us not to hide behind our knowingness.

• • •

Encountering O'Keeffe's paintings for the first time, one might be struck by how small the majority of them are. They are often modest in size and intimate in scale. An intimacy which is curious. O'Keeffe's habit of cropping in on the image, of holding a feature of the landscape, a bone or a flower, inside the painting, bestows on them a specific focus, a tight focus, giving the works a very particular quality of controlled compressed energy. Yet, the images do not jump out of the paintings; they do not feel constricted as many truncated paintings do. They feel comfortable and at ease with their modest dimensions. We, on the other hand, have become used to encountering and looking at large paintings. We have come to accept largeness as being synonymous with ambition in painting. The quality of size gives us that synthesis we have come to expect of a unified look and felt experience. That sensation of the painting rubbing itself against our gaze. So, where does that leave us in looking at modest-sized works? How to physically engage with a small painting, to not simply look into it, but to sense its material being, to sense and engage with that pulse?

• • •

I cannot think of many of O'Keeffe's paintings without also thinking about hands. Perhaps this is a legacy of seeing the photographs of O'Keeffe's hands by Alfred Stieglitz, but it also may be to do with the paintings themselves, with the feeling of enclosing and embracing, of wrapping up and enveloping with a tenderness and fragility that is so present in the work. The flower paintings especially seem to say something overtly about this, holding the look of the eyes and at the same time inviting the caress of the hands. The paintings solicit a tenderness to which I as painter can respond.

Franz Kline, the American Abstract Expressionist, said in an interview that, for the artist, art was not about taking but about giving. This begs the question, what is the difference between a form, a shape in a painting, that gives and one which receives?

• • •

O'Keeffe grew up in a period of great changes in painting. In Europe, such artists as Edvard Munch, Gustav Klimt and Wassily Kandinsky were pushing form and space in painting into new places. They were abandoning orthodox perspectives and folding forms in and out of the picture space, establishing new territories for the painter to paint in. At the same time, they were creating for painting a new kind of psychic arena. Painting went directly into the interior world of the artist and collided head on with the established exterior, descriptive world. The concerns in painting became as much as anything about reconciling this conflict. O'Keeffe's generation had time to reflect on the conflict and to begin to distil it. Her understated and calm paintings quietly let us into an interior world, which hovers between a particular form and the shape it may flatten into, as it folds into the canvas. Within this gap we sense the psychic body of the painting.

...

The form, the shape, the line, there is always the reduction back to a fragile edge: an edge which, although precise and emphatic, is paradoxically only ever just there. It is a brittle edge, parched and dry like the desert. Ironically, O'Keeffe, who placed a strong emphasis on the drawing in a painting, spent much of her life in the circle of photographers. Here, she was confronted with a very different sensibility and aesthetic to that of painting, for the photograph, contrary to the drawing, finds line by contrast, the shadow and the silhouette. Much of photography at the beginning of the twentieth century touched on this area of light, the silhouette and its aura, the ectoplasmic nature of the body and the candescent light emanating from it. This also became an issue in painting; one has only to think of Munch. O'Keeffe, as well, made significant use of the silhouette, most blatantly in the city nightscapes and the 'cross' paintings. Less directly perhaps in other works, although they also often have a clear sense of form, be it a skull, a doorway or a hillside being silhouetted, set against a clean background. With O'Keeffe, such silhouettes have a dryness and compactness, a stillness suggesting nothing will ever move again, like a bleached boulder fixed in a bed of sand. Or, as William Carlos Williams would say, 'the world of actions is a world of stones'.[1]

One could call this quality of stillness in O'Keeffe's paintings *composure*. For reducing to, holding and fixing, that quintessential moment of the meeting of form and content would seem to be one of the major concerns in her work. Yet, this reduction is not a synthetic reduction as, say, in Minimalism, for O'Keeffe is not afraid of her subject matter; her forms stay complex and real. Rather, this reduction, which is perhaps better understood as a stilling or a tuning of the image to its point of absolute self-composure, is where something definitely is present, but equally is not. To a moment of absolute absence yet presence, where absence becomes more weighted than presence, which only painting seems able to actually achieve. The photograph constantly longs for this state; one can in some photographs almost sense the image aching for this composure, but at the threshold the photograph always hesitates. For the time of the photograph can never be experienced and actually found like the time of the painting. Each and every painting finds its time, another time, its own time.

Yet O'Keeffe's contact with the photograph pervaded all of her work: how she cropped her images tightly, so that they appear sometimes extracted, like that first moment of looking through the viewfinder of a camera. Even the brittle, drawn line in the paintings, precise but acutely vulnerable, was probably a painter's reaction to the merciless grain of the photograph, which aims to deny the line, to push everything evenly and uniformly back into the defused blur of the photograph's emulsion paper.

...

In the book *Georgia O'Keeffe: Some Memories of Drawing*, the artist speaks of one work as being about a headache and another as being about 'well maybe a kiss ...'.[2] O'Keeffe's imagery is on the surface rarely ambiguous and never ambivalent. The paintings, especially after her discovery of New Mexico, are lean and pared down. The desert, like the northern landscape, seems to engender a natural visual poverty, a reduction down to basics in a good sense. One of the reasons the paintings are so disarming and beguiling is because they are so evidently what they are.

A window, a doorway, the hole through a pelvic girdle or two black centres in oriental poppies, the paintings are full of holes. In painting a painting, the artist takes up that age-old challenge of applying the simple means of image-making in order to cross the threshold from the blank canvas into another space. Where he or she lands becomes the painting. In crossing the threshold and entering the painting, there are things that are revealed to us, and some things that perhaps are revealed to no one. Part of the painting's task is to prevent us from getting to know too much.

• • •

A particular painting by O'Keeffe I feel connected to is *The Lawrence Tree*, the Indian red of the trunk and upper branches spreading up and out like tentacles against a deep-brown canopy of foliage silhouetted against a white-flecked blue night sky. Like the dream of the worms, as E. M. Cioran would say.[3] Anyone who has been to New Mexico knows that insatiable desire to lie down, look up and gaze, and then sleep *inside* the night sky. Living in northern Europe, where the night sky is usually shrouded, we are not used to the horizon being so open and expansive, pulsating with stars, thousands and thousands of them, against pure blue. The sky then becomes something full bodied within the world in which we live, rather than a vague atmosphere.

Travelling through New Mexico, one is struck by how true O'Keeffe's colour sense was to the actual landscape. The desert reveals those weird combinations of yellows, pinks, purples and greys that we see in her paintings. Those strange natural forms, the hills and arroyos, which she cropped out and made into paintings, are precise features in an otherwise expansive open landscape. They give the desert an architecture, a connection back to the body and a particular sense of place, which seems to have become an increasing concern for O'Keeffe the longer she worked there.

• • •

What are we to make of an enlarged, slightly cropped detail of a flower? As an image in painting, the flower has had a chequered history, never aspiring to the still-life status of the glass or even a bowl of fruit. It was always deemed decorative or the consequence of suppressed sexual longings. In the nineteenth century such intrepid explorers as the British-born Marianne North spent years travelling the world painting flowers in all their exotic variety. The flower was then neutral territory, unoccupied within the domain of the male-dominated art world. But North's paintings have come to be seen as Victoriana, their significance ignored and recognised only by the sheer number painted and her insistence they be kept together and housed in a specially commissioned gallery at Kew Gardens in London. However, her travels and painting reflected one woman's ambition to leave behind the constraints of Victorian England, not primarily an encounter with painting. It took the likes of Claude Monet and Gustav Klimt to subsequently bring the flower fully into the arena of painting, Monet turning it into a field to literally paint in, Klimt ornamenting the human body with it, physically and emotionally. Both, holding flowers, spread their muscular arms out as far as they could go, turning the flower into an expansive field for painting. What is significant about O'Keeffe's flower paintings is that she closed in on the flower, understanding its intimacy, the delicacy of actually looking into and through it. She was not afraid of touching the petal and the stamen and all that implied. O'Keeffe tried to make the flower, the painting, transparent, to light it from the inside. William Blake in his epic poem *Jerusalem* speaks of 'the limits of opacity', as if to suggest that the act of revealing was an inevitability of life, despite all attempts to obscure or cover up.[4] How in seeking the inner life of a form in its transparency it was possible to disclose another state. To find this fragile other state, where form is resolved, clean and clear, yet open and yielding, is still a challenge in painting.

• • •

The relationship between the materiality of things and light would seem central to the quality of O'Keeffe's paintings. They are always suffused with a clear pristine light, which would appear to caress the forms into being. It is a cleansing light, hinting at being all-pervading, as if to say, imagine a world in which there is only omnipresent light, in which everything, even thought itself, is mingled with the same intense light. It is a white light. For whiteness carries the light into O'Keeffe's paintings and sometimes it sticks and becomes colour. However, white as a colour is always furtive, anxious and eager to move away before one gets too close. If other colours can be held still and even suggest a sense of form or place, white remains abstract, suggesting only a sense of space. Given a chance, it will always drift away.

• • •

Clouds, ladders, a pelvic bone, even a road, the forms in O'Keeffe's paintings are always ascending, invariably floating, for floating is a way of resisting the horizontal without asserting the vertical. The French religious thinker Simone Weil believed that two forces rule the universe: light and gravity.[5] The one elevating, the other rooting us back to the ground, or as Bob Dylan would say, 'It's gravity which pulled us down and destiny which broke us apart'.[6] All painting acquiesces to one or the other of these polarities, to a sense of either elation or of being rooted. The impetus behind perhaps all painting is the desire to rise above the mundane condition, compromised by a need to hold onto and define the material world. Painting ceaselessly reflects this conflict.

'Thinking about Georgia O'Keeffe', published in *Louisiana Revy*, Louisiana Museum of Modern Art, Humlebæk, 42, no. 2, February 2002, pp. 26–29.

For Kehnet Nielsen – In Praise of Painting
(2002)

Sometimes when the daylight is fading in the studio with the onset of night and the paintings are receding into silhouettes, becoming mere ghosts, I know their place. At the same moment I also know where I stand in the world. I sense, Kehnet, that it is the same for you, and I wonder about the night and about light and that potent moment, and what that means for you. I do not want to ask, because I know such questions are not, as such, questions for the painter, but rather are simply an intimate part of what it is to actually paint a painting. Yet, the question is still there, and when I look at your work I am drawn towards a thinking stemming from the paintings themselves.

'Painting comes out of darkness', Kehnet Nielsen has said.[1] The painter either paints into the light or paints towards the night; these are the two options available to him. It is a curious anomaly that for a country such as Denmark, indeed, perhaps for the whole of Scandinavia, with its omnipresent light, so many of its good painters should withhold the light. Hold it back as if its full glare would be too much for the eye to take. Vilhelm Hammershøi certainly did not want to let it out. Edvard Munch squeezed it into a battery-charged glow and Asger Jorn crushed it literally inside colour. More recently, for Per Kirkeby light was like glacial meltwater, clouded and fogged. It is as if, for northern painters, too much pure light cannot be borne, the summer's night and the winter daylight are all that can be tolerated.

When I look at Nielsen's paintings, I think of James McNeill Whistler, another painter who also held in the light. I think of the two incredible milky-grey full-length portraits that hang in the Frick Collection in New York and I think of Nielsen's denial of the possibility of pure white. The way he always turns it off, pushes it over another colour, so that it is unequivocally clear it has been used, is being used. For Nielsen, paint or colour cannot be pure; rather, they have lived a life to become the painting. Equally, in dark paintings, such as Whistler's *Nocturnes*, the paint surface has to be physically punctured to let the light out, for the light is sealed off, trapped behind the surface of the painting. No longer available to us, it must find, and we must sense, whatever cracks and gaps there are in the paint surface in order for the light to make its presence felt.

On the wall of a friend's house is a framed text from a daily newspaper. It reads: 'In the absence of light it is possible to create the brightest images within oneself'. Within oneself – I sense, Kehnet, that you do not want to say too much in your paintings and that, if possible, you would rather say very little. Perhaps you even strive to say nothing. For one so easily forgets in this crazy modern world of brash media and overselling that a painting's role may be to say nothing at all, but simply to eloquently be.

Paint is never out of focus; it is always first and foremost the material stuff that it is: paint. A blob of paint is just that, a blob of paint. The situation only begins to get more complicated when the transition occurs from paint to painting. Reflecting upon Nielsen's paintings I am drawn to think of a fellow countryman of mine, John Constable, with whom I know Nielsen feels an affinity. Constable's handling of paint was direct and lumpy. He had none of the virtuosity or smoothness of handling that one finds sometimes in, say, his contemporary J. M. W. Turner. If Turner pushed paint towards a feeling of the hermetically smooth surface, as the history of the aesthetics of painting dictated, then Constable, like Gustave Courbet, presented the antithesis, painting as a consequence of the honest, awkward mark. The dilemma for the painter then becomes how to hold onto such an obdurate mark and the surface of the painting, acknowledge it for what it is, yet move beyond it. Clyfford Still, an artist who resolutely declared paint as foremost paint, said, 'I never wanted colour to be colour, I never wanted texture to be texture, or image to be shapes. I wanted them all to fuse into a living spirit'.[2]

In relationship to this obdurate mark, I wonder, Kehnet, if there is what I can best describe as an underlying uneasiness in your paintings, and that it is somehow unavoidable? All painters need a problem to paint and good painters tend to have good problems. Part of the creative process is in turning what appears negative into something positive, squaring the implicit conflict. Without that underlying struggle painting becomes merely academic and mannered. Paul Cézanne's work is suffused with a kind of clumsiness, a stumbling to find the image in paint. One senses that painting was never easy for him. This is partly the quality we are responding to in looking at the work, for we recognise and acknowledge our own awkwardness. At the other extreme, Pablo Picasso's virtuosity and speed of working can raise doubts, at least for me, as sometimes it looks too easy, or when there is clumsiness there, this can appear contrived, theatrical.

Constable and Courbet were both naturally awkward painters. Perhaps on the one hand this had to do with the actual physical problem of putting paint onto the canvas, but on the other hand it also had to do with what Yves Klein referred to as the tyranny of the paintbrush – the problem of how to avoid the clichéd, the ubiquitous brush mark, or the paint mark as signature.[3] Certainly in the twentieth century these things have been significant issues for painting. Jackson Pollock poured and dripped his way out of the problem. Josef Albers painted all of his *Homage to the Square* paintings meticulously with a small palette knife, in order to avoid the look of the brushed mark entering his work.

I get the feeling, Kehnet, that you also want to paint a painting that refutes the brush mark, a painting in which the paint must find another way of getting itself onto the surface of the painting. Yet, and it is an important yet, you want the painting to be emphatically organically made, to be in no way synthetic. All of those prods and jabs that tentatively grope towards the painting must be clearly present. The painting has to hold all of these uncertainties within it. Whether they are buried under the surface or scraped off does not matter, they must still be there, a part of what the painting is. For they give the painting the quality that Still referred to as 'a living spirit'.

In an essay published in a catalogue accompanying an exhibition of Nielsen's paintings, referring to an observation made by Philip Guston, Paul Erik Tojner writes about gathering and spreading.[4] About how painters either gather in their work, or else how they spread things out. He is right; indeed they do. I certainly know that I am a gatherer. I have even written about gathering symmetries like eggs in a basket and thought of titling paintings Gatherings. Nielsen, on the other hand, is a spreader. Of course, it is only natural that he should be a spreader, after all he trained and worked for some years as a glazier. Trapping a sheet of glass within a frame and then edging it in with putty was his trade. He moved constantly across from one edge to the other and back again. So, when Nielsen took up painting, it was inevitable (and in that sense Nielsen is a natural, there is no artifice) that the relationship between the surface of the painting and the edge should be critical. For his paintings spread constantly from edge to edge and, like the trapped sheet of glass, they seal off one side of something from the other. They close us off and as much as anything they are about that closure. Establishing another space, another place beyond where we stand, where what we think we see cannot be heard and we also are unheard. Mute, we can only look back.

For something, anything, to spread it must first have been in a gathered state, concentrated. Equally, for something to be gathered together, it must first have been spread out. The two states are part and parcel of the same conundrum. But what is it that is being gathered or spread? Certainly in painting it is not just the material substance that is the paint itself. Neither is it simply the formal process of image-making, of tightening up the image or pulling it apart, although this is how the painting, the image pictured, may appear. For the look of a painting is one thing, but the painting's full embodiment is another. It is far more fundamental. This embodiment, either gathered or spreading, is a reflection of the way the painter understands, sees and grasps the world and begins to make sense of it. This is not something concrete, tangible; instead, it is made up of abstractions, made up of intuitions, instincts, feelings and insights. It is about abstractions and that is why, ultimately, the painting is abstract. It can be no other way.

Published in *Kehnet Nielsen, Saudade*, Karsten Ohrt and Thorsten Sadowsky (eds), exh. cat., Kunsthallen Brandts Klædefabrik, Odense, 2003, pp. 11–15; edited version reprinted in *Kehnet Nielsen, Painting Out of Time 1980–2011*, Ove Mogensen (ed.), exh. cat., Museum Sønderjylland, Kunstmuseet i Tønder, 2011, pp. 161–9.

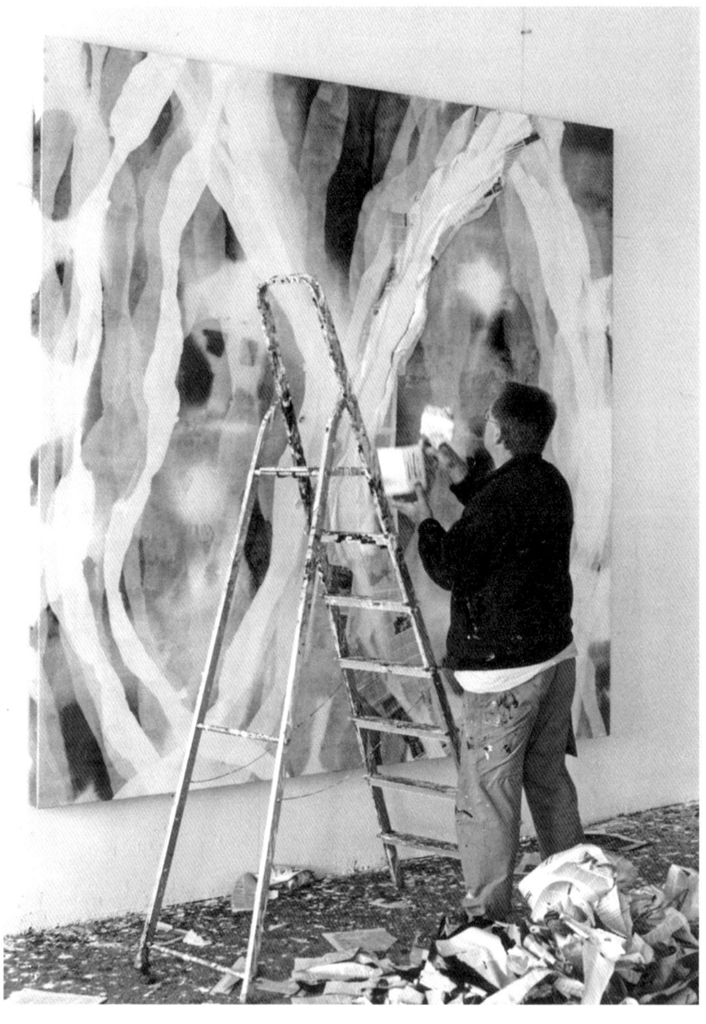

Talking Painting
(2004)

As a painter invited to talk to students about their work in the painting department of any art school in Britain, one is expected to have a critical perspective on more or less anything that is being made by students. One is expected to have a liberal eye and ear, when frequently the work has little to do with painting. In engaging with students in such a way, we enter into a kind of 'art speak' whereby everything is given equal status, where boundaries become confused and any clear reference to painting becomes just another facet of a vague, generalised discussion about art. As such, there is little tight or focused debate concerning painting itself. Because of this tendency, perhaps it is sometimes a good idea to remind ourselves that the history of European art is first and foremost a history of painting and its counterpart, sculpture: these two orthodoxies. We should also keep in mind that when push comes to shove, most contemporary art will validate itself through these orthodoxies and by conspicuous references to them, as much as it may appear and claim to be radically different. Yet in this erudition it frequently deflects from, obscures, what is the core of painting, which is to be a statement unto itself, that is, first and foremost a painting.

In his book of critical writings, *Testaments Betrayed*, the Czech novelist Milan Kundera speaks about how we no longer as a culture go back to, or deal with, original material, but rather revert to commentary and interpretation as our means of understanding. With reference to Franz Kafka, Kundera says:

> There is only one way to understand Kafka's novels; to read them as novels. Rather than searching the character K for a portrait of the author, and K's words for a mysterious coded message; to pay careful attention to the behaviour of the characters, their remarks, their thoughts, and try to imagine them before your eyes.[1]

'Before your eyes'; paintings stand still before our eyes. In looking at paintings the task is not to understand them, nor to read meaning into them, but to accept them as experience, to 'be' with them and to begin from there.

Our society and our culture are increasingly predicated on the supposedly known. We now comment on everything; very little is left unsaid. Knowing something or someone has become what we value, almost our first currency. We barter our way through life with it in one form or another. The mystery of the unknown, on the other hand, is now more or less considered worthless. Yet, attempting to at least familiarise ourselves with those things we cannot know is perhaps one of the great freedoms still available to us.

In painting a painting one does not set out to paint what one knows but rather tries to touch those things that one does not know and perhaps cannot be known. Implicit in the unknown, and what we cannot know about paintings, is a stillness and a silence. Our lives are now flooded with images that remorselessly bombard us with what we 'should' know, and which steal our time. Perhaps one of the things that paintings can do for us, if we are prepared to be still in front of them, is to give us back our own sense of time and the independence which goes with it.

Published in Ian McKeever, *In Praise of Painting: Three Essays*, Michael Tucker (ed. and introduction), Centre for Contemporary Visual Arts, University of Brighton, 2005, pp. 60–2.

Light

(2004)

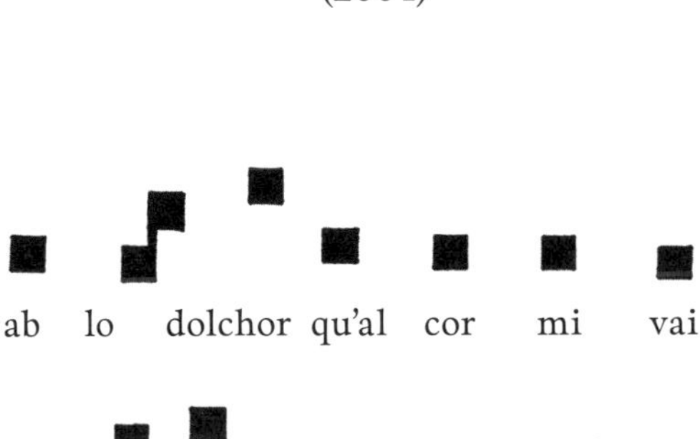

AB LO DOLCHOR QU'AL COR MI VAI

that the body of light come forth
from the body of fire

The last time I visited the Louvre, I spent the afternoon in the very long gallery that houses the Italian paintings. It begins with the Duecento and Trecento painters such as Duccio, Giotto and Simone Martini and continues chronologically up to the seventeenth century. What struck me, as I walked up and down this history of painting, was how much it was about fading light, and that the history of painting is also a history of the loss of light. For slowly but surely, from the omnipresent intensity of divine light in early Byzantine painting, which preceded the emergence of Italian painting, to the obscuring chiaroscuro of such painters as Titian and Caravaggio, the light is squeezed out of painting to become finally a mere candle flicker. A world once full of light becomes a world of shadows. When light does eventually re-emerge, as intense light, it is in another country, France, in the nineteenth century. However, by then the light of God has been replaced by the prosaic light of day.

In the tradition of the Byzantine icon, the icon lives in a world of light, an absolute light. This is paradoxical, in that the icon knows or acknowledges no source of light, either internal or external, yet there is light. Icon painting considers light as something not external to objects, nor as belonging to some primordial substance such as the sun. Rather, iconic light establishes and builds things itself. In that sense the icon is executed upon light. It is as if we and the world we inhabit were to be actually made of light. Vincent van Gogh alluded to this quality when he said, 'I want to paint men and women with that something of the eternal, which the halo used to symbolise, and which we seek to convey by the actual radiance and vibration of our colour'.[1] Robert Grosseteste, the thirteenth-century Bishop of Lincoln, in his treatise *De Luce*,[2] said more about this when he wrote of light being the first corporeal form, that light was the maker of matter, just as the American architect Louis Kahn did, when he wrote, 'I sense Light as the giver of all presences, and material as spent light'.[3] For Kahn, material is potentially lightless, becoming the shadow of light. We could say that, as the material world of today has become more 'what matters', the need to form it, give it shape and make it visible has necessitated that we withhold more and more light. As if, paradoxically, the more we know and have, the less light there remains to illuminate anything. The writer William Burroughs envisaged a world where the ceaseless taking of photographs – the quick click of the camera – is stealing each time a piece of light: in the end, all natural light will have gone.[4] We will have consumed it all and will be living in perpetual darkness. Our only means of illumination, what artificial light we can conjure, will be thrown back on the millions and millions of photographs that congest our lives and have become the only means by which we view the world, photographs which have indeed become our world view.

Painters either paint towards the light or they paint towards the night. There will be either more light, or there will be less. Johannes Vermeer was a painter who seemed to insist that light infuse the human spirit. We can palpably sense its increasing emergence; it glows. In his work, the light source is never revealed; it is always hidden yet it permeates everything. In that sense, his paintings connect to the tradition of the early Italian painters and the Byzantine icon; to the light of being rather than the light of day, where objects are never seen in shadow but are fully illuminated by whatever light there is. Every nook and cranny are somehow lit and greys never find a place, but everything remains in full colour. Imagine a world of omnipresent light, of no gradations, how would we see and measure ourselves, how would we make images of ourselves? We are blinded by too much light, just as we are by too little.

If Vermeer painted towards the light, then an artist who painted towards the night was the Dane Vilhelm Hammershøi. Like Vermeer, Hammershøi was a painter of the human figure as stilled life. However, rather than finding that moment of potentially omnipresent light, he squeezed out of the painting all the light he possibly could, pushing all colours into greys and reminding us of Ludwig Wittgenstein's observation that 'Grey is not poorly illuminated white'.[5] In Hammershøi's work light recedes and we face the possibility there will not be more. In looking at his work one gets that same sensation as when sitting in the studio at dusk looking at a painting with the light fading; that point at which colour slowly goes out of the work, detail becomes lost and one form is silhouetted against another. Then one experiences paintings in another way, they become soft, lose colour, but at the same time take on another definition. It is as if they become shadows of themselves, laying one shadow on top of another until eventually all is lost in darkness.

The Swedish poet Gunnar Ekelöf sensed this moment of building dark upon dark when he wrote:

> It is the dark, which contains all the colours
> Not the light
> [...]
> What else are colours but shadows
> Or shades of light?
> Lay colours on top of each other and you get black
> The purest vision
> Is pure shadow
> The opposite of light.[6]

Perhaps for some Scandinavian painters the full light of the sun is more than they can take. This quality of turning inwards away from the light, instead of towards it, is probably one of the qualities that distinguishes the northern Romantic tradition from its southern

Classical counterpart. From the safe interior of a 'lived-in' space, looking out through the window to a clear light-filled vista, the Classical world can be idealised. It can be both proportioned and apportioned and finally made into a system. While for the Romantic painter, always shying away from the fullness of day and looking into the half-light of his interior personal space, such distance and distinction from the world around him are unrealistic: he can never see beyond himself. More than anyone, the Norwegian painter Edvard Munch captured the restlessness of the long, sleepless northern summer nights, of daylight followed by more light, another kind of light, stealing the night. For Munch, light was the fading northern glow, a fading phosphorescence that seemed to envelope everything in an electric aura. His figures at times appear charged like batteries. It is as if they were electric.

In the Munch Museum in Oslo is a small ink drawing entitled *Professor Jacobson electrifies the famous painter, Munch*, with the added inscription, 'and induces male positive and female negative power in his enfeebled brain'. The drawing depicts the seated, exhausted artist framed on one side by a table supporting a battery and chemical flask. On the other side the doctor is mopping Munch's brow; at the doctor's elbow, a nurse awaits with electrical terminals in hand. Rolf E. Stenersen, who was a friend of the artist, recalls in his book *Close-up of a Genius* the time when Munch called him over to his house to replace an electrical plug that had accidentally come out of its socket.[7] Apparently, the artist had a deep-rooted fear of electricity, which is understandable given that he was exposed to electric shock treatment, and yet no other painter in the twentieth century has painted so much that appears to be electrically charged and radiates such static. His figures frequently seem to hum and hover as if surrounded by an energy field, a kind of aura, like poor Walt in Paul Auster's book *Mr Vertigo*, who, having spent years mastering the skill of levitation, is then confounded by the problem of how to move laterally once up there.[8] Equally, Munch's figures often appear to have mastered the first lesson, but then like Walt are stuck in limbo, heating up while waiting for another external force to move them on.

The relationship between light and heat, light and energy, is intriguing. I have always found it somehow surprising that every place on the surface of the earth receives the same number of daylight hours in a year. It is only that they are distributed differently. For the equator it is twelve hours of daylight and twelve hours of darkness; for somewhere on the Arctic Circle it is midnight sun in summer and long dark days in the winter. However, this difference is not only one of the qualities of light, but also of heat and potential energy.

> 'Whoever is near me is near fire'
> Psalm 88

In the watercolour *Capaneus the Blasphemer* from William Blake's version of Dante Alighieri's *The Divine Comedy*, Capaneus is being struck by lightning for defying the god Zeus. Blake was able to impart his figures with a monumental stone-like quality. They are statuesque, yet at the same time appear to have a restless inner life force. Blake did not take his models from life but from casts of Classical sculptures and brought them back to life in the work process as if they were living stone. He imbued his stony figures with an inner heat, whereby at times they feel red hot. Blake, of course, was working before the harnessing of electricity, and perhaps because of this, the impulse to activate the figure seems much more elemental. Lightning, fire and water all appear to be integral parts of the primal ooze from which he conjured life into being, as if some form of alchemical force were needed to convert stone to blood. Often Blake's figures remind me of the 'Mud Men' in the Flash Gordon films I used to see as a boy at the Saturday morning film matinees. Men who mutated between rock and flesh, emerging, only to disappear back into the rock face without sound or trace at the first sign of any intruder.

For Blake, light and heat seem synonymous. There is an elemental quality to his work, which constantly pushes and pulls between the transience of forms and potential energies, between an inner energy and an outer force. It is a world where light and heat constantly commingle and where shadows appear to have little time to settle. What Blake seemed to be striving for was a world without shadows, a universe fully revealed. But unlike the light of the icon, or the paintings of Vermeer imbuing a world with unity and stillness, with omnipresent light, Blake's sense of light is trapped in the restless heat of forms, and to find release it must force its way out. It is a light that we sense as contained heat, an animal heat, and as such every living thing must find its own primordial glow. All must offer their own suppressed heat to be amplified to bring light into the world.

I have always liked Rudolf Steiner's insight that light has the nature of thought, darkness that of will.[9] In Blake one senses this duality, the recognition that perhaps sometimes things have to be willed into being, and that in the resulting heat, light will be found.

• • •

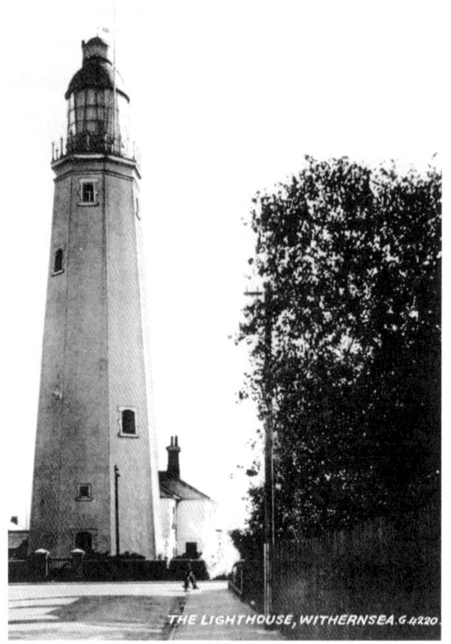

It sits at the end of the road. From the house I cannot see it. As I head down North Road and approach Arthur Street, where the road straightens out it comes into full view. The road seems longer than it probably is, the lighthouse sitting at the far end like a guardian giving a weight to one's step the closer one gets. When Roger Fry asked Virginia Woolf of the significance of the lighthouse in her novel

To the Lighthouse, she gave him short shrift. 'I meant nothing by the lighthouse, one has to have a central line in the middle of a book to hold the design together'.[10] The spine of a book, the centre fold, the book's pivot, as one turns from page to page. The white sentinel as I turned daily upon meeting it, left to go into the town centre and right to the school. From the house towards the light; to house the light. Light's capacity to become an architecture, to appear solid in the world. To find the inner light in a painting. Not picture its presence; instead to make it an emanation from within, 'that the body of light come forth ... And that your eyes come to the surface'.[11] A painting's insistent surface, the plane to which it repeatedly pulls back, on which as if by a miracle the light can be housed.

The lighthouse rises 39 m above the ground, its brick and concrete hexagonal construction sheathed in bright white, towering up above the squat buildings that surround it. Built inland in 1892 to avoid the instability of the shifting sands were it located out at sea, it has weathered nature's trials and tribulations with greater dignity than did the short-lived pier. All that remains now of this magnificent folly is the twin tower entrance, known locally as Pier Tower, which stands with its crenelated profile, set against an open sky looking more like a cut-out from the neighbouring funfair slightly further along the promenade than any pretence of authenticity. The pier itself has long succumbed to the battering of waves, storms and the sea's unrelenting and unforgiving moods. In its heyday, it stretched out 365 m into the open sea, a magnet for the tourists, which one can see from old photographs frequented the town, to among other things walk on the stretch of wooden planking, suspended above the murmurings of the sea below. Absorbing once out at the pier end, even if only fleetingly before they turned back to face the reassuring land, the magnificent light sky and sea conjured up between them, which verged on the primordial. A light sometimes so intense and tangible one felt one could grab a chunk of it in the hand and put it in one's pocket, taking it home to then release into the more mundane air of one's daily life, watching as it began to glow and hover before dispersing into a million luminescent flickers and then be gone. Pockets of light. As a child one's trouser pockets were either full or half-empty, the sea never far away a seemingly infinite source of replenishment. Even with the most heavily leaden skies solid with cloud and the sea black, foreboding, a tiny particle of light would find its way into an empty corner of a pocket, and accompany one on the way home.

It is 144 steep spiralling steps up the lighthouse to then enter the lamp room, in the centre of which sits the lens. Weighing 3 tons, its multifaceted surface is a crystalline cylinder of infinite mirrors, belying its weight as it floats on its bed of mercury. It turns almost frictionlessly, as its once wind-up mechanism, now motorised, keeps its regular rotations alive. The lantern's bulb generates the light, all 800,000 candle power, which is focused into a beam through the lens and is said to have a range of 27 km. In the evenings as I lay in bed as a child, this shaft of light would dance across the bedroom wall, its regular rhythm seeping into me as did the rhythm of the neighbouring sea, and I would imagine a pathway of brilliantly burning candles, all 800,000 of them, as inviting as Dorothy's yellow brick road along which, if only in my dreams, I could venture and roam.

Published in part in Ian McKeever, *In Praise of Painting: Three Essays*, Michael Tucker (ed. and introduction), Centre for Contemporary Visual Arts, University of Brighton, 2005, pp. 62–6.

Black
(2004)

Sometime in the mid-1970s the French philosopher Michel Foucault signed an agreement with his publisher to write a book entitled 'The Black and the Surface', a project that was never realised. Such a tantalising phrase for the painter, 'the black and the surface', summoning up, as it does, both the limitations and all that is possible with the painted surface. For the painter must find a way into the surface, go beyond picturing, which paradoxically both submits to the surface and denies it, and turn blackness, the blind alley of looking, into another way of seeing.

In his *Letters on Cézanne*, Rainer Maria Rilke threads the colour black through the text like a leitmotif.[1] As such, it never gets heavy or black as mood but remains a living part of painting. The reddish-black of Cézanne's wine bottles, the mirror-black of Francesco Guardi and the effect of a light being switched off in Edouard Manet: black can take on positive qualities we rarely ascribe to it. In that sense paintings are one of the few areas in which black can actively live.

Black as a colour gets fat fast, it takes on a body quickly and absorbing that body into itself it soon becomes opaque. Leave black transparent and it is no longer black. Stand close to a large black painting, as opposed to a white one, and it feels like the difference between standing close to a brick wall or a high hedge. One will yield, the other not. White is never so white that we cannot see into it, but black can be so black that we cannot see out of it. When treated as a colour instead of its opposite, black is somehow always more than the sum of the other colours.

However, it is difficult to see pure black, just as it is difficult to see pure white; both are always tinged. When lit, both will deflect away from certitude. Their absoluteness lies more in the mind than in any intimations of black and white we might see. In the black-stockinged legs in Giovanni Battista Moroni's *Portrait of a Gentleman* in the National Gallery, London, or the black of a Robert Motherwell painting from the *Elegies to the Spanish Republic* series, the colour black moves easily and at times imperceptibly between material and metaphor. In his own writings Motherwell referred to the unexpected contradictory natures of black and white as pigments, which any painter knows well.[2] Pick up a full can of black and it is far lighter in weight than all the other colours; pick up a can of titanium white and it is significantly heavier. For the painter, black begins light, taking on another heavier sense of weight as it becomes extended by use.

Kurt Kocherscheidt: Between the Wall and the Floor
(2004)

Sometime in about 1988, while browsing around a bookshop I came across a small publication concerning the influence of Romanian wooden church architecture on the sculpture of Constantin Brâncuși. The next day, without reading it, I posted the book to Kurt Kocherscheidt. A few days later he called me and during our conversation asked why I had sent it to him. I cannot remember the reply, but it was brief, and we quickly returned to talking about other things. Although when we met, Kocherscheidt and I spoke often about painting, that brief exchange on the telephone alluding to his own concern with sculpture was the only time we ever spoke about the matter. I always sensed that for him the wooden sculptural works were part of a private dialogue with himself as a painter, and that I should leave it as such.

I understand very little about sculpture; I never know how to come to it. With paintings I know where I stand. I like the relationship between a painting's sense of frontality and my own peculiar frontality. Through that physical relationship of looking at, of being in front of a painting, I can sense my own being. Stepping backwards or moving forwards to look, shifting to the left or the right, I am always aware that the painting and I must at some point face each other: the painting and I must eventually come face to face. Sculpture, however, instead of focusing me leads me to disorientation. In circling a sculpture, I too begin to circle around myself and more often than not rather than finding focus and composure, I wander away from myself. Sculpture makes me restless. Paintings on the other hand give me a sense of my own body, give me back my body. Sculpture, and here I should say not all but most, would seem to steal it away from me.

It has often occurred to me in looking at paintings and sculpture that there are painters who think like sculptors and sculptors who think like painters; that there are sculptors who think flat, so to speak, but whose work comes out three-dimensionally. Here, I might recall some of Anthony Caro's seminal works of the 1960s, such as *Early One Morning* (1962) or *Yellow Swing* (1966), sculptures which have specific viewing points. Equally, there are painters whose work struggles constantly towards three-dimensionality. This is not the pictorial depiction of space we normally associate with image-making, but rather the artist would aspire to and will into being a real space for painting, one which is so indelibly connected to the forms painted that it can be no other way. Kocherscheidt willed such a space for painting. His paintings were an endless struggle to find and to hold onto such a space. It was therefore natural that he should begin to see and then make those implicit forms in his paintings literally three-dimensional. Yet there is, as anyone who attempts to paint such 'concreteness' will tell you, a strange edge here, for the painting will remain what Max Kozloff identified as being 'metamorphic'.[1] It will always be fictive, a flat surface in need of being seen in another way in order to be realised. It is partially this illusiveness which beguiles the painter, in that he paints forms and space within the fictive confines of the picture plane, while holding onto the belief that it might just conceivably become a 'real' space. For the painter this uncertainty gives any notion of space an edge of potential danger. Space is held in a tentative and at times fragile balance whereby at any moment it could inexplicably revert back to the deadening flatness of the canvas or alternatively evaporate into nothing. All could be lost. Sculpture, conversely, is a 'volumetric entity' occupying a fixed space; it will begin by being physically present and the sculptor starts with this assurance.

So, when the painter crosses the threshold from depicted form and space into the real world of actual concrete form and space, how do we also negotiate that transition? How do we connect to that selfless act of faith? Or is it an act of transgression, which the painter was forced to undertake, forced to invite as a sudden violent rupture: the point when form is actually cut out, loses its ambiguity and becomes concrete in the world? In essence, this is what Kocherscheidt did: he cut out the forms already explicit in his paintings and began to make them materialise in the world. He took the courageous step to challenge his own language of painting to be capable of living in, and of being redeemable within, the prosaic and banal world of the concrete object.

When I first got to know Kocherscheidt in the early 1970s, we both had studios at St Katharine Docks in east London. And we were both tentatively groping towards a language for painting. He, the debonair European, at ease in a large city; I, the young naive man from the countryside, in awe of all around me. Yet, already during this period he was working on cut-outs: works built up from cartoon characters and organic forms cut out of thin sheets of plywood, which were then drawn upon and lastly arranged like silhouettes on a narrow theatrical stage. For many years I had one such profile leaning against the studio window. During that period Kocherscheidt enthused about comics, particularly the unusual and quite rare kind that could be read both ways round. Turn the first half of the narrative upside down and with miraculous incredulity the characters and story line could be continued the other way up. The ambiguity of the image, its capacity to jump onto another level, was already something he was immensely curious about; a concern which permeated all of his subsequent work. Although the jump into the large wooden cut-outs of *Englische Acte* and *Felder* appears now radical and unexpected, the cut-out had been something that had underpinned the formative years of his work in London.

In working on a painting, the painter takes the flat but yielding surface of the canvas and, for want of a better expression, tries to make the forms he creates in the painting 'body-forth'; to make the emphatically flat surface of the canvas appear to have form, appear to have a real body. Ludwig Wittgenstein in *Remarks on Colour* makes the distinction between two kinds of colour: the colour on the surface of things, as paint is, and colour that goes right through things, as orange colours a carrot. For the painter it is clear he is working with paint, surface colour. However, for the sculptor things are different. For colour can go right through the material, can be the material out of which the sculpture is made, or it can sit simply on the surface. That the sculptor should consciously ornament a material, be it wood, metal or stone, with colour is to add to the work another element, another shape, which brings about a shift in our understanding of it.

In an article written in the 1940s David Smith refers to the sculptor's potential use of colour, how historically colour 'had been an important factor in the best periods of the past. Yet for centuries, bronze had been dead dark, and marble, dead white'.[2] In his choice of materials, wood and oil paint, it is tempting and perhaps not too far-fetched to relate Kocherscheidt's work back to the great European tradition of medieval polychrome sculpture. To that interface of two disparate languages where we find the passage of time has shaped another meaning. Kocherscheidt never covered his sculptures completely with paint. They are never painted out to become another surface. There is always retention of the material's true nature. The slightly irregular stacking of the planks that formed the profile of his sculptures is echoed by the bands of brushwork applied over them. Probably the most painterly are the two earliest works *Englische Acht* and *Felder*. While in the later sculptures the paint is more partial, less prone to close the surface underneath, the wood still breathes. It is perhaps curious to speculate as to what extent the paintwork keys the works back to the wall, pulls the works back to painting, or to what degree its pictorial qualities invigorate the work's dimensions.

In the autumn of 1990, Kocherscheidt and his wife Elfie Semotan visited London for the opening of an exhibition I was having at the Whitechapel Art Gallery. While there, the one thing he was insistent we did was to visit Kew, the Royal Botanical Gardens. He wanted to see some big trees, of which Kew Gardens has some fine specimens. Spending a leisurely afternoon there, Kocherscheidt lamented the fact that it was not possible to see such old and majestic trees in his native Austria. Clearly, he was touched by being surrounded by the presence and power such large trees can generate.

It is one of the qualities of wood that it engenders a sense of human scale; even large trees seem to speak to us in a very human way. In that sense wood is not an engineered material like steel or even concrete, two materials which seem to have no specific scale to them, but rather can be infinitely extended. Wood, on the other hand, and our understanding of its growth through the life the tree has led, enables us to know the material in another way. We have grown up together, so to speak, and that connection stays with us in coming to a wooden sculpture. As Mario Merz commented 'a tree occupies mainly time', the same time we also inhabit.[3]

Kocherscheidt's affinity with this material, and his decision around 1986 to work with it, must to a large extent have grown out of his circumstances. In the year after they married, he and Elfie acquired a house at Grieselstein in Burgenland, close to the then Yugoslavian border. Although it was several years before he was able to seriously work there, all of his sculptures with the exception of *Tor der Winde* were made at Grieselstein. The location gave the artist ready access to the necessary wood and, equally importantly, the sympathetic skills of the carpenters Peter Pilz and Karl Feyerabend, who helped him cut out the forms and assemble the works. Perhaps time also was a factor: as anyone living in the countryside is aware, the pace is different to that of the city. The space engenders another kind of time: the time to sort out, arrange, stack, cut out and assemble, which in itself is a different sense of time to that of painting.

I am sitting in the study gallery of the Ny Carlsberg Glyptotek in Copenhagen. Before me are long rows of Greek and Roman heads that one takes to be portraits. Yet, are they indeed portraits as we have come to understand that term, or are they archetypes? And has the passage of time, with the loss of a nose, an ear or a chin, turned them into something else again. Equally, in looking at a Kocherscheidt are we also looking at a portrait? Not in a literal sense, or that ubiquitous notion that all artworks are somehow a portrait of the artist, but more the idea of a true archetype. Indeed, was Kocherscheidt searching for an archetype, for a sense of the body that would not only carry his body, but all bodies within it?

From the head to the torso, the body takes upon itself the same symmetries. All of Kocherscheidt's sculptures are of a human scale. They invariably throw us back to a sense of our own body, our own peculiar symmetry, and reflect our own 'standing' in the world.

In speaking about Gustav Klimt and Egon Schiele, two greats of Austrian art, a tradition Kocherscheidt was acutely aware he was rooted in, then his preference was firmly for Klimt. Certainly, one can see an affinity between the two. Just as Klimt squeezed his figures tight up against the surface of the canvas, as if pressed against a sheet of glass, Kocherscheidt also squeezed his forms flat against the canvas. Likewise, in the sculptures, the forms suggested are pressed back against the wall, as if unable to break through an imaginary screen that prevents them from committing themselves completely to three-dimensional space.

Klimt's truncation of the body in his figures would also appear to have been an influence on Kocherscheidt. For both frequently treated the body as a block, in a statuesque sense, as sculpture, rather than as a fluid limbed being. Both built upon the territory that

Auguste Rodin opened up in allowing a part of the human body to be seen as a living fragment, as if it were an object invested with a life force; a still-life that has the potential to be a lived life.

I have often thought that the forms in Kocherscheidt's work, both in the paintings and in the sculptures, move between a sense of the human body and that of a still-life. It is as if the psyche of the body, the human spirit, were trapped within the form of an object, becoming stilled-life. Perhaps here the word trapped is significant, for in Kocherscheidt's work one feels a strong sensation of holding in, of being embraced. The elements in his paintings, especially in the later works such as the *Waldblock* series, accentuate an isolation, a closing down of the form within a constrictive surround. On the occasions this form does appear to be breaking out as in *Ohne Titel*, bulging against the orange edges of the canvas, there is still an incipient constraint, a holding in. From a painted form to the torso, then to the chest, there is remorselessly the sensation of restricted movement. Like constricted breathing, the forms in Kocherscheidt's paintings hold onto this action of in and out with tenacious persistence.

'The work of art should end within itself', Rilke wrote in reference to the sculpture of Rodin.[4] For the painter, however, there can be no ending; paintings are always beginnings. Is this one of the limitations of painting that drives the painter to take up the challenge of sculpture? Is this one of the reasons that pushes the painting off the wall to make the distinction which David Smith referred to as a separation of but 'one element of dimension'?[5] And in that one element of dimension, is it possible for the artist to sense an ending, to come full circle and feel a sense of closure? Kocherscheidt's slow movement away from the wall in the thirteen sculptures he made in the short period between 1986 and 1992 appears inevitable within his work. It could not have been any other way. Through his paintings we can better see the sculptures and through the sculptures we can better feel the paintings. In the narrow gap he forced open in moving from the wall to the floor, he affirmed what we should have known already from looking at the paintings: that he was always facing out to meet us.

Published in *Kurt Kocherscheidt: Catalogue Raisonné*, Vienna and New York, 2005, pp. 345–62.

China

(2004)

Lost in the crowd of shoppers on a busy central Beijing street stands an elderly monk. He has with him a bucket of water and a large Chinese brush on the end of a long wooden pole. He dips the brush into the bucket and begins to draw onto the pavement with the water in bold calligraphic characters the first line of a traditional Chinese poem. As the characters appear on the pavement, wet and dark against the lighter colour of the dry concrete around, the shoppers step aside, carefully walking around the poem, only to regroup again once beyond. As the monk moves further down the street drawing line by line of the poem, the first line begins to evaporate, slowly disappearing in the summer heat. As it does, the throbbing crowd steps back onto what is now dry pavement, only to disperse again as each new wet line of the poem appears. At a certain point the monk stops his work and stands waiting. It was the last line of the poem. Then slowly even this line too dries out and the poem is gone. And once again, the monk is lost in the bustling crowd of shoppers.

Five weeks in China – it is like standing on the beach with one's feet in the waters of a vast sea.

Not understanding a word of the language allows one to begin all over again, to be for a moment both unhearing and unheard – there, but then again, not there.

The museum in Taiyuan. A sign above the door reads, 'Watch out knock head'.

A second sign placed on the plinth of a beautiful stone sculpture of a reclining leopard reads, 'No stroking'.

Notes
(2005)

It is one of the curious contradictions of painting a painting that to do it one has to be on one's toes, on edge. However, what one is trying to do is to find the centre. But then can we only sense the centre by its edge? Is it only folly thinking one is edging towards the centre? Certainly, the more I think and feel my way into a painting, the closer to an edge I feel I am moving.

When process becomes too pronounced, painting becomes purely factual.

Neither vertical nor horizontal – but floating.

Is guilt a consequence of gravity?

I have thin skin; it feels porous. I am not sure exactly where my own body ends and the rest of the world begins. I am not absolutely sure even where you finish and I might begin. When I look at the work of a painter like Edvard Munch, then I sense he understood this state in which the body does not end at the limits of the skin, but in a territory beyond, which is hard to describe and at times impossible to call one's own.

One evening I watch a video profile of Noam Chomsky. Am I drowning in words or are they the ripples of an oceanic mantra, lapping against the edge of my mind? The next morning, I am on the train reading the journals of the film-maker Robert Bresson. Such brevity. I long for such economy. But how to find it; and how to reconcile the other side of oneself which lets all spill out? ... walking backwards – drowning in the ocean or walking on water – time and time again ...

I know that dryness leads to symmetry and that wetness until absolute will resort to the asymmetrical.

'Sentinel and vigil' ... a single phrase may be enough for a beginning or an ending.

'Light falls', such a strange expression.

Birds cracking snails on the roof; counting crows.

Extracts published in Ian McKeever, *In Praise of Painting: Three Essays*, Michael Tucker (ed. and introduction), Centre for Contemporary Visual Arts, University of Brighton, 2005, pp. 80–2.

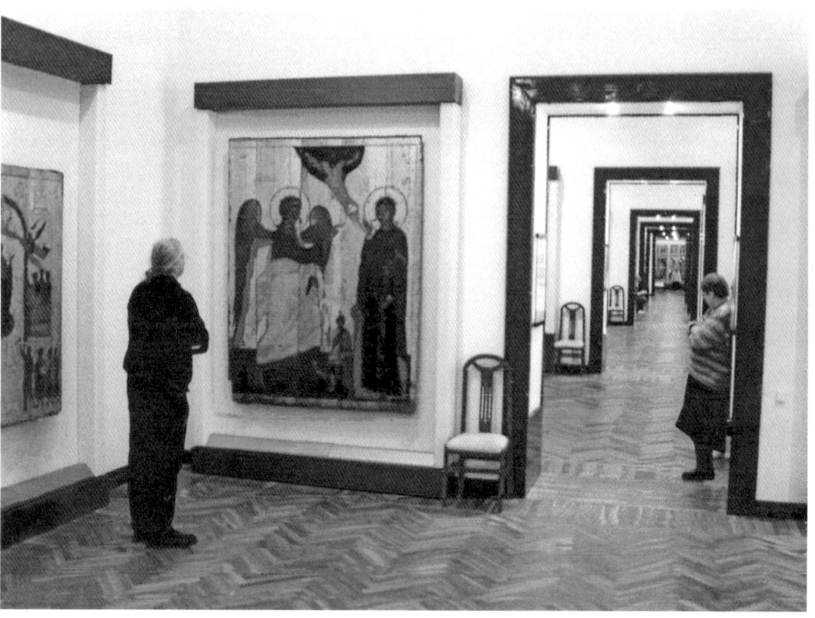

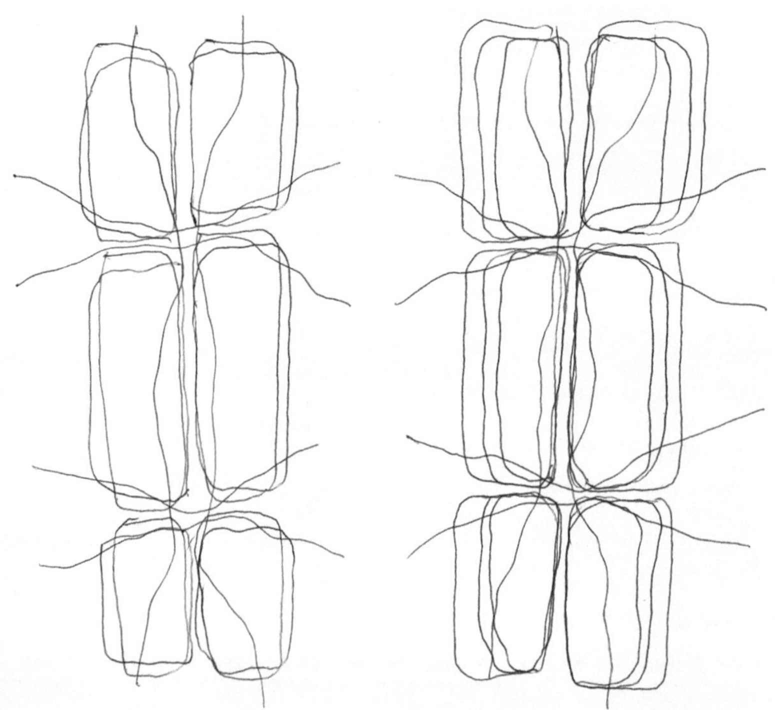

Painting and Countenance
(2005)

I

Pinned to the back of the bathroom door is a poster of a painting by Sandro Botticelli, entitled *Portrait of a Young Woman*. It depicts, in profile, the head and shoulders of a young woman wearing a black dress. My wife put it up several years ago, and it has remained there ever since. This is how I first got to know the painting. It was many years after I saw the poster that I encountered the actual painting quite by chance in a modest exhibition of Botticelli's works during a brief visit to Florence. Seeing it there I knew immediately why the poster is still pinned up. On another door, the one leading from the studio to the storage area, a solitary postcard of a small painting by Vilhelm Hammershøi is stapled, again depicting a young woman in profile, and again by coincidence wearing a black dress. I came across this painting while strolling around the art museum in Odense, finding myself repeatedly drawn back to look. What is it about some paintings that they are able to get right under the skin? Often, they are the paintings that one would least expect to do so. How and why do we find such intimacy with certain works? At times it feels as if they have been painted specifically for us. They leave the mass and weight of art history behind them and become an inexplicable part of one's life.

Two paintings, two young women wearing black dresses, heads turned in profile to the right. In both, one is drawn to follow the line from the curve of the dress up to the throat, then around the contours of the face, over the head, and down again, tracing the curves of the pinned-up hair down to the nape of the neck and then back to the dress. In both, an exquisite line. A tender, fragile line made with what can only be described as love. Why do we find it so hard in Britain to speak about our emotions in relationship to art?

In Botticelli's *Portrait of a Young Woman* especially, there is a quality of line that seems extraordinarily pure. Such a pure fragile line, in which we can sense both vulnerability and strength. Then, one immediately knows what it is to be human. Free of bombast and brute force, it is a line that takes us to an edge where beauty becomes painful, and we know why only certain things can contain grace. We also know that it is only possible to paint such a painting if it has love secreted within it.

In Hammershøi's *Portrait of a Young Consumptive Woman* the line is softer, its edge lost in the blurring that so often accompanies oil paint. Its fragility lies more in its illusiveness. When I first saw this modest painting, which measures only 31 x 27 cm, I was struck by its delicacy. It is a painting that can almost be cupped in the hands and, indeed, one desires to do just that. It is the same size as a small devotional icon; however, icons seldom, if ever, show depictions in profile.

Full face or profile. In writing about the difference in reference to the icon, Paul Evdokimov speaks about the profile interrupting communion, inaugurating a fading away, a flight leading to absence.[1] In more general terms, I wonder if there are painters who paint 'head on' and painters who paint 'in profile', so to speak. Is it the difference between the gaze and the glance? Equally, in coming to look at a work, do we also either gaze or glance, and can we only gaze back at what is already gazing at us?

Face to face. There is something emphatic about the self-portrait of Edvard Munch staring out at us from the canvas *Between the Clock and the Bed*, just as there is in the self-portraits of Lovis Corinth, of which in later life he painted one a year (in itself a wonderful simple idea). I have always been curious as to where the necessary distance lies for the painter in order to paint such an image. That edge, which separates him from what he paints, and the nature of the discipline, of seeing oneself as subject matter. We approach self-portraits differently from how we come to other portraits. I use the words 'come to' because looking seems so passive an idea and good paintings do not give us that prerogative. Instead, we have to find a state of attendance; we have to be present.

> But now the young girl
> Is all enveloped by blue.
> She sits on the throne,
> She becomes august
> With a simple majesty,
> Suddenly
> A winged figure
> Appears before her,
> but, from a higher place.
> It is the angel, the announcement.
> The air, the visible catch fire.
> In the heat Giovanna dozes off.
> Oh, he will paint: later, when the time is right.[2]

In this short section from the epic poem *Earthly and Heavenly Journey of Simone Martini*, the Italian poet Mario Luzi refers to what is perhaps Martini's greatest painting, the altarpiece *The Annunciation*. Painted by Martini and his brother-in-law Lippo Memmi in 1333, the work depicts the visitation of the Archangel Gabriel to the Virgin Mary, with St Ansanus and possibly St Margaret in the two lateral panels. It is thought that Martini painted the central panel and Memmi the two sides. The painting, commissioned originally for the altar of St Ansanus in Siena Cathedral, is now in the Uffizi. On the occasions I have seen this painting I have found myself at a loss as to how to walk away from it, how to begin to leave.

Between the Archangel Gabriel and the Virgin Mary stands a vase of lilies with the message 'Hail Mary full of grace, the Lord is with thee', arcing above. Gabriel is leaning in from the left and Mary away to the right. The centre of the painting (except for the vase and text) is empty, yet the space feels pregnant. It is as if everything else in the painting is in attendance to this absence, to this moment that allows for the Annunciation. To paint a painting in which what is said is not overtly there, in this case, cannot be there, but only intimated, is difficult. When we trust the gap created by this absence to carry more weight than what is present, we know that we are in the realm of great painting. It is possible to make saints out of wine bottles, as Rainer Maria Rilke never ceased to remind us.[3] To make something miraculous from little more than intimation.

II

In 1946 Barnett Newman made a brush drawing of a circle, the central area of which was left empty with the black ink brushwork feathering away from this void towards the edges of the paper. The same year he did another ink drawing in which a central vertical is again left unpainted with the two side areas to the left and the right feathering away in black ink. They are perhaps the first two works by Newman that leave any reference to the pictorial behind. Yet, one drawing goes further than the other, for the circle holds an absolute that is also its limitation. We cannot get beyond thinking of an implied suggestion of heaven or earth. This will invariably fill our vision and even as an absence it will evoke a particular sense of presence. To hold any notion of the infinite we have first to circumscribe it, name it, call it the numeral 0. For Newman, as for most of the Abstract Expressionists, the symbolic still lingered. To go beyond this, Newman must displace heaven and earth, eliminate any pictorial notion of this and arrive, no matter how tentatively, at a sensed absolute, trusting that meaning can be invoked in an apparent absence.

> 'One is the number of solitude; two is the number that separates, and three is the number that goes beyond separation.'[4]
> Paul Evdokimov

Newman painted *Be I (second version)* in 1970, the year he died. It is in many ways one of his simpler paintings, a thin vertical line bisecting the canvas to create a tripartite composition. It echoes the structure of *Onement I*, the 'first' of Newman's paintings and the canvas he recognised as being the breakthrough to his mature style. Although Newman painted many works with more complex structures of four, five or six vertical divisions, the basic one of three, which 'goes beyond separation', somehow seems to say something fundamental about his work. It informs in a way that more complex configurations only seem to echo. Newman attempted something few artists do, especially painters: to begin all over again, to start from the beginning. *Adam – Eve – Day before One –* and *Now*: the titles alone evoke a beginning through the actual act of painting. He stated in his extensive writings something to the effect that content was determined at the very onset of making. Alternatively, one could phrase it differently by saying one cannot really speak about it; one can only paint it.[5] Yet what is curious about this apparent conflict between saying and making is that Newman was perhaps the most intellectual of all the Abstract Expressionist painters. By this I do not mean the theoretical, as there is no apparent theory behind the work, but rather an insistence upon seeing the intellect of itself having the capacity to carry subject matter, to give the painting a latent emotional charge, as opposed to the more explicitly emotionally charged paintings of Mark Rothko. Viewed in these terms it is as if Newman endeavoured to paint the act of thinking, its immateriality, as an embodied and weighted abstraction mirroring the vertical presence of the human form.

In his novel *The Wings of the Dove*, Henry James writes of the character Kate Croy, 'she had stature without height, grace without motion, presence without mass. Slender and simple, frequently soundless, she was somehow in the line of the eye'.[6] The line of the eye, its sweep and capacity to hold still, to be in the moment. The vertical line of a Newman painting, staying true and without interruption, meeting the line of one's eye, all reference to the horizontal banished. The painting stands as we stand before it, and perhaps for a moment takes on countenance.

Published in part in Ian McKeever, *In Praise of Painting: Three Essays*, Michael Tucker (ed. and introduction), Centre for Contemporary Visual Arts, University of Brighton, 2005, pp. 87–92.

White
(2008)

Stepping into the bathroom, four white walls, all painted the same brilliant white, except not now. The one lit by the full glare of the sun is luminescent, the wall to the right less bright, its white tinged by the green of the landscape outside. Opposite, the wall half in shadow feels like a white relaxed, while the wall in which the window sits, in full shade, gives life to the others. The ceramic tiles of the shower modulate their white as if the colour were singing; the shampoo, poured out, reacts like the colour of the albumen of a poaching egg as it turns from liquid to white form. The rough and smooth sides of the towel give different whites, one withholding, while the smooth side spreads its white with pride. A porcelain handbasin holds its white slowly, and as water fills it goes from certain white to white seen at a glance. The bar of soap holds its white in the same way a candle does, as if within it there is an inner light, a profound white, which with each washing, as the bar wears down, one will get closer to seeing and touching but of course one never does. The toothpaste tube and its cap are two different whites: the cap a harder, cleaner white, the tube a white, softer and more greyed, showing something of its purpose to be squeezed and to reveal the full refreshing white of the paste. On the windowsill stands a white orchid, its full petals set against the daylight behind. A single petal as white as perhaps any white can be, through which the light glows, is translucent with life, breathing light and white as one. And where one petal overlays another, a white so dense and rich is formed that one has to remind oneself that this white is simply the name of the colour.

Dressed, I go downstairs and have breakfast. I once tried to count all the different whites in the kitchen, starting with the ceiling, walls, doors, skirting boards, then moving onto other larger white areas, wall tiles, radiators, shelves, butler sink, dishwasher, gradually going down in size, the teapots and roll of paper kitchen towel on the windowsill, then on to the shelves, cups, saucers, mugs, plates, bowls. Of course, the list is endless and becomes increasingly so as one realises that virtually every surface and object carries its white in another way and as light changes what was one white becomes another. In the end the project took on a Sisyphean comic element; one could imagine oneself spending the rest of one's life counting whites, making an inventory in homage to white, never knowing if a white seen today was the same white seen a month or a year ago and, if so, how one would identify it, by what means one would document these whites, arrive at even the most rudimentary cataloguing system. Venturing such thought then realising that in all probability one would never get beyond the kitchen door, becoming increasingly cocooned in a shrine of white, like a glistening white marabout sitting isolated on the Moroccan desert foreshore, seemingly oblivious to what surrounds it as waves lap in, clouds glide overhead and footprints are left in the sand. The simplest movement of a cup, a teapot to another place, even if only by a few centimetres, would be enough to change the white, induce another inflection, warmer, cooler, tinted or shadowed, as if moment by moment the world were made anew by the happenstance of circumstance. Confronted by the impossible, of chasing fool's white, the white that would be all whites as one,

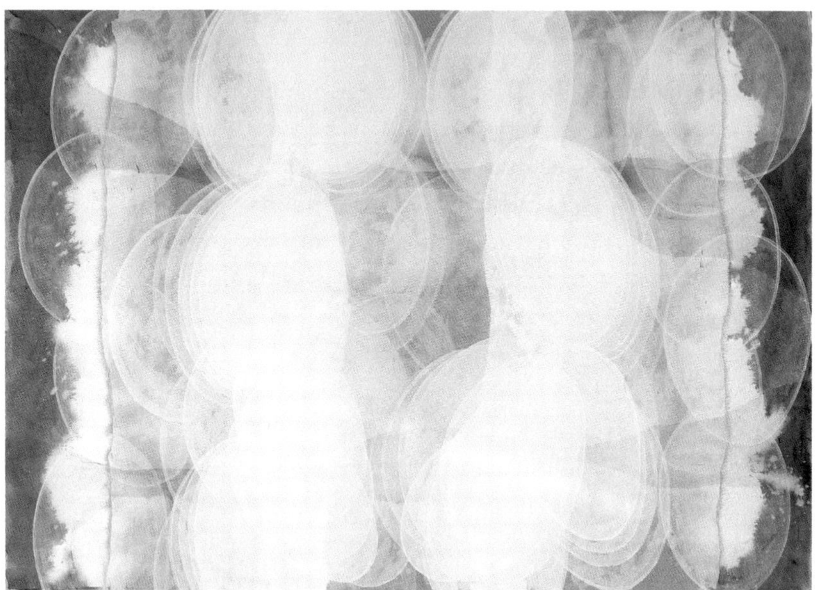

it became enough to sit for some more moments after breakfast each day and watch the myriads of whites hold and fold their way in and out of ever-changing intensities and reticence.

I have come to think that looking is a form of meditation and that our eyes, ever greedy to grasp the world around us, restless in their insistence to see, somehow reduce the mind's freedom, clog it up, and that stilling the eye is also to still the mind. To sense a stillness in

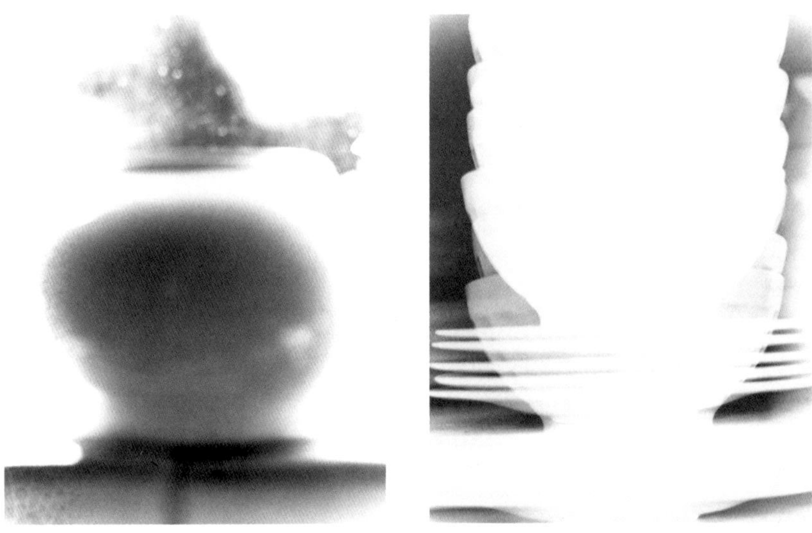

looking, not at what is fleetingly out there, which given half a chance would hoodwink us at every turn, but in the eye's inner looking, where eye and mind still into one. I remember once travelling with Gerlinde in Spain and sitting one late afternoon on the hotel terrace overlooking the valley to the distant clear horizon beyond. The sky was of a clean light blue except for an intense small white cloud that hovered above the horizon line. As I watched it, the cloud would for a minute or two suddenly disappear, as if a fade on a slide projection, only to then return to exactly the same place all over again. This sleight of hand, of going and coming, continued for a good hour or so. I never did understand the meteorological phenomenon of the cloud's strange conjuring trick, its seemingly effortless comings and goings and the increasing sense of familiarity it brought with it. Yet with each new appearance this increasing familiarity engendered a sense that it was getting closer, neither moving up nor down, neither left nor right, simply getting closer. Before it finally disappeared behind the building for good, I imagined that it was upon us, not passing overhead but instead directly coming to meet the eye, there to be sucked into the eye, becoming the most exquisite white imaginable. A white that was perfect white and containing within it all the whites there could possibly be.

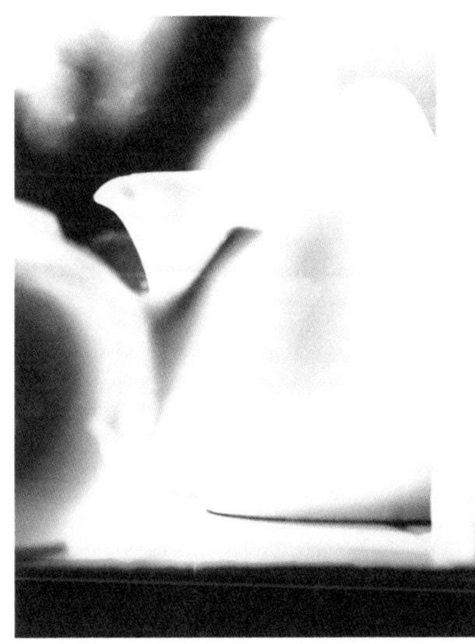

White's generosity. Pierre Bonnard's whites, which hold a freshness and a place to rest the eye. How his paintings push white away from itself, yet manage to retain its pristine nature, its capacity to hold itself at a distance from the other colours. The white tablecloth, its pale-yellow stripes allowing one to ease oneself into the picture plane, or the white of a door, modulated by the warmth of an ochry yellow, the eye moving across the painting from the cooler almost mauve white of the radiator to the door, then on to the inflected white of the wall to the left, whiter yet still somehow infused with the expectancy of colour. Francisco de Zurbarán held white in a subdued milky state as if it were the colour of grace. Its omniscience endowed with the weight of tradition and calling, the robes of Cardinal Albergati, of the Blessed John Houghton, St Hugo of Grenoble and of St Arnald in the Museo Provincial de Bellas Artes in Cadiz, in their rectitude and folds of servitude allowing their heads to seemingly move out of this earthly stupor into the realm of the spirit, as if detachment were already in progress. In James McNeill Whistler's painting *Symphony in White, No. 1: The White Girl*, Joanna Hiffernan's full-length flowing linen dress turns white into a receptacle. White's capacity to receive. It is perhaps the most generous of all the colours, more willing than others to call forth another name, be immersed in the spectrum of colour and life. The white of a Robert Ryman painting, his insistence that he never set out to paint a white painting, giving the painting a distance, preventing it from being snared in the pictorial and the prosaic, pushing white back to the practicalities of painting, of putting one paint mark next to another paint mark. Releasing colour and painting from the weight of reference and meaning and sliding it, as if an act of sabotage, towards a silent neutrality, becoming a painting with the aching distance of a work by Paul Cézanne.

Wave and Other Sensations
(2010)

The chair leant inwards, its back resting on the edge of the table. The underside of the seat exposed, set in dark shadow against two white legs. Summer seemed a long time coming. But the light was good. There was plenty of glare. Pockets of it spilled out into the air, hiding definition. He screwed up his eyes to see. Standing in the doorway he felt the need to absorb something of this discomfort. He waited, letting his creased eyes fix and take in the glare, then turned into the shadow and walked inside.

He sat. Looked. His gaze moved slowly across the floor to the wall beyond. He leant back into the chair, eyes focused on the painting on the wall directly across the room. As he did, it began to pulse in and out of focus. His gaze wandered away from the painting and eased itself back down to the paint-splattered floor. From the gap between where the wall met the floor, a gentle and at first almost imperceptible ripple began to immerge. Growing in size and momentum it waved its way towards him, bellying up like a huge bulging gut. Approaching him, now shoulder high and moving fast, it pushed him hard back into the chair, passed through him, then beyond. In that instant he felt both fear and elation, that same sensation when as a child he stood on the beach and looked out to sea. As if it were heaving up to meet him, higher, taller than himself, engulfing. Then the floor was flat again, and as his head tilted upwards and his eyes retraced their way back up the wall, the painting came out once more to meet his gaze. He sat. He waited, then slowly got up, unthinkingly walked back to the open door and looked out.

He turned, walked back in, looked at the painting on the wall. Waited. Sometimes the space breathed in and sometimes it breathed out. This quality of space he could both understand and accept. The idea of flatness, on the other hand, mystified him. He could comprehend a more immediate flatness, the polished plane of a tabletop as he ran the palm of his hand over it, or the floor of a modest room, whose distance he could stride without a loss of time.

Both could be grasped, held within the rhythms of his body. Beyond that an ill-defined flow took over, which either engulfed him or left him adrift. A strange state reassuringly tangible yet without clear form.

Geometry, the meeting point of flat planes, he could understand as an idea. After all, things had to meet somewhere. The vertical, the horizontal, which seemed so close to the constructs and limits of thought itself. They gave things an edge. Ideas could be wedged against them or alternatively spread out flat against the plane. Flatness, he thought, gave the world a kind of certitude, whole philosophies could be stacked up or leant against it, and that one simple angle suggesting the perpendicular against the horizontal could turn corner into culture.

He picked up a book and began flicking through it. On an otherwise stark white blank page a photograph was reproduced in the bottom right-hand corner. Its placement on the page made it look like a footnote. On the opposite page the caption read, ‘Barbara Morgan, *Light Waves*, 1945, vintage silver print (photogram) 24 x 18 cm’. The image drew him in. Its central dark block, running top to bottom, riven with flowing skeins of white, suggested emerging, energetic light, electric. To either side, lighter vertical bands hemmed in the darker central section. It looked like a painting. From the small reproduction he could get no sense of the photograph’s grain yet could still feel its lingering optical depth.

Flicking on through the book he stopped at a page reproducing an ink drawing by Barnett Newman, *Untitled* (1948), and was struck by the connection. From half-light to intense light. The dense blacks of the brushwork set off against the heavy cream of the woven paper. The centre, a narrowing wedge of white, slicing the paper in two from top to bottom. ‘Light turning to solid’, he said to himself, paused, then, ‘Let the light flow’. Light would seem to have been an important part of what Newman was striving for in his work, he continued thinking. Yet usually, we are directed to the more formal aspects of his work, the vertically divided canvas, the proportion of one section to another, or to the implications of his Jewishness. Trapped between a reductive minimalist rhetoric and the esoteric, always secure in language known. However, the titles of Newman's paintings – *Primordial Light, White Fire, Shimmer Bright* – he thought suggested something less about structure or the intellect.

He looked across the room to the open door. The light angled in. To make it concrete, palpable, had that been Newman's aim? Divest the light of its furtive optical properties and stand it solid and erect against the verticality of his being. Make it solid in the world. Concrete, yes concrete, he thought again, the word seemed hard and flat enough. To push the painting back to the solidity of a flat plane was a strong desire in any painter. It took the painting somewhere else, set it apart; separated from all around, it could find its own place in the world. Away also from the artist, especially the artist.

Published in Ian McKeever, *Black and Black Again ... Paintings 1987–2010*, exh. cat., Museum Sønderjylland, Kunstmuseet i Tønder, 2011.

Morocco
(2010)

I am back in Morocco; it has been many years. The first time, I left Liverpool from Speke Airport simply with the plan to travel. Rucksack, tent and walking boots, thinking I would be going north. Instead, the only flight leaving that day takes me to Malaga and from there I catch the ferry over to Melilla. Then travelling along the coast to Oujda before heading south to Bouarfa, then Figuig along the Algerian border. It now seems such a long time ago; the photographs I took then are still waiting to be processed. Still in their 35 mm small black plastic tubs. I simply did not know what to do with 'Morocco'. But then it was the same with Italy back in 1967, looking at Giotto's frescoes in the church of Santa Croce in Florence. I could have been staring at the moon, it all seemed so far away. There is the saying 'what goes around comes around', certainly for me this would seem to be the case.

So, I am back in Morocco rereading Paul Bowles's novel *The Spider's House*, the quintessential Western writer about Morocco. Like his fellow countryman Henry James, he used another culture to find himself. Used the foreignness of place to find a voice. Both Bowles and James harnessed distance to reflect on and to speculate as to what it means to be sensate in the world. Touching that brittle edge of identity and the loss of self within the unfolding mesh of circumstance. Both writers employed dialogue, the human voice, to think aloud, their characters voicing more than the prittle-prattle of conversation in order to express ideas. Often deep ideas with real philosophical undertones, and yet this is always expressed with ease, as if to say, 'isn't this how we speak with each other'?

Larache; I have to get out of here, Chefchaouen that is. The plan was to stay two or three days, wandering around the town looking at the Andalusian influences, but it is overrun with Japanese and Chinese tourists. The next group we pass carry even larger cameras than the last. The town, which is not big, boasts three Chinese restaurants, and somehow reminds me of Dali in the southwest of

China. It has something of that laid-back, let it all hang out druggy feel. So early the next morning we leave, taking the bus south to Quezzane, then head northwest, arriving at Larache on the coast in the early evening. The coastal towns of Morocco are curious, a strange juncture of ocean meeting arid land. One minute you are standing on an almost deserted beach looking out to the sea, the next almost cheek by jowl with people in the medina. The air off the ocean carries an abrasive wind that is both refreshing and scouring.

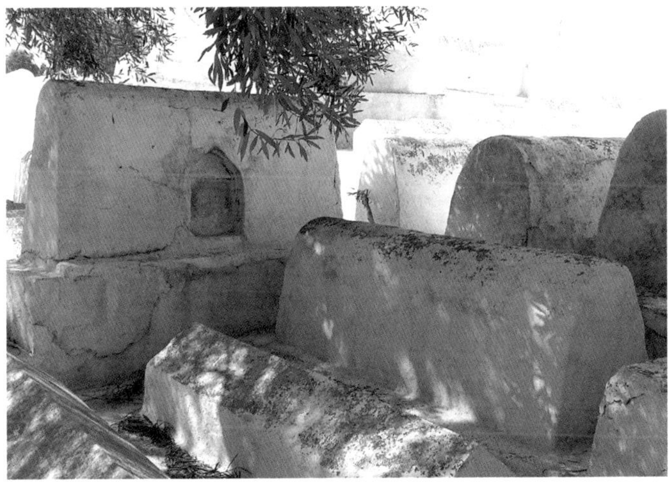

At the southern edge of the town overlooking the ocean is the Christian Cemetery. Jean Genet is buried here. I never read the essay he wrote, 'What Remains of a Rembrandt Torn into Four Equal Pieces and Flushed Down the Toilet', but how can one not smile at such irreverence.[1] Or his suggestion that Alberto Giacometti's sculptures should be offered to the dead and buried with them. Trapped in their apparent perversity, such ideas hold the kernel of what has become a forbidden truth. Touch a possible meaning in art that goes beyond the niceties and politeness of the norm, hark back to a more rudimentary, one is tempted to use the word primitive, justification for the making of art which usurps art's incessant love affair with the museum. Later, in 2017, the Spanish writer Juan Goytisolo would also be buried in the same cemetery. Goytisolo spent many years living and travelling in the Maghreb. Like James and Bowles he too was self-exiled, except perhaps in his case it had more to do with a profound sense of displacement. How else to react, when as a boy you are taken to the tomb of your mother only to see the space which has been reserved for you from birth.[2] The desire to walk away from a life laid out before one is strong in some people. Fear of the known can be so much greater than the uncertainties of the unknown.

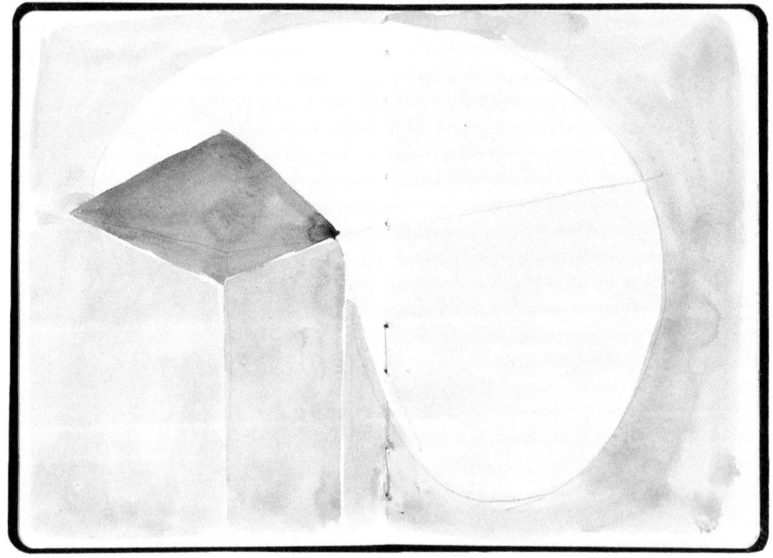

For some writers, displacement is the shifting of continents; for others, it is simply the relocation of the chair. The Danish poet Inger Christensen wrote, 'With my back to my poem, to myself, I go away from myself, from the poem, my word, and even further into my word, into my poem, into myself'.[3] Separation, one either craves it or resists it. Goytisolo, in his novel *Marks of Identity*, charting his early life in the form of a fictive biography, lays out his need for exile. To find a word devoid of a past as if but a seed, to try to own the word, to own oneself, and then to lose oneself in the finding, one can only marvel at the courage of it.[4]

Meknes; staring up at the ceiling. On the long list of lying on my back, stomach churning, it is not a great one, there have been better. Mardin, on the other hand, was a good one, carved and mellow faded painted wooden beams, the plastered areas between each irregular, all slightly differently moulded. Aleppo was good too, very high, a tall room, and although the ceiling was simple, one could somehow feel an echo of the exterior walls out onto the street, their beautiful alternating ribbons of light and dark stone creeping into the room and across the ceiling. Göreme was domed, after all it was a cave dwelling, with a plain unadorned cross painted on the ceiling in faded

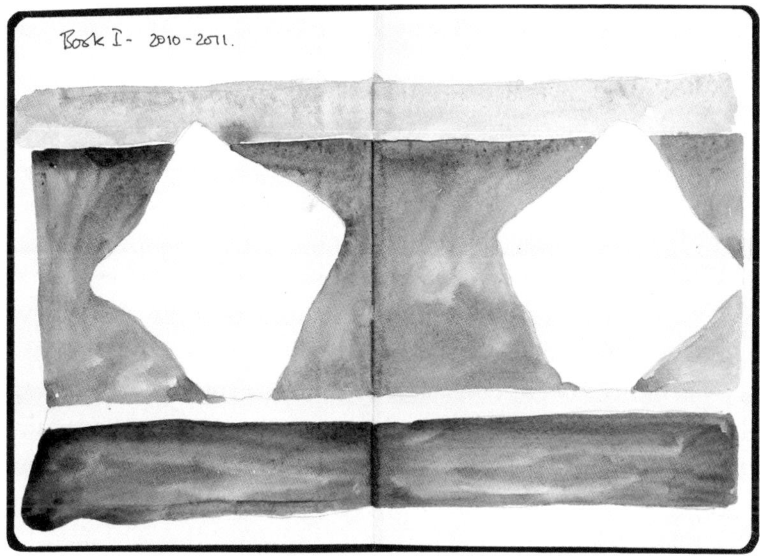

reddy-ochre. It was as if amid all the grunts and groans of stomach cramps this silent blessing would see me through. Chengdu was not so much a ceiling as intervals of knocks on the hotel bedroom door to see if I was still alive and the distant noise of the crowd at the nearby football stadium, and Melilla, well if the room did have a ceiling, I never saw it.

Tasnacht; at some point I had to come here, to this small town in the southern part of the High Atlas. Just to put my foot down in the place. It is making me start to think I am like one of those people who go around the Scottish Highlands Munro-bagging. Tasnacht, it sits in my mind like some kind of Eldorado, the quest for the holy grail. Of course, the actual reason is far more banal: a book about Berber textiles from this region by the Austrian specialist Kurt Rainer simply titled *Tasnacht*.

Tangiers; it has to start somewhere, the preliminary ritual of being shown all the tourist rugs and what have you. Usually a couple of words, haik or adrar, help things along, but it is important they are not said too soon, these things take time. Eventually, the dealer gets out of a locked cupboard a beautiful old adrar, a woman's headscarf, or veil as some say. In this case it is one used specifically for a wedding ceremony, measuring about 120 x 90 cm and made of the most exquisite soft off-white wool. Held up against the light it is almost transparent, the play of warp and weft beautifully nuanced from one section to another. The two long sides of the adrar are painted with traditional henna ideograms; the shorter selvedge ends edged with cotton weft, lighter in colour than the wool and resisting the henna, from which delicate tassels hang down. We talk price. It is expensive, which is alright. This can change. As it is already late evening and I am tired, I ask if I can return in the morning to see it afresh and in daylight. This we do, except instead of being shown the adrar we had looked at the previous evening I am shown several crude versions. It is clear we are getting nowhere, so I ask to be shown the specific piece I had seen before, of which I have a picture on my phone. Alas, I am told, it was sold first thing this morning. As we begin to take our leave the owner says in perfect English, in otherwise what has been a very stilted conversation, 'well, you can't always get what you want'. I am just about to ask him if he is a Rolling Stones fan, then think better of it. I do not know whether to laugh or cry.

Occasionally, very occasionally, one senses in one of these textiles something of what can only be described as a spirit. Ah! that bogeyman of contemporary life, the spiritual. The feeling one gets when going into some buildings, as if one is taking in the aura of its use and occupants. At its strongest it is an energy of light. One can get the same sensation sometimes from a garment or textile; it holds its luminous past. Perhaps it is my strict Catholic upbringing that makes me harbour such thinking. The cassock, in its white and black starched austerity worn as an altar boy, too prim to be more than an intimation of a sign, yet holding as it did the contradiction that to be of such a realm of light a soiling must have taken place. The Turin Shroud, its immaculate emergence as an image out of the soilings of life, an image made in the absence of life with its ethereal faint glow.

In such moments of looking, one stands alone no matter how many people are thronging around. To be solitary, to stand in the modest inner courtyard of the Al-Attarine Madrasa in Fez, or under the expansive glistening Mozarabic ceiling of the Sala de Dos Hermanas at the Alhambra, and feel a presence so strong that it brings tears to the eyes. The painting too in some crazy way is a textile. It begins with running one's hand over a pristine stretched canvas surface. The smell of cotton duck or linen seems to pass through the hand to the nostrils as one feels it yielding under the pressure of touch. In that slight yielding is a giving so big that in this moment it contains everything and more of what will become the painting. Its presence will grow out of the delicate caress and response of this first touch.

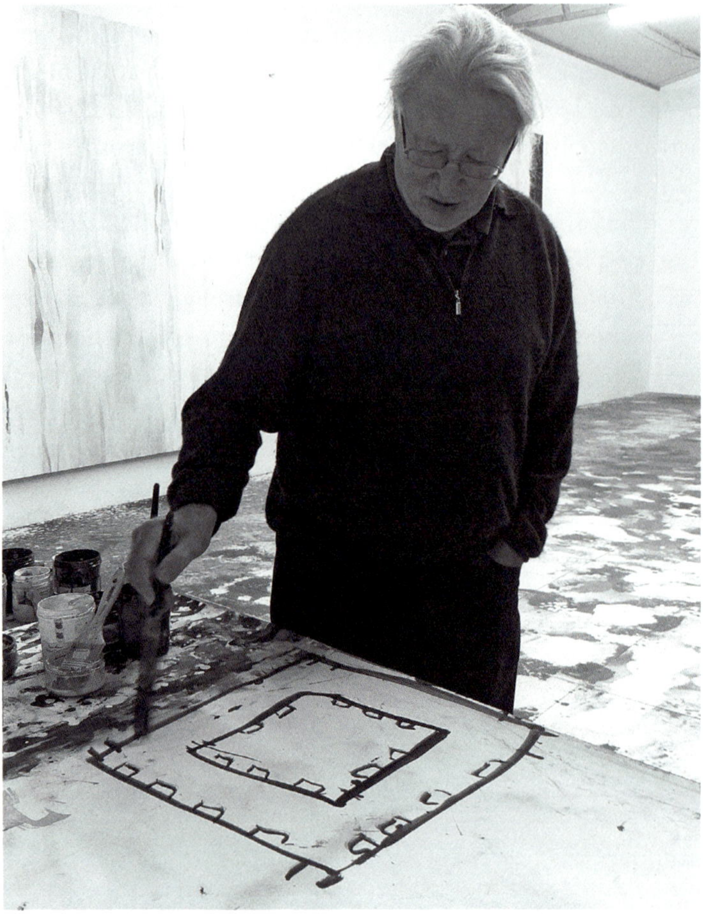

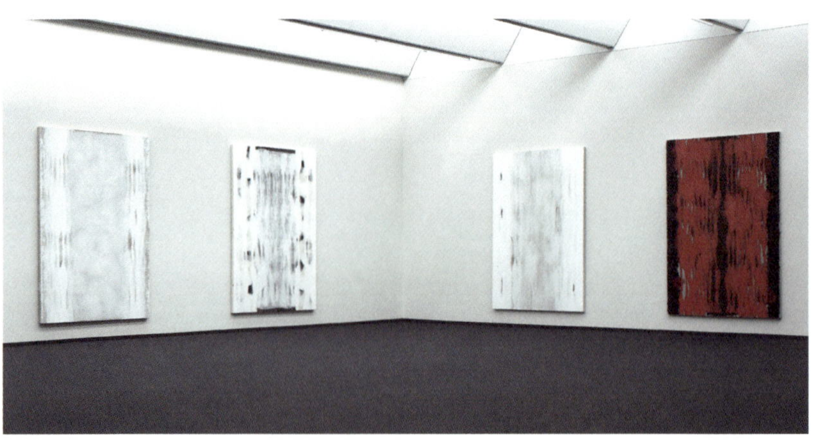

Notes II
(2010)

To seek the inner light, it seems such a crass assertion to make. Pathetic in its attempt to call forth something that is such an anathema to our current way of looking at things. Embarrassing, but who if not the painter can indulge a little aspiration towards what appears to be ridiculous in the face of our current preoccupation with smothering the world in facile knowingness? Eduardo Chillida burrowed into the block of alabaster to call forth the light. Fra Angelico slid it between one colour and another so that it shone across the whole surface. Barnett Newman squeezed it into a vertical shaft, and Mark Rothko, who perhaps desired to reveal the light more than any artist in the twentieth century, shielded it from his eyes, as if its pure intensity would be too much to bear.

Time

Let us begin with a simple thought: meaning is always held in time. Something means one thing one minute and something else the next. We give weight to meaning yet at times it feels weightless. It is always a case of time and time again, from one moment to the next. It is impossible to grasp time as a continuum. Instead, we dip in and out of it as if scooping a cup of water out of a river. Yet to paraphrase Joseph Brodsky, time unlike water seems to flow horizontally through our lives.[1] Time, although most of the time vague and ungraspable, is one of the things that sits deep within painting. Deeper than any notion of space, which is always in itself imbued with time. Fast space, slow space, big space, small space, deep space, shallow space, clean space, confused space, they all hold time as a prerequisite to their perception and understanding. Time is what gives a painting its feel. Trusting that it will find its place in the painting allows it to be more than just a picture and become a painting.

Form

A form that is circumspect, which holds off from making itself explicit, in simple terms one might call a shy form. Hugging the wall, refraining from stepping out into the crowd and hurly-burly of art, a form which does not wish to chatter. To support such a form is to accept its indifference to the need for specific meaning. Its position is crude, rudimentary, in that it is ill formed. If it has an elegance then it is in its poise, held through its stillness, its quietude.

Holding back, the ridiculous contradiction imposed on the painter, of wishing to bring into the world something concrete, graspable, yet denying that impulse the space to exude by the act of painting itself. The flat surface of the painting is like an impenetrable wall. Try as he may, the painter cannot get into it, nor can he get out. Always, always, he must reconcile himself to that dumb surface.

Light

We are in the full light of day; it is a soft even light. Shadows in the folds of fabric, in the angles of limbs, are easy in their inflection of a darker tone. Shadow is not allowed to be drama, nor to have an inference of meaning beyond what it is, a softening of light. One would think light's presence in the painting is dependent upon contrast, the play of light and dark; here it is declared as being present even in shadow. The painting has what can only be called its own intrinsic light. A light not borrowed but coming directly from the mind's eye, making it sovereign to the painting itself. There is neither declaration of time, nor of mood, of situation nor of circumstance; rather, it is light as abstract thought, as a state of being.

Surface

An email from Kehnet in which he writes about his early days as an invigilator at the Statens Museum in Copenhagen, looking at the 'silent graspy surfaces' of the paintings of Vilhelm Hammershøi. Given that surface is in essence what a painting is, it is surprising how little it is spoken about. Glossed over, so to speak. Yet for the painter it is where the painting begins and where it ends.

Proximity

'The world was something different from what he thought it. It had come nearer, but in coming nearer it had grown smaller'.[2] The closeness of things, that strange contradiction that the closer we are to something the less we see.

For many years the photograph chased the painting. More recently, it has become a case of the painting pursuing the photograph, hunting it down to either eat it or love it to death. Thinking back to the four black plastic tubs containing their 35 mm films that have never been processed and never will be. Their time long gone as if a mirage hovering like a veil between what has been seen and can only be imagined. Always with photographs there is this gap between what is concrete in the film and the filament of what was and will be seen. Its arrival held through time, the time of waiting, photograph taken, film processed and print made. So mundane an activity, yet holding within it its own intimate reflective sequence, evolving towards the image. The mind has time to think between these gaps, time to forget what was actually seen and come to terms with what the photograph can be. Looking is held still and seeing changes as the image evolves from film to print. Now, of course, with the digital camera, images jump into life the moment they are taken. Without gaps or time for the mind to think, the image steps into the shoes of reality just like that, becoming more real in its immediacy for some than reality itself.

What if, he thought, instead of painting on the surface of the canvas each day he painted directly on the wall, just painted the wall white from top to bottom. It already had numerous layers of white paint on it, from being repainted to cover over the various splashes of paint and smudges from the daily act of painting. Perhaps, he wondered, if every day he painted the whole wall twice a day, how thick would those layers of paint be after a year, one or two millimetres, half a centimetre? How long he wondered would it take at such a rate to paint himself out of the studio?

Darkness folds into itself; black has a tendency to do the same thing. Attempting to pull it away from this introspection is part of the challenge of using it as a colour. One wants to make it breathe, to open out into the world.

Edges are more enigmatic in the large paintings. They cease being details and begin to have the capability to evoke meanings.

When something is physically out of one's reach, the nature of the visual experience changes. Looking comes more to the fore; at the same time one becomes more aware of one's physical relationship to what one is looking at. A strange contradiction is set up. The gap between looking and the physical experience of its supposed absence somehow becomes more pregnant with feeling. Perhaps on one level this gap between looking and feeling is the beginning of abstraction.

Kurt Kocherscheidt: The Sense of an Ending
(2013)

1992, it is early November. I am in Vienna visiting an old friend, the painter Kurt Kocherscheidt. We had planned to travel together to southern Hungary; however, Kocherscheidt's health is not good, so instead we are staying in the city, chewing the cud as they say, and generally mooching around. It is good to see him. After a couple of days we decide to go over to the print workshop of Kurt Zein on the other side of the city. Kocherscheidt has recently finished some woodcuts he would like to sign and having worked in the workshop with Zein the previous year I am keen to see him again. It is a lazy jovial day and midway into the signing Zein suggests that he prepare an etching plate and that Kocherscheidt and I spend the rest of the afternoon working on a print together. There is no pressure, so we start. Kocherscheidt begins by drawing onto the centre of the pristine plate a solid shape resembling a Parma ham. This is then aquatinted so that it will print strong black. Now it is my turn. In contrast to Kocherscheidt's flat solid form I take a chisel and gouge in hard dry point a line version of the ham, resembling a loosely gridded cage floating above and away from the solid form below. Zein proofs the plate; however, it is too clean except for the double image, even with the coarse dry point. So, we take the plate out of the workshop into the courtyard below and stamp it hard face down, grinding it into the surface of the rough concrete ground. Zein cleans off the debris now sticking to the plate and reproofs. We mull the print over for a while and decide it is finished. Later in the day, while sitting talking and looking at the final print, Kocherscheidt jokingly comments that the image, with the lighter gridded drawing hovering above the solid form, looks like the spirit of the ham is about to leave the body. We laugh about it, but with hindsight it seems charged. For two days later, Kocherscheidt is rushed to hospital in Vienna, then the following day to Wels, and while undergoing emergency surgery for his long-standing heart condition he dies. He is gone; he was 49 years old.

...

What does it mean when we speak about the late works of an artist? For a painter like Willem de Kooning, who died well into his nineties, it is clear the late works are those of an old man, taking on the quality that Virginia Woolf referred to as 'the power of taking hold of experience, of turning it round, slowly, in the light'.[1] For it is as if late works can take on a silvery translucent sheen, appearing to be already divested of the corporeality of life, becoming almost transcendental in nature and evoking a freeing of the spirit. With old age, we can, and do, surmise a certain otherness that lies beyond our own current years, one which only great age is able to instil. This state is perhaps best summed up as an inner wisdom, one that augurs the arrival of the closing of the day, distilling as it does, in the process, an irrefutable and inimical last statement, without need of further amplification. A statement that, often with painters, contains a recapitulation of the artist's earlier concerns, the cycle of life seeming to be complete, coming as it does, full circle.

But what of the artist who dies younger, for whom we cannot speak of the fullness of the life, of the work, in the same way? Of whom we must predicate our understanding of the work as a rupture, a break, whether sudden or of a longer duration, and irrespective of how it came about, which nevertheless gives us another and different sense of an ending. How do we perceive it? And in the late works of such an artist, is there something specific to those works that intimates and illuminates a final closure? Or are we simply by default vicarious witnesses to that imminent ending?

...

When I look at the late paintings of Kocherscheidt, I think in particular of a painting by Francisco de Zurbarán in the National Gallery in London, a painting I return to repeatedly. It depicts St Francis on his knees, dressed in a rough brown habit, clutching a human skull to his chest. The feel of the painting is of a sombre warmth. It is painted in an overriding palette of browns, a colour many painters find difficult to work with. Edvard Munch referred to brown as being used by the painter to conceal,[2] an easy way to unify the surface of the painting. Yet in Zurbarán's hands brown is alive and well and can at its best inhabit an earthy glow. Kocherscheidt's pervasive use of brown in his work in the 1990s, however, suggests something quite different, an increasing sense of foreboding. It is the other side of brown, accentuated by a simplification of forms and a general darkening of his overall palette. With Kocherscheidt brown is a colour we cannot quite put our finger on, in much the same way as we find it difficult to identify the colour(s) in the late paintings of Mark Rothko. With both painters one feels that the light is being squeezed out of the painting, and we are left with a leaden earthiness, a strong gravitational pull downwards. It is as if the physical nature of paint and its inherent colour is pushed hard up against an obdurate and ill-defined subject matter, reluctant to reveal itself, a subject matter that at the same time feels somehow soiled, too closely wedded to the visceral sense of blood and sweat of the human body. The physical nature of paint becomes a metaphor for the rawness of life. Then painting ceases to be about the painted image, and instead becomes primarily paint as material, as a manifestation of the human condition. No gap is left between paint and painter in which to embroider comfortable meaning.

•••

1993, it is early spring. I am visiting Franz and Eva Morat at their home in Freiburg. They have over many years been enormous supporters of Kurt Kocherscheidt and his work, as well as very close friends. We are sitting in the kitchen talking when Franz asks me which paintings were hanging on the walls in his studio when I visited Kocherscheidt the previous November, his very last paintings. I try to remember but cannot be sure. I can remember that there were not many paintings in the studio, perhaps eight or so, and that they were not big, at least for Kocherscheidt. There were four or five on the walls and the others scattered around on the floor, leaning against the walls. It felt like the artist had spent time shuffling the paintings around, trying one next to another, the way some painters do, to get to know the works. The paintings had the feel of having been painted quickly, perhaps each in one go. Kocherscheidt was incredibly prolific during the last three years of his life, making 65 paintings in 1990, 26 in 1991 and 44 up until his death in November 1992. The last nine paintings I saw in the studio during my visit were probably made after his return in the autumn from a summer in Grieselstein, the family's country home.

Two of these paintings in particular I find intriguing: they depict what looks like a seed pod, or some kind of valve, set against a uniform ground. They are painted in brown on a lighter more ochre background, their colour giving the 'objects' a peculiarly leathery feel. As such they take me back to the paintings by Kocherscheidt from the late 1970s and early 1980s in which small objects appeared to be placed randomly together to form a group, resembling a still-life. What those early works had, however, was an easy casualness, even a playfulness, not evident in the last paintings. Rather, in the late paintings the object, a single isolated object, has been placed flat, hard and tight against the almost monochrome ground. They do not look or feel like still-lifes; they are more emblematic, as if lifted out and abstracted, yet somehow still curiously precisely objectified. When I first saw these paintings, I was perplexed, and even today I find myself held at a distance from them. For they seem to contain and engender a state of anxiety, as if something is being overly scrutinised, yet unknowable, at least to the viewer.

The expression 'through a glass, darkly' springs to mind.[3] That sensation of looking at something, yet not seeing it clearly. All good paintings set up some kind of block, a means of obscuring, so that we cannot fully get into them. Meaning is inaccessible beyond a certain point, our contact dissolves, and we are left bereft. Thrown back on our own devices, or not, as the case may be. One of the reasons good paintings are so beguiling, and that we keep going back to them, is precisely because they do not reveal all, or let us fully in. We are held at a distance. Hence, we return again and again, in a vain attempt to get closer. The curious quality about the last paintings of Kocherscheidt is that they do initially appear to be 'letting us in'. We feel we are being intimate with the painting and the object depicted. For all their gruff earthiness they are explicit and welcome us. Yet paradoxically, this access is only fleeting, then we are thrown back to paint as paint, that lumpen brown viscous material again.

• • •

In a letter to René Schickele in 1930 Joseph Roth wrote 'only time and not talent can provide us with distance'.[4] All paintings hold time. It is one of their redeeming qualities. Beyond the image, if indeed there really is an image, time is what gives a painting true meaning. Beyond any formal or abstract concerns of the artist, it is what weds the painting back to our lives as viewers. It is the means by which we come to a painting and also how we begin to leave.

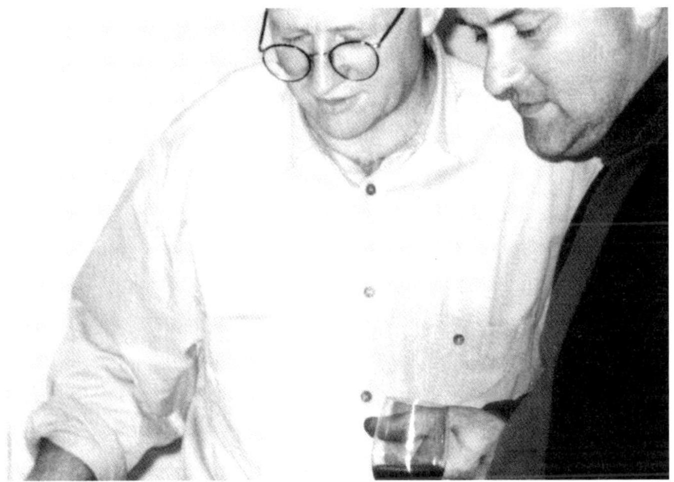

Dear Elfi, Hartgrove, 5 January 2013.

Where to begin?

How to speak about certain things? How to bridge the distances between different times in our lives? Times charged by the events of one's life, then blurred or made crystalline by time's furtive presence.

It is Vienna, early November 1992. I am visiting you and Kurt. It is evening. We are sitting at the dinner table eating, with Ivo and August. Kurt and Ivo are having one of those typical sparring sessions common between father and son, I as a father know well. The young buck and the bear staking their claim. At one point in the evening, I look across the table to

Kurt and for one fleeting moment I cannot recognise him. His face is gaunt, detached, somehow less. Then the moment is passed.

The next day, joining you in the hospital waiting room, after visiting Kurt, I have tears in my eyes.

Later, months later. The kind of later which holds even this moment within it, yet feels like it never was, we meet again in Vienna. You look so fragile I hardly dare touch you. You ask me about that time sitting in the hospital. Did I know that Kurt was dying? I had no answer.

Later again, much later, with time between, standing in the basement of the Morat Institute in Freiburg, stuffed as it is with books and paraphernalia, I ask Franz about a bronze face mask lying on the table. 'Why, don't you recognise him?', he exclaims, 'it's Kurt, his death mask'. I am confused and thrown, I cannot see him. Then it dawns on me that it is the same face I saw momentarily at the dinner table, all those years before. This recognition jolts and frightens me, then, slowly releases me.

Our lives are made up of infinite cycles which pulse and flow like the sea. Sometimes, just sometimes, a small bubble will surface and in that delicate encircling form we have the chance to see and perhaps understand.

With affection,

Ian

Published in *Kurt Kocherscheidt, Im Fluss der Bilder, Malerei*, exh. cat., Josef Albers Museum, Quadrat Bottrop, 2013, pp. 126–31

Painting on the Threshold, Richard Diebenkorn (2015)

Paint is slippery stuff. It drips, pours, spreads, pools, thickens, thins, slips and slides; once out of the tube or can, it is almost formless. Unlike most materials used by artists, which retain something of their inherent form in the making process, giving the artist an intrinsic structure to build upon, paint, its fluidity, rubs right up against the artist's sensibility.

This makes for a raw engagement, one often difficult for painters to get their hands on. Much of painting's history over the last 200 years has been about this predicament: paint's elusive nature and how the artist either tames it, or lets it run wild. For paint either heats up the artist's temperament, encourages excess, or else it is held in stasis by the artist, somehow stilled as it is applied to the canvas. Either way, most painters struggle with this beast in one way or another. For painting is first and foremost a declaration and display of temperament. Before all else, it is this we feel when we engage as a viewer with a painting.

The American artist Richard Diebenkorn painted *Ocean Park #79* in 1975. It is one of an extensive group of abstract paintings, all with the title *Ocean Park*, which he made between 1967 and 1985, eight years prior to his death in 1993. They evolved, one leading to the next, their collective identity slowly becoming discernible with time. There are now 125 such paintings. They represent what is considered to be the third and last phase of Diebenkorn's oeuvre. The *Ocean Park* series was preceded by an overtly figurative middle period, which in itself followed on from an early phase of work in which the paintings were again abstract. However, they were abstract in a different way to the later *Ocean Park* series, in that they were rooted in the biomorphic forms of the Abstract Expressionists, more specifically in the work of fellow Americans, the painters Arshile Gorky and Robert Motherwell.

If the early abstract works by Diebenkorn are composed of flowing interlocking forms, then the *Ocean Park* series is distinctly angular and urban. Although appearing counter-intuitive, in going from abstraction, to figuration, then back again to abstraction, the trajectory of Diebenkorn's work does in fact pursue a clear enquiry into the nature of what, in painting, abstraction might be.

By contemporary standards, in comparison to, say, the consciously theatrical megapictures of Anselm Kiefer or David Hockney, *Ocean Park #79* is not a big painting. It measures 236.2 x 205.7 cm. Indeed, its size could be said to hold a relative modesty, a characteristic common to Diebenkorn's work. Higher and wider than a doorway, yet still having a sense of the scale of the human body, perhaps the height and width of a man with arms raised high or spread wide, this human scale seems important to the painting. The paintings in Diebenkorn's *Ocean Park* series seem actively to want to pull us back to our own physical place in the world, to find an intimate contact with the viewer, whereby it becomes a specific one-to-one, body-to-body relationship. The body that is the painting and the body that is our own.

A painting is a door. It is also a threshold. Grace Hartigan, the American painter, said, 'I want a surface that resists, like a wall, not opens like a gate.'[1] We could say that one of the fundamental differences between American and European painting is how space is handled. American painting tends to be flatter, the image, if there is one, more emblematic, a quality typified in something like Jasper Johns's *Flag* paintings or the stylised still-lifes of, for example, Wayne Thiebaud. Space in European painting, on the other hand, tends to be more nuanced, and there is greater spatial depth. Diebenkorn is often referred to as having a European sensibility because of his use of space. The paintings in the *Ocean Park* series do have a flatness to them, as has all his work, yet at the same time the space in them is finely nuanced, oscillating between the sensation of looking down, as in an aerial view, while at the same time looking straight ahead, suggesting a doorway, a space we can enter.

A pronounced vertical and horizontal view is presented to us. In most of the *Ocean Park* paintings horizontal bands are running predominantly across the upper part of the painting, these being met either by vertical columns or a more open, generalised space, imbuing the paintings with a strong architectural feel (*Ocean Park #116*, 1979). One is reminded of the look of the frescoes of Pompeii, or of some early Italian painting, where figures meet architectural features and both become subsumed in a broader composition, attaining, as Roberto Longhi wrote in reference to Piero della Francesca, a reduction back to 'demonstrations of surfaces'.[2]

It is curious that the more paint one puts on a painting, building the surface up, the less depth the painting has. It reverts to becoming material, flat paint. After all, a blob of paint is first and foremost just that, a blob of paint. It is also often the case that as a painter gets older, the application of paint gets thinner, more sparse. Think of the late paintings of Edvard Munch or Henri Matisse. Less becomes more, and transparency begins to annul the materiality of paint. With Diebenkorn's *Ocean Park* paintings the accretion of transparent thin washes of paint gives them a sense of inner space and light.

Paintings either breathe in or they breathe out; equally, they are absorbing light or releasing it out into the world. In Diebenkorn's paintings, especially the *Ocean Park* series, one senses strongly the dry brittle light of where the desert meets the ocean. A crystalline light, noticeably different to the moisture-softened light we have here in the British Isles. Diebenkorn said, 'I arrive at the light only after painting in it, not by aiming for it'.[3] For the painting to hold the light, as opposed to depicting it by the means of chiaroscuro and shading, would seem to be what Diebenkorn is aiming for. A state in which the space in the painting is self-illuminating, almost transcendent. Such omnipresent light takes us back to Italian Duecento and Trecento painting, to a light before the slant of the shadow and human tainting, a time when form was held as pure colour.

The American painter Willem de Kooning in a statement about his understanding of abstraction compared it to the look on a German sailor's face.[4] Georgia O'Keeffe, another American artist, when asked about an abstract drawing she had made, replied that it was about a headache.[5] Our usual understanding of abstraction in art is that artists begin with something visually realistic in the world, and then somehow modify it, simplify it away from its original recognisable form. But are there other ways to understand abstraction? In his book, *Early Christian Art*, Frederick van der Meer writes of, 'this constant double image – prefiguration and fulfilment, shadow and reality, past and present', words that are redolent with the complexities of attempting to paint an abstract painting.[6] For the painting must find itself, and hold itself, in a condition whereby figuration is never declared and fulfilment is withheld, yet it must suggest a presence; a precarious state, a sort of waiting to be.

The term 'prefiguration', as used by Van der Meer, is perhaps helpful in understanding the nature of the abstract in Diebenkorn's late works. If our conventional understanding of abstraction in painting is that the image somehow moves away from the concrete object, be it a chair, an apple or indeed the human body and becoming in the process more abstract, then prefiguration suggests something prior to the object actually being perceived. A painting that is formed in the artist's mind before the concrete world appears, in which any notion of representing is preceded by felt experience. Certainly, in the architectonic spaces set up in the *Ocean Park* paintings, there is a sense of expectancy, as if the space is waiting for the figure to materialise, to come into being. Yet, curiously enough, we somehow know it will not arrive, and the empty space in the paintings takes on a significance whereby absence becomes more weighted than presence (*Ocean Park #43*, 1971). This pregnant space is not new to painting. One need only think of Simone Martini's incredibly beautiful painting, from 1333, of the *Annunciation* in the Uffizi in Florence. Flanked on the left side by the Archangel Gabriel and to the right the unsuspecting Virgin, the empty central area of the painting is, literally, pregnant with expectation. The *Annunciation*'s 'abstract-ness' is the subject of the painting.

Perhaps related to this is a sense of time. For paintings are as much about holding time, their own time, as they are about form and space. The time it takes for apparently empty, abstract space to begin to hold potential meaning or the waiting for meaning to configure itself. Of course, wedded to this is also a sense of stillness, a slowing down. Have you noticed how fast-painted paintings are seldom quiet, rarely hold still? The art critic Adrian Stokes wrote, 'The great work of art is surrounded by silence.'[7] One senses in the *Ocean Park* series that this was something Diebenkorn was striving for, to still the painting, whereby we too, as viewers, are invited to be still. They are meditative paintings, in no rush to reveal themselves. Paintings that need time.

In our contemporary world of ceaseless moving images, where pictures bounce forth to meet us as soon as we get up in the morning, there is a fundamental question of what painting is for today. Many contemporary painters now embrace the new technologies and the pace of the modern visual world, run with the pack so to speak. Indeed, much of Postmodernism's *raison d'être* has been about assimilating the canon of painting into its fold. However, for some painters, and Diebenkorn is certainly among them, there is always one fundamental question: what is specific to painting, sovereign to painting, that allows it to find its own place in the world? To stand alone, to be of itself, above and beyond references to other visual media, whereby we are left with no crutches, but have to face the painting emphatically as painting. This question asked now, in an art world that is so self-consciously knowing, and where a belief in painting per se is treated with scepticism, might appear naive. Yet the question is still pertinent, and the reason why the paintings of Richard Diebenkorn are so relevant.

Published in *Royal Academy of Arts Magazine*, no. 126, Spring 2015, pp. 50–5.

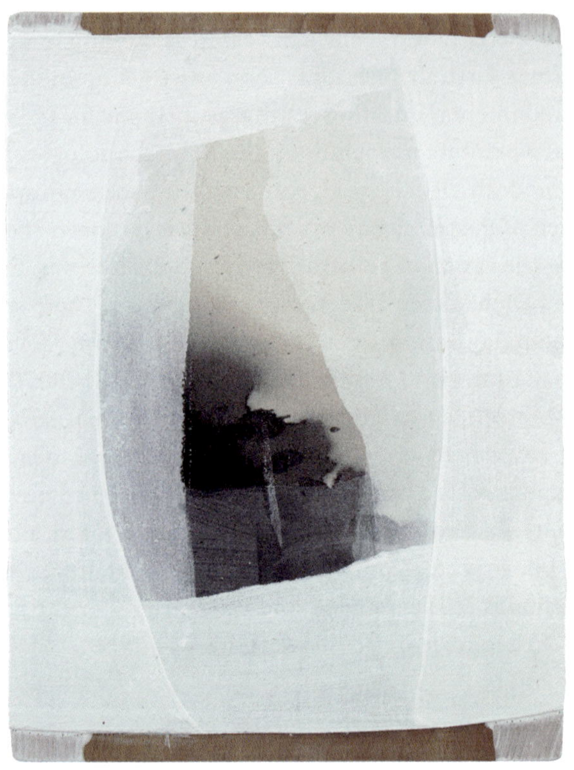

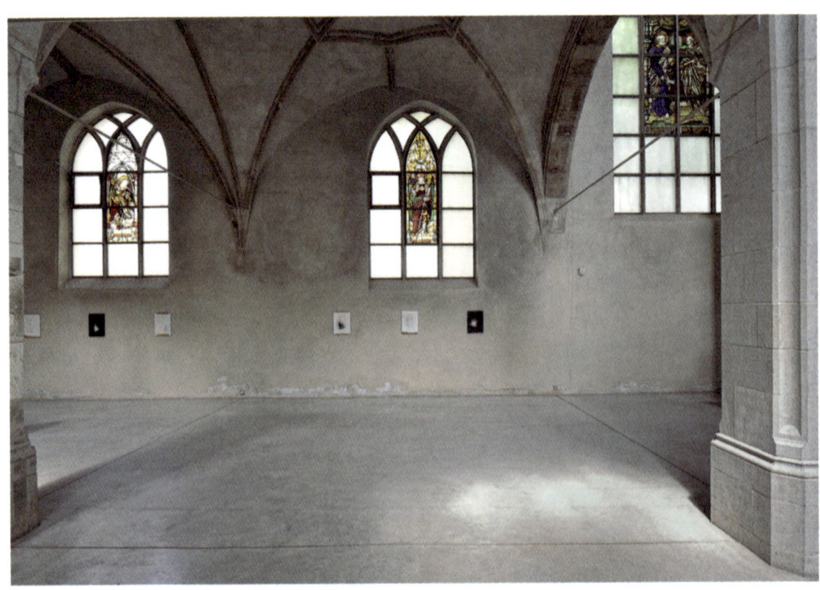

Wood, Paint and Recycling
(2015)

I have always liked the conjunction of wood and paint. Perhaps this goes back to my childhood, kitchen cupboards scuffed and chipped with constant use. The paintwork scrubbed clean revealing a mellow fusion of wood and paint. I now seek out this union wherever I can find it: churches, old buildings, furniture, junk shops. To be more precise, it is the junction of white paint or plaster with warm wood, set against other surfaces. As in the Sala de Mexuar in the Alhambra Palace, Granada, where the warm rich surface of the underside of the wooden ceiling rafters meets the rich off-white of plasterwork. Also in Spain, in the roof cavity separating the older horizontal timbers of the outer roof and ceiling from the later domed false ceiling in the Convento de Santa Clara, Salamanca. The hidden fourteenth- to fifteenth-century Mudejar ceiling glows with the play of wood and colour. The reds in particular, deep vermilion, seem polished until luminous.

I have always discarded works that I feel are going wrong in the process of making, preferring to start again rather than salvage what looks like a lost cause. I like works to look clean and clear rather than a car crash. Certainly, over the years this need has become more pronounced as the paintings have become more pristine and the transparency of their making more evident. In the early years I simply disposed of these abandoned canvases. Later, sometime in the mid-1990s, I began to keep these rejects, rolling them up and storing them away, thinking that one day I might better understand their incalcitrant nature, find a way to revisit them.

The desire to use wood and paint together has been an area I have returned to many times over the years, usually without success, the works either being too woody or too formulaic. It is a very different experience to paint on a flat wooden board as opposed to a canvas. The board unyielding, pushing the paint too quickly back to its materiality, as opposed to the flex and bounce of the canvas. The brush prefers the yield of the canvas, the paint goes in rather than sitting on the surface, giving the paint a different pace and feel.

In 2012 I was invited to make an exhibition at Kunst-Station Sankt Peter, Cologne. Sankt Peter is a Catholic church in the centre of the city, which although still consecrated is largely empty and given over to a programme of contemporary exhibitions. I had seen two or three exhibitions there prior to being invited; all in one way or another tried to compete with the building, take on its size, and all had on one level or another failed. How can one compete with the physical mass of a large church, especially with paintings? Their very being is dependent upon another notion of size, which is not architectural, not about housing the human form, but more echoing it. There had to be another way and so I went small. This took me back to the rolls of abandoned canvases and to wood.

For the exhibition I made a series of small plywood, painted canvas panels, all 45 x 33 cm, using fragments from my discarded rolls. I cut the painted canvas sections so that when glued on, the plywood areas of the wood were left exposed, using the cut edges of the canvas as a kind of drawing where paint meets wood. Some were left just like this, others reworked over with paint, again using the brushed paint edge as another line where paint meets wood. In the autumn of 2014, 28 of these works were exhibited in Sankt Peter on the two adjacent walls of the nave below the window height, with the title 'Hours of Darkness – Hours of Light'.

Thinking back, recycling works is not something new within my work. Both the *Sand and Sea Series* and the *Field Series* of the 1970s recycled drawings left out in the landscape to weather, documented with photographs, the photos subsequently being assimilated back into a final work. Equally, in many of the early *Diptych Series* of 1981–91, one half of the paintings was painted over a previously abandoned landscape work, the other half painted new. The final *Diptych* was a play between one half of the work newly emerging as an image, while the other darker half, usually more heavily painted, was the pushing back of an existing image until almost obliterated. Coming and going, so to speak. The 'Hours of Darkness – Hours of Light' painted panels contain something of this dialectic.

Same Old Story
(2015)

Trying to get an angle on what might constitute the core identity of the British painting tradition is like looking for fool's gold. It has no hard centre. What has become identified as British painting, School of London figuration, the work of Lucian Freud, Leon Kossoff, Frank Auerbach, is steeped in German Expressionism and Austrian angst. Their painting is in essence about as British as a slice of Sachertorte or a Berliner pastry. Although emigrating to Britain when young, these artists brought with them their own tradition and sensibility and largely stayed true to that tradition, held Britishness at bay. Perhaps that is why the only 'true Brit' in the group, Michael Andrews, looks curiously out of place. This is not in any way to denigrate these artists, their significance is there to be seen, but only to make the simple observation that their work is not nurtured out of a British sensibility.

Does this matter, one might justifiably ask? No, but then again, yes it does. Good art, painting, is rooted; it grows out of something. That something has to be real, the ground substantial enough to support growth. One cannot make good art while on holiday, so to speak. No matter how 'international' art may now appear to be, good art is directly fed by the culture out of which it grows. The two are intertwined. Attempting to place art somewhere 'out there' in free fall for the sake of political correctness is to diminish it.

Perhaps a truer manifestation of a British figurative painting tradition is evident in the earlier work of the Bloomsbury Group, painting with quite a different character to that of the School of London. Less raw, more polite, lacking in psychological and emotional depth, a painting more at ease with itself and the world. The paintings all too easily settling into the armchairs of the educated privileged class. A painting that did not wish to disrupt. Disruption, when it did occur, was left to a writer, Virginia Woolf, who took the human psyche into far deeper and uncomfortable territory than any of the painters dared to go. The painters may have seen the lighthouse, but none ventured to enter, climb the stairs and turn on the light.

Instead, they held things at arm's length, turned art into a comfortable engagement. A polite exchange with the audience that still influences much of British art even today.

This softening and gentrification of external influences could be said to be what constitutes a recognisable British painting. The St Ives painters, Peter Lanyon, William Scott, Roger Hilton and Patrick Heron, did this with the work of the American Abstract Expressionists, just as the generation of British Pop painters domesticated American Pop art. Visit the National Gallery in London and it is room 33 before one comes across British painting in the eighteenth century. In getting there one has walked through the early Italians, Duccio, Piero della Francesca, then on past Titian, Rembrandt and the full weight of European painting. In many ways the National Gallery's incredible collection of paintings distorts our self-perception of our own Johnny-come-lately contribution within the broader Western painting tradition. We adopted that tradition by proxy. We adopted the Wilton Diptych (almost certainly Flemish or French) or the work of Hans Holbein as being somehow quasi-British, just as in naming Diego Velázquez's painting 'The Rokeby Venus' we somehow claimed greater ownership than simply having it. We wed it back to being of that place, while at the same time mumbling under our breath that if we had not had the Reformation then we too would have had a Piero della Francesca, an Albrecht Dürer or a Johannes Vermeer. Of course, the reality is we really did have the Dark Ages. There simply was not enough light to paint anything of significance, and no artists here to paint the paintings even if there had been.

When painting did emerge in Britain with any vigour in the eighteenth century, then it was with a certain pallor. A propensity in its colouring towards earth colours, especially brown. Just think of the paintings of J. M. W. Turner, John Constable or George Stubbs. This was inevitable. Britain is built on clay and mud, whereas Italy, say, is built on clean rock and has clear skies. Italian painting was never going to lapse into murkiness; hard rock would make certain of that. It seems British painting had no alternative but to slip into the muddy ooze from which it grew. A world of defused light and vague atmosphere. Painting, like a nation's psyche, grows out of the land on which its people walk.

In speaking about brown, Mark Rothko referred to it as a colour used to obscure, suggesting it was a means of fudging, of avoiding clarity. Perhaps there is some truth in this. British painting emerged at a time when the broader European tradition was itself pushing colour out of the painting, getting a little fuzzy around the edges. It was engaged with more overt expressiveness, eliminating the cleanly pictorial and moving towards a concern more with abstraction, the point where feel takes over picturing, so to speak. Yet interestingly, British painting in making its way through these transitions never did seem to find its own identity or clarity. The distinctive voices in British painting have always been the oddballs, Turner standing out from the niceties of Thomas Gainsborough or Joshua Reynolds like a sore thumb. His work is still conspicuously ill-fitting and separated out as presented at Tate Britain. Or William Blake, his pictorial inventiveness often being seen as more eccentric than worthy of elevation.

Abstraction has always been an anathema to the British sensibility, which craves a narrative. Without a strong storyline the British mindset seems incapable of following anything except the most rudimentary. This almost pathological need runs right through everything: political discourse, the media and the arts. It is a blind spot that has impoverished everything from the debates around Brexit, to how the arts are presented in the media. Everything is story-led; core concepts, the abstract ideas behind something, are offloaded as being excess baggage. Yet, most stories are themselves excess baggage, usually having a soft core. At best, they can shelter deeper thought, but are more often than not only a way of deflecting away from that which truly matters. Here one need only think of popular culture, the media in general, and their propensity to denigrate the serious, to trivialise, almost as an act of faith. Understanding this, separating out the story 'about' from that which something really is, should be a part of our critical understanding of the world. Yet for some reason in Britain we prefer to ignore this. Making light with a bit of a story is a far more comfortable place to be.

Bounce

(2017)

'It's slap bang hard up against the surface', he says.
    'Are you sure?', I say.
'Well, you wouldn't get a sliver of paper in there, it's that tight', he says.
    'Let's have another look', I say.
'Well, what do you think?', he says.
    'Perhaps we should start again', I say.
'Do you think it will make a difference?', he says.
    'Who knows?', I say.
'Hang on, you're right, I can see something now', he says.
    'Yep, but can you get inside?', I say.
'Don't know, let's see', he says.
    'Give it a try', I say.
'There's something in there, I can feel it', he says.
    'That's a good start', I say.
'I'll go as far as I can', he says.
    'Why not?', I say.
'Who'd have thought there would be so much space', he says.
    'Always is, once you're inside', I say.
'Now I can see right in, it's big', he says.
    'What d'you see?', I say.
'Looks like a body, all scrunched up', he says.
    'A body?', I say.
'Yep, a body', he says.
    'Anything else?', I say.
'All kinds of stuff, here take a look', he says.
    'You're right', I say.
'Damned body's gone, what now?', he says.
    'Must be something', I say.
'All a bit vague', he says.

'Normal', I say.

'Feels strange', he says.

'Different every time', I say.

'What next', he says.

'Can you get a hand on the red?', I say.

'Hum!', he says.

'Try it', I say.

'The white's in the way', he says.

'White's like that', I say.

'The stuff is everywhere, won't let me through to the red', he says.

'Easier than black', I say.

'Wouldn't know about that', he says.

'Trust me', I say.

'Thought I had it then', he says.

'Had what?', I say.

'The red', he says.

'And', I say.

'Nothing', he says.

'Try that body again', I say.

'Nope, it's gone. There's a blobby thing now', he says.

'Can you get hold of it?', I say.

'Nope, keeps moving', he says.

'Try pushing it towards the red', I say.

'Easier said than done', he says.

'Come at it from the other side', I say.

'Maybe, nope, now that's gone too!', he says.

'Another day', I say.

'Another day', he says.

Visiting Joan Mitchell

(2017)

1984, a visitor to the studio. At some point in the conversation the name of the American painter Joan Mitchell crops up. I admire her work, although at the time her paintings were difficult to see in Europe. I had always assumed that being American she lived in the United States, but no, I am told, she lives just outside Paris, having moved to France some years earlier with her then partner the French Canadian painter Jean-Paul Riopelle. A few days after the visit a postcard arrives with the telephone number of Mitchell, suggesting that should I be in Paris I give her a call.

The following year while in Paris with Gerlinde, from a phone box I try the number. A gravelly female voice responds, 'what do you want?'. After a brief conversation Mitchell invites us out to visit her. We take the train to Vétheuil and upon arrival at the house are invited into a largish room furnished simply with a long wooden table, benches either side. Mitchell is petite, with fringed black hair and large horn-rimmed spectacles, which make her look even smaller. A cigarette hangs out of the corner of her mouth. She places at one end of the table a bottle of wine and two glasses; we sit at the other. She then excuses herself saying she will be back shortly. Two German Shepherd dogs that had accompanied her as she greeted us upon arrival remain in the room, sitting alert between us and the wine. It seems wiser just to sit and wait.

Returning, Mitchell abruptly asks me about other painters. She has just come back from the Venice Biennale where Howard Hodgkin is representing Britain and is keen to know my thoughts. I have the strong feeling I am being tested. What to say? I have never been drawn to the work of Hodgkin. She asks why? How to put it, it is a particularly British thing. The paintings' insistence upon an anecdotal narrative to carry the work panders to all the worst indulgences of the English sensibility, which has an almost pathological need for a storyline and an element of voyeurism in order to engage. Hodgkin's paintings shamelessly serve this need.

The colour sugary sweet. The dauby self-conscious brush marks too present as the artist's 'signature'. The work is safe and often as comfy as a sofa. Little seems to be risked in the paintings; they are polite. Mitchell listens, then asks about other painters: Emilio Vedova, whose work is very current, the Germans and some American painters. The questioning goes on for some time. She then suggests we go into the studio and look at the paintings.

Over the next two or three hours, Gerlinde and I are shown works, Mitchell giving me that 'don't you dare' look whenever I suggest I help carry the larger paintings to the wall. She does not say much, and I mostly look. It is a real pleasure to see the work, a generous encounter. As Gerlinde and I prepare to leave, Mitchell suggests we join her at the local restaurant for dinner, which we do. One of the dogs lies under the table. The dinner talk is much about the predicament of being a woman painter in the macho climate of 1950s–60s America. Clement Greenberg's overarching influence and his resistance to female painters. I begin to understand something of what drove her to settle in France. But, of course, it is not that simple, it never is. We leave, and I keep in touch with the occasional postcard or letter.

To speak about a female painter, be politically correct, one must be gender neutral. Leave the woman, or the man for that matter, behind. Or in the case of a woman, proactively foreground this aspect. I find both approaches difficult to take, too prescriptive. I am attracted to the work of certain female painters including Joan Mitchell, Georgia O'Keeffe, Hilma af Klint. Drawn I sense strongly to a quality in the work that I do not see in male painters. A man simply could not have made the works they did. The work has something other, beyond what a man can do. Just as no man could have written the novels of Virginia Woolf or the poems of Anna Akhmatova. This is not to say that their works are dependent upon gender difference, they go beyond this difference; rather to simply acknowledge that difference gives difference. A difference I find incredibly rich and intriguing. I grew up in a fatherless household with my mother and two sisters. The female psyche enveloped me. It was something in my life I learnt to value greatly and take as a given. Perhaps here I am getting into dangerous waters and digressing from what I set out to say about

Mitchell as a painter, but political correctness can at a certain point become indifference, lazy thinking.

Siri Hustvedt in an essay on Mitchell refers to her large paintings, and some are very large, as being hermaphrodites, arguing that there is a fragility, a femininity, to some of her brushstrokes, while the size of the paintings posits the masculine.[1] I can get where Hustvedt is coming from in wishing to de-gender Mitchell's work, yet I find this take on the work too simplistic, too dependent for support on gender stereotypes; too prone to lapses into well-trodden clichés. Several women artists have produced large ambitious paintings, one need only think of O'Keeffe, af Klimt or Agnes Martin. The nature of the painted statement sometimes necessitates size, irrespective of gender. Equally, there have been many male painters with what we might call a fragile touch, think of Fra Angelico or much of the history of early Italian painting. If difference does exist, and I think it does, between male and female painters, then perhaps its presence is not so overt as the marks made or the size of the canvas, but sits much deeper in the work. At levels that get too close to our own psyche for comfort, which blur rather than polarise. Touching areas of what it means to be human, which most critical writing prefers to shy away from, the felt experience. Here, one need only think of the tendency in art magazines for the writer to be divested of the sense of self, of an 'I', to be replaced by a protocol of self-impartiality. What is speaking is the magazine, not a person.

Standing in Mitchell's studio, what strikes me first is the lightness of the painting. These are not 'heavy' paintings. Big, yes, however they are not pulling back down towards the ground. I try to identify why this is. In the large horizontal paintings, the sense of looking is almost cinematic. They resist the gravitational pull down, while the 'image', for want of a better word, is somehow still held, no matter how tentatively. The paintings have that same suspension of space which is present on the cinema screen. It is a curious quality, there and not there, fleeting, different from much of American painting: in contrast, say, to Mark Rothko's hovering forms that are strongly secured against an implied base line; or Jackson Pollock's drips pulling directly back to the land and the human psyche; and Willem de Kooning's anchorage back to the human body. Perhaps related to this difference of weight and fixity in Mitchell's work, in relationship to much American painting, is a sense of lightness in the colour palette and paint handling. Nothing is pressing. The paintings are less emblematic, more European in their acceptance of doubt and uncertainty.

As a second-generation Abstract Expressionist Mitchell stayed true to the gesture, while many others of her generation eventually shied away from it. Think of the overtly figurative late paintings of Philip Guston, or the schematic 'Unfurleds' of Morris Louis. The painted gesture can be both profound and trite. The tipping point from one to the other is very fine. The good painter knows this; the bad painter does not. In my time with Mitchell we never spoke about making. That seemed a given. Just as meaning in a painting is a given, it does not gain from being further articulated, at least not directly in front of the painting.

Claude Monet comes to mind in looking at Mitchell's paintings. Especially the more gestural, open works, such as the long horizontal *Water Lilies* (1919–20) in the Musée Marmottan in Paris or the vertical *Weeping Willow* (1920–21), which is also there. Both are late paintings, created at a time when Monet was losing his sight and seeking help from opticians brave enough to experiment with lenses that might help him see his paintings fully again. To see and to see again is apt in thinking about Mitchell's paintings, for they have the quality of first looking. Every time of looking is the first time. This quality gives the paintings a certain European-ness. It is different to much American painting, in which the 'look' is often emphatically stated. The look is what it is. A more nuanced, similar quality to that of Mitchell's paintings is present in the works of Cy Twombly and Mark Tobey, painters who, like Mitchell, spent significant lengthy periods living in Europe. One senses a look beyond a purely American take on things. In the case of Mitchell this difference can also be located in a different sense of time. A multilayering of time that effaces any explicit rush to surface meaning.

An aspect of this European-ness is also evident in how the paintings are structured, the feel they evoke. Both Mitchell and Twombly rarely occupy the whole canvas with active paintwork. There is usually what we might term a neutral zone upon which the action of painting situates itself, be it the white of the primed canvas with Mitchell or with Twombly often a discreetly painted ground. Neither artist paints edge to edge. This aspect of leaving empty could be said to be one of the pronounced qualities in the work, allowing an open-endedness counter to much American painting which posits emphatic edges.

In the case of Twombly this neutral ground functions as the blank sheet upon which the artist's 'script' is written, the words side-stepping and throwing off our usual understanding of resolved pictorial space Weight is taken off the pictorial, displacing it, with one language inflecting another language. The cusp of transfer from one to the other invokes meaning poignant with both a sense of loss and possible revelation. Time past, time present, both intimating a knowingness that is then cut short by the blunt dumbness of the paintbrush. With Mitchell the gap in the canvas between empty and occupied is less knowing, less of culture and more of nature. The nature of a sensate being and ensuing temperament. The paintings are not guarded by culture as they are with Twombly. To fill the painted canvas edge to edge is to declare a boundary. This gives the painting a specific authority. In seldom using this approach Mitchell refrained from positing closure and separation. The paintings are always open, never feel hermetic, are actively breathing. There is always plenty of air in them. The paintings veer towards the floating elusiveness of pure consciousness, rather than any concreteness of knowing.

Over 30 years later I am standing in front of Mitchell's *Salut Tom*, from 1979, in the Royal Academy. It is a monumental painting measuring 280 x 802 cm, filling most of the wall. The large horizontal paintings of the 1970s, such as *Salut Tom* and *Clearing*, are for me the artist at her strongest. The scale of the canvas allows her painting language to fully open up, to breathe. *Salut Tom* is made up of four vertical-format canvases abutted; *Clearing* of three. The device of dividing a long horizontal painting into discrete sections solves the practical problem of how to physically carry the work around the studio, as well as having a formal purpose. It allows the painting to be both one and episodic at the same time; for time, or times, to be of differing durations within the same painting. In these large multi-part works Mitchell never attempted to disguise their composite structure.

She accepted this as an aspect of what the paintings are about and worked with it. Here, again, I am drawn to a comparison with Monet's late horizontal *Water Lily* paintings, which have a sense of accumulated time across a single viewpoint. With Mitchell this accreted time is further extended by variable viewpoints within the same painting. In *Clearing* both the left and right panels contain the same roughly squarish black form at the top of the panel and the more open mauve form lower down. Yet their placement is distinctly different in location and feel. It is as if one is walking around two related objects, with each new perspective giving yet another angle on the basic relationship. Echoing but not reflecting. *Clearing*, being in three parts, is not a traditional diptych, nor is it a continuously unified field, split into three, as in Monet; rather, it appears as an aggregate of both differing times and viewpoints. Here, I am drawn back to the analogy with the cinema screen and films' capacity to simultaneously invoke space and time as being past and present upon a single surface. In a similar way, Mitchell's paintings intimate the vagaries of memory and the fragility of the actuality of being present right now. They are a call to attention, pulling her paintings ever into the present.

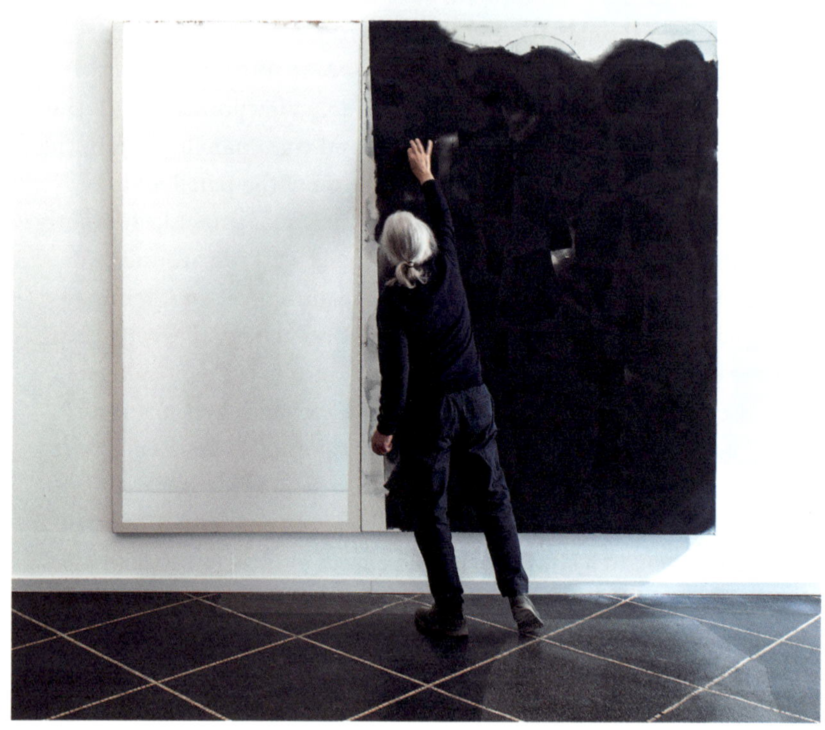

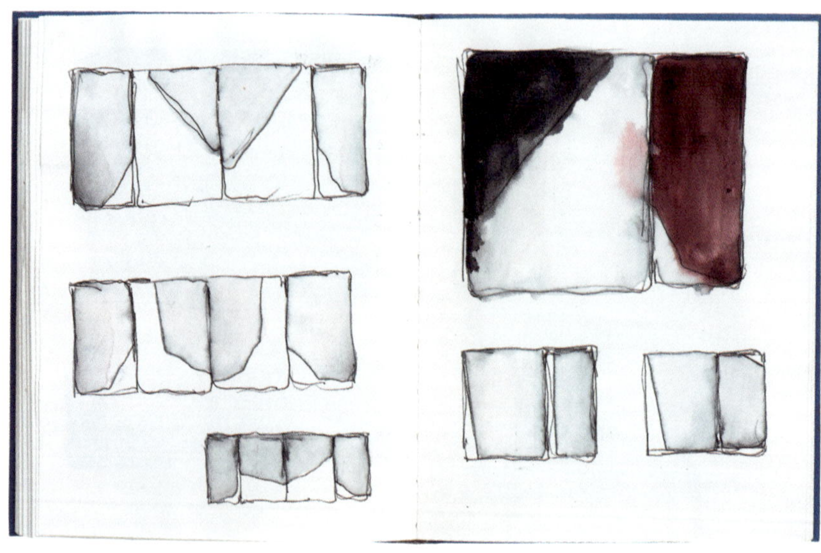

Time and Time Again

(2018)

If only he could hold meaning in his hands, he thought; if only meaning were that solid, had matter. Unlike thought that seemed so light, meaning had gravity, a sense of weight. Perhaps not easily measured, but nevertheless a weight and a form; it was graspable. He imagined taking a thought, any thought, folding it as he would a piece of paper, compressing it until it became meaning. Then holding that meaning in his hand, feeling its concreteness, its measure. Afterwards, then slowly unfolding it wide open again until meaning was no longer there, gone, and his earlier thought had reappeared. Or perhaps another thought, with which he could start the whole process of folding and unfolding all over again.

He wondered why meaning was always smaller than thought. What happened in the shrinking transfer from one to the other? Did the shift of thought to meaning open up another kind of gain? Or was that transfer with the passing of time simply the gaining of weight? He knew that time was important in this exchange, yet could not see how. Time was too big, distant, remote even, to be held in any space meaning might occupy. It was so much bigger than space. And anyway, time never settled, never committed to one place, it was always just passing through.

Time and time again, like his piece of paper, he tried to fold the thought, to give it weight. Compressed, it now had meaning yet strangely was displaced outside of time. He held it in his hand, feeling its weight, observing its form. Then slowly he began to prise open the parcel of meaning. Now open, he waited. Waited for time to become thought again.

He looked at the painting on the wall. Thought leant into meaning. It would change things. He did not know how. He could sense it changing shape, becoming more rounded. He would not rush it, no, let it settle. There had been a time when he would have. Not let things settle down first, that is. Now he gave into the lean. Felt its implied heft and mass. Up against it meaning became solid.

Ceased being between things and became state. He could feel it as he rubbed against meaning. The rub gave it both form and solidity. The refrain from the song 'Lean on Me' came to mind. Now settled, his thoughts drifted.

Published in *Ian McKeever/Tony Cragg. Malerei und Skulpturen*, exh. cat., Skulpturenpark Waldfrieden, Wuppertal, 2020, p. 14.

Eye to Eye: Reflections on the Self-portrait and Helene Schjerfbeck
(2018)

> 'For I have always found it impossible to resemble myself from one day to the next.'[1]
> Philippe Ricord

'I never go around mirrors ... it tears me up to see a grown man cry', he sang to himself as he looked into the mirror. The face staring back at him, presumably to others always the same face, was to him barely known. He never could figure out whose skin he was in, for sure it was not his. But then he would not recognise his own skin were it ever to wrap itself around him. How did others deal with this he wondered? Did they too feel this discomfort, a rub that never eased? Never spoken about, lived with. Or was he one of just a few who had what felt like a body on loan. A body he did not fully trust. Committing to something he did not fully know or trust seemed reckless. So he withheld, as if only ever partially present in the world. A part of himself held back, unsure if he had the resilience to endure, survive total immersion.

Most of the time he felt truly lost. Things around him, people even, polluted him. Turning him into mere flotsam and jetsam floating aimlessly, without meaning. Becoming just a part of the vague, directionless flow of life. Any meaning that might crystallise itself into something concrete, graspable, eluded him most of the time. So, when in those odd moments it did materialise, he hung on to it as if his life depended upon it. He turned away from the mirror, casting one last glance into those eyes.

...

It is 1975. I am in Helsinki, participating in my first group exhibition abroad. It is an exhibition of SPACE artists, the London-based studio collective, at the Taidehalli, the city exhibition space run by the Finnish Artists' Union. The city feels dour, grey, emerging as it was from being politically sandwiched between Sweden and the Soviets.

Each of the visiting artists has been allocated a Finnish counterpart as minder-cum-guide. Mine is Timo, a painter photographer, who also writes, perhaps a couple of years younger than myself. We get on well. On one of the free days Timo takes me to the Ateneum Art Museum, which houses part of the Finnish national collection of paintings. It is my first introduction to the history of Finnish art. Difficult; I have no reference points. However, Timo is good, he knows his country's painting tradition, and he helps me to ease my way in. Some works come easier than others: the large snowy landscapes of Akseli Gallen-Kallela, for instance, I can thread back to a broader context with relative ease. At one point we find ourselves in a gallery of smallish paintings, still-lifes, landscapes and portraits. It is the work of Helene Schjerfbeck, Timo enthuses. I am both curious and nonplussed, unable to make head or tail of what I am looking at – why the fuss?

Over the following years, Timo and I become good friends and I am in Finland fairly regularly. On such visits at some point I invariably find myself standing yet again in front of Schjerfbeck's paintings. They have become a Finnish marker for me. One of those things we use when travelling to tell us we have arrived, be it a croissant in Paris or the mounds of fresh mint in Marrakesh. Paintings, too, can anchor one from museum to museum, country to country. I have only to stand in front of Vilhelm Hammershøi's small *Portrait of a Young Consumptive Woman* in Funen Art Museum in Odense to know I am slap bang in the middle of Denmark and its culture. For me, in Finland this has become Schjerfbeck.

It is the self-portraits that particularly hold me, keep me guessing. They emit a strange discomfort, which has to be reciprocated. Discomfort as such is not the problem; after all, looking at art is not a comfort blanket. Even if the sensation of looking is pleasurable, satisfying, it should at least have that quality of not being fully available. One should be left with a lingering ache, like unrequited love. But there is something about self-portraits that gets closer to the bone. Makes looking, eye to eye, somehow harder. Puts one in that embarrassing position of being caught out as the only one looking. Not even the painter in painting the self-portrait is outside looking on, giving us another set of eyes. He or she is literally in the painting, depriving us of that usual reassurance of being complicit in looking.

We cannot step into the artist's shoes as the artist is in the painting, looking back. We are locked out.

How does a painter begin to grasp any notion of painting the self? What is he or she looking at? What does it look like? I can understand the idea that every artistic statement is somehow a reflection of the artist's psyche. A statement left in the vague twilight zone of glance and glimmer. Yet to paint the self as semblance, as somehow fully appearing in the world, mystifies me. How is it different to painting another person, or even a table or a chair, come to that? How does the artist objectify the self? Where does the painter begin, and what is then held in the painting's fixity? Who is it the painter is looking at, eye to eye?

The history of Western portrait painting begins in profile. Eyes do not meet. The head is refined into a beautiful silhouette. Both Piero della Francesca's *Portrait of the Duchess of Urbino* and Fra Filippo Lippi's *Profile Portrait of a Young Woman* present the sitter in profile with the inscrutable quality of a delicate flower. Too fragile to get close to. As immaculate as any portrait on the cover of a twenty-first-century glossy magazine. Beyond approach or reproach. It is only in the fifteenth century that the Italian portrait under influence from the north slowly begins to turn its head to gaze back at the viewer. Meets the world full on. This changes things. Changes not only the nature of the portrait, but also how we look at paintings. The painting ceases to be something we behold, becoming something in which we have a shared interest. We are now in conversation both with the portrait and the painting, eye to eye. The painting and the portrait have become a reciprocating part of our lives, too.

In a modest book titled *Piero della Francesca, or The Ineloquent in Art*, from 1954, Bernard Berenson discusses the nature of portraiture. One so easily forgets with what lucidity and eloquence such writers as Berenson wrote:

> I am tempted to conclude that in the long run the most satisfactory creations are those which, like Piero's or Cézanne's, remain ineloquent, mute with no urgent communication to make, and no thought of rousing us with look or gesture. If they express anything it is character, essence, rather than momentary feeling or purpose.[2]

'Character, essence, rather than momentary feeling or purpose' – let us ponder this thought by Berenson. Schjerfbeck's first self-portraits, painted when she was in her twenties and thirties, show a young woman self-consciously looking back at the viewer. The works have an innocent earnestness, expressing a desire to be present right now, in the moment. Later self-portraits from the middle of her career reveal much greater reserve and restraint. Both the person painted and the painting are organised into fitting composure. A restraint clothes these paintings like a stiff Protestant collar, and we are held at a distance not evident in the early portraits. There is something in these paintings that makes me think of the photographic portraits of Georgia O'Keeffe by Alfred Stieglitz. O'Keeffe's self-conscious stare and presence divest the photographer of his role, throwing the making back onto the sitter as actively creating an image of the self, as do so many contemporary celebrity images. This somehow flips the photograph over into a controlled, by proxy, self-portrait: a quality self-portraits also seem to hold of doubling back on themselves, of being in and out at the same time.

Things change again in Schjerfbeck's late self-portraits. The paintings are more ragged, edgy; composure goes out the window. What we are seeing is not just the ravages of time, but also a loss of self. Everything is hollowed out. The paintings exist in a state between fatigue and indifference, as if looking through a glass darkly, any notion of a portrait appearing as a distant echo rather than a reflection. During the last two years of her life the artist painted around twenty such portraits. The works have a sense of being more a cipher than a portrait. Here I am thinking of the 'portraits', the *Mystical Heads* by Alexej Jawlensky, from 1917–18, which as such are not portraits, but rather archetypes similar to the way saints are depicted in Russian Orthodox icons. The artist becomes a dispassionate medium, a transmitter; the ego is absent. He or she is somewhere beyond the painting, unreachable. What is being painted is simply that which needs to be painted. Here, we are touching upon Berenson's reference to essence and character, the mute and ineloquent. That unknowable space which we each, as individuals, can inhabit, in which we are present as self, uncontaminated by exchange with the world. This emptying out can manifest itself, in painting, as the paring back of paint and 'image' to its minimum, a quality found in the late paintings of some artists. This is a quality that is equally present in other later works by Schjerfbeck, especially the still-lifes. For the still-life and the portrait are never very far away from each other; both are a stilling of life.

A timeline. Sometimes helpful to get a sense of where an artist stands. Helene Schjerfbeck was born in 1862 and died in 1946. She was a contemporary of her fellow countryman Gallen-Kallela and also a close contemporary of Vilhelm Hammershøi (b. 1864), as well as Edvard Munch and Hilma af Klint, who both died in 1944. Looking further afield, Piet Mondrian and Wassily Kandinsky, who also died in 1944. While af Klint, Mondrian and Kandinsky were influenced in their early work by Madame Blavatsky's theosophical movement and the spiritualist zeitgeist of the time, and while Munch engaged with the fashionable investigation of the protoplasmic nature of the spirit, Schjerfbeck appears to have stood outside such esoteric concerns. Equally, she avoided immersing herself in Nordic mythology and folklore as did Gallen-Kallela. Instead, she shared a closer affinity with the relatively private position of Hammershøi: a looking inwards towards the more domestic, the norms of daily life.

...

Walking from the hallway to the bedroom, he lost the thought. It was that fleeting. Between the clock and the bed, so to speak. This is the title of Munch's self-portrait of 1940–42, *Self-Portrait, between the Clock and the Bed*. The painting literally depicts Munch full on, standing between his bed and a grandfather clock. It is a painting that does not so much look out, contrary to Munch's gaze, as one which internalises the passage of time. Turns the gaze inwards. This internalisation separates the northern Romantic movement from its southern Classical counterpart. The Classical world proportions and apportions. It is a view from the inside looking out, both temperate and idealised. Coherent sense is made of the world. The unknown relegated to the world of myths. The northern Romantic tradition knows no such harmony or boundary. Instead, things are left to the individual. Looking inwards, the self must grapple with life's meaning. Make sense of a situation as hostile as it is homely. These two differing worlds feel like separate parts of the brain. Two distinct possibilities as to what it means to be human, to understand. How could it be otherwise? The north goes from long, oppressive, cold winter nights, to summer days that never end. Days relentless in their stifling glow. Days to be shied away from. While further south one is invited out to meet the warm embrace of the morning's light. The night will be welcomed in its own good time. We are made of where we stand in the world.

Where we stand in the world. So close and yet so far away. The raw edges of our being can either shield ourselves against what is out there or lay us bare. 'Polish your eyeballs', he said to me. Most of the time we see things through a haze. Just occasionally do things come into sharp focus, the eye crystal clear in its looking. Then the mind is free. We can see beyond what we already know. The painter looks, incessantly trying, usually in vain, to get to this clarity. To the point where meaning is not a given, but is to be newly seen, felt, as if for the first time. That strange reflection in the mirror is perhaps one point where the painter can begin to do this, to glimpse, to see, to paint and to know again for the first time.

Published as 'Face to Face: Thoughts on the Self-portrait and Helene Schjerfbeck', *Royal Academy of Arts Magazine*, no. 143, Summer 2019, pp. 46–51.

Robert Smithson: Paterson
(2019)

He leant the rucksack against a rock, slid his hand deep down into the side pocket and pulled the book out. Unable to face reading it in such an elemental landscape, or perhaps more accurately, rereading it while spending days trekking over the loose moraine, he knew what he should do. Bending down, he wedged the book between sharp rocks and then began to pile more rocks on top. Now buried, this seemed to him to be a fitting end to his engagements with Michel Foucault's *The Archaeology of Knowledge*.[1] Somewhere he had read that Greenland is home to some of the oldest rocks known to man. Out there on the tundra would be an appropriate ending to what had been a long engagement.

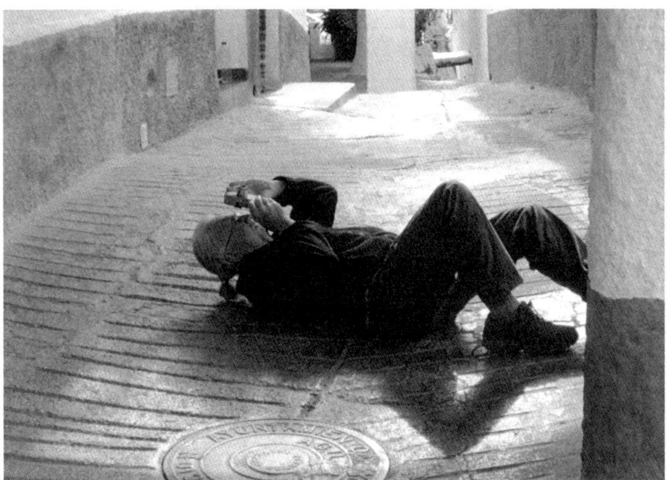

As a young man several books had stirred him, suggested ways forward, signposted a road to take. Foucault's writings, especially his thinking around monuments and documents and their ability to morph into each other, had been one such lead. Usually it was thoughts, or lines of abstract enquiry, which set him off. Not so much seeing other works of art, but ideas, or a simple thought, opening up clues suggesting the visible. These were enough.

Robert Smithson's writings had been another strong thread. If in the end he had to leave Foucault out there on the Arctic tundra, then with Smithson it was different, more complex and perhaps deeper. His initial affinity with Smithson had again been abstract ideas, entropy, sedimentation, a sense of geological time and process as being analogous to mapping one's own mindscape. That strange edge between a thought held for just a second yet suggesting sweeping timescales, geological timescales, compressed into a word. Smithson was a master of piling up millennia of time and dumping them at your feet on the floor as a modest pile of earth or rocks.

Sometimes he asked himself what use were other paintings to the painter? The conceit expressed by Clyfford Still when he wrote concerning his work that it was 'not proven by a continuum [...] I am myself – not just the sum of my ancestors'.[2] He could understand this thinking, for sometimes paintings were simply not enough, other roads had to be found to get deeper into the work. Beyond the inhibiting surface that paint often declared in equal measures of generosity and restraint.

•••

Distance held in time. He remembered reading something Paul Bowles had written in his novel *The Spider's House*, about space always being smaller than time. That space could never be as big as time. This idea seemed to hold a world within itself. The distance between one place and another, or the time of just standing still. The vastness of William Blake's grain of sand held in the hand, the enormity of time, moment to moment.[3] He thought again of Foucault, of how years ago on a cycling holiday in France they had passed a village called Foucault. He had photographed the roadside sign, as a personal homage to the man. His second copy of Foucault's *The Archaeology of Knowledge* was still on the bedroom shelf unread. It was one of those books he needed to have around him, like certain works by Martin Heidegger. Both writers were unflinching in their insistence upon thinking aloud, in treating thought as an evolving process, as a state of being in the world. He found this open-endedness appealing, how a thought process in itself could be the substance, as opposed to being the mechanism towards a given end. Such open-ended thinking was like music. A friend had mentioned to him that he had read a potted history of Western philosophy, and that the two pages allocated to Heidegger had allowed him to understand the philosopher's position. He laughed to himself and wondered about the comparison to music and what one would gain hearing a symphony by Ludwig van Beethoven reduced to a ditty. He thought of the full weight of a piece of music. A weight held in time. How would that time hold its form? And where was gravity in this, its pull, revealed in the distance of time, a distance pushed against, shrunk to the near.

Smithson's writings and works declared the inevitability of gravity; its constant slippage and slide was unavoidable. Of course, this interest had been an integral part of sculpture from the mid-1960s to the mid-1970s, especially in America. One need only to think of the thrown lead sculptures of Richard Serra or the broken-glass stacks of Barry Le Va. Both sculptors had insisted on the inevitable thrust down to a final settling on the ground. Yet, if they held this state by process and material weight, Smithson somehow through his writings wrapped gravity's pull more into a state of mind. One particular work by Smithson had stayed with him. He had never seen it; he knew it, as he suspected most people did, only from photographs reproduced in books. It was *Asphalt Rundown*, made in Rome in 1969, and showed a tipper truck offloading a pile of asphalt down a steep embankment, its black mass settling into a fluid elongated tongue as the gravity seeped out of it. It reminded him of the molten volcanic lava flows he had seen frozen onto the mountainsides in Iceland. And it made him think about painting, its physicality. He could jump from the poured skeins in the *Veil* paintings of Morris Louis, to the ovoid black forms in Robert Motherwell's *Elegies to the Spanish Republic* paintings, weighted and anchored, then on to the near rise of Mark Rothko's floating forms, as if by a miracle. Yet even they intimated a gravity, a physical pull to the ground, needed this to assert their loftiness.

All substances are susceptible to the downwards thrust of gravity; paint is no exception. Indeed, given its liquid state it is more susceptible than most things in making gravity visible. Yet, as a physical phenomenon it tends to be given little thought in painting. Contrary to sculpture, where weight and mass are often placed to the fore, painting's pictorialism and flatness are all too easily given over to a kind of suspended animation. The acceptance of a fictive space of make-believe fixed to a wall.

He needed to resist this conceit of painting and find through the act of painting something more rooted. A sense of paint's own physicality, not as a demonstration of bulk, but somehow as an equivalent to thought. To place the weight of a thought as paint, its very idea on the surface of the painting, becoming more than mere paint on surface. Ideas are held at a distance, he thought to himself. A distance, which nevertheless has to be located, fixed; left to themselves they hover without taking root. He imagined Heidegger tending his thoughts as one would a garden, digging, planting and pruning his thinking, letting his philosophy grow organically. Never finished, it was a work in progress. Painting was the same. One thought overlaying another, or allowed to slide and gather, the painter trusting that gravity's inevitability would hold any evolving form.

• • •

Paterson, his bus. He drives it daily, Monday to Friday, bus number 23 to and from Paterson. Listening, as he drives, to the seemingly inconsequential conversations of the passengers, hopping on, chatting, until they then hop off again. Maybe some of the passengers are new, but mostly they would appear to be regulars. What changes are those passengers who are sitting within earshot of Paterson while driving, and the conversations that ensue. Each morning, before setting off on his daily route, Paterson sits in his driving seat and writes his reflections into the notebook he keeps in his metal lunchbox along with his sandwich and flask. Then off he drives, turning the same corners each day, stopping at the same traffic lights, and waving a casual greeting to the other bus drivers heading the opposite way. He is Paterson, the main character in the film by Jim Jarmusch of the same title, *Paterson*.

The film is a warm and gentle homage to the great American poet William Carlos Williams and his seminal epic poem *Paterson*.[4] Published in five volumes between 1946 and 1958, the poems chronicle the lives of the inhabitants of Paterson, New Jersey, in a combination of verse interspersed with extracts drawn from local newspapers and letters sent either by Williams or received by him. In its epic scope *Paterson* is an elegy both to small-town life, its poetic resilience, and to Williams's social concerns as a doctor to the plight of many of its inhabitants. The work in its scope and depth elevates people and place to the quality of myth, that distinctly American ability to lift the normality of life to being almost epic.

But back to Paterson, his bus and the week of his daily run that is the time frame of Jarmusch's film. For Paterson, his bus is as a snail's shell, the house in which he is safe to travel through the world. From his driver's seat he sees and hears it all, yet feels secure in the knowledge that as the driver he must not be disturbed from his task in hand. The bus allows him to be present, to participate in an exchange with the wider world, while at the same time shielding him from engaging too far. He must appear to others to be not there. Paterson and his bus could be said to be an astute observation by Jarmusch on the creative process. The need for the artist on the one hand to be engaged, yet equally desiring to hold off so that things can be seen with fresh eyes. Part of the discipline of being an artist is in setting up and holding onto such mechanisms of distance. It does not matter how it is done – hiding behind the camera, the studio as ivory tower, the refusal to speak about the work, or the invented persona – one way or another the artist will find an equivalent to Paterson's bus.

> *Paterson*: Book 1, Preface
>
> To make a start,
> Out of particulars,
> And make them general, rolling
> Up the sum, by defective means.[5]

How did he know? How could Williams understand so completely the act of painting a painting? Was it so close to that of writing a poem, 'by defective means', the stupid, blunt limitation of paint on a brush? He was reminded of sitting late one night at the dining-room table with Niels in Copenhagen, endlessly batting to and fro the limits of the word compared to the limits of paint. Of course, they got nowhere, the word stymied by its inability to release itself, and paint, well without the word to back it up, more often than not just downright dumb.

Apparently, Williams was Smithson's family doctor. Smithson was born in Passaic, but grew up in Rutherford, New Jersey. Williams was born in Rutherford and practised as a doctor there. The River Passaic flows through Rutherford, then on through the city of Paterson, where it displays its majestic waterfalls, to continue and emerge out into Newark Bay. The Passaic, the word has something of the antediluvian about it, time and time again being held within it. In Book 1 of *Paterson* Williams refers to 'A man like a city...',[6] suggesting that strange and unfathomable coexistence of separation and unity between a sense of the self and the greater collective body. One can sense a similar duality in the writings and works of Smithson. The need to locate the local as a tight specific, this then flowing in and out of the sweep of the more general. This can be seen in Smithson's *Sites and Non-sites*, the concern with the disjuncture of taking stuff out of its natural environment and placing it in the confines of a gallery space, setting up by displacement a dialectic constantly pushing and pulling to find a form. In 1967 Smithson made a series of photographs entitled *The Monuments of Passaic*, depicting the industrial detritus lining the Passaic River. Some of the photographs show industrial pipes discharging 'fountains' of waste into the river. Another image is of abandoned pipes lining the river shore. This he entitled *The Great Pipes Monument*. Yet another image depicts derelict pontoons, their usefulness long expired. It is a landscape positing the dystopian, yet within it Smithson finds a beauty, is alert to the possibility of a viable aesthetic. As, in a similar way, Williams had posited in *Paterson*, the normality of place, its detritus and peoples' everyday lives elevated to the near sublime. The Passaic River and the Great Waterfalls of Paterson become a filter, a metaphor through which the flow of time and its capacity to purify can give things new and richer meaning.

...

The sea, that feeling of claustrophobia he always felt when out on a boat. Endless expanse all around, yet one could go nowhere, unless one could walk on water. He was curious about other people's thinking, those who said they felt a sense of freedom out on open water. This he could understand intellectually, perhaps as a way of freeing the mind, letting the sea flood in and wash the mind clean, so to speak. Freeing it of all the norms of life's daily rhythm. Perhaps this was what people meant by freedom. He could sense this walking on the beach staring out into the endless sea and sky. Yet to be free he needed to be able to put one foot in front of the other. His body had to be able to walk into that mindscape.

A body of water, endless. He thought of J. G. Ballard's short story 'The Terminal Beach', which narrates how the oceans have become covered in a fine film of plastic particles, a continuous membrane that prevents surface evaporation taking place.[7] As a consequence, all the earth's land masses are suffering a drought, fresh water sources having dried up. People have gravitated to and congregated on beaches, trying desperately to convert salt water to fresh water. A tiny strip of beach with access to the sea being all important to survive. The irony of it, a world dying, done in by plastic, the fictive imaginings of a writer in the 1950s now becoming a near reality. And he himself, as a painter, worked with plastic, acrylic paint, building up the paint surface layer by layer. Never wanting to close it off, seal it, instead keeping it open so that it could breathe, allowing life to be still within it as a painting. Perhaps in the end this is how it would be with the oceans. They would be covered with a woven web of plastic, analogous to the internet, a web that would articulate the oceans, giving them another surface definition. The gaps between the warp and weft, allowing evaporation to take place, and for life under water to survive. He imagined the earth from land mass to land mass covered in an articulated web of fluid plastic that began to take on meaning, this being a mirror of the increasingly dense digital web which cross-crossed the skies. The fine particles of evaporating water from the oceans linking the two webs as light bounces back and forth from one to the other. These shafts of light becoming in themselves a language by which we connect and understand the two.

...

Surface to surface. From the surface of the sea to the surface of the sky, they are the same thing held in different densities. The sea is like a fluid mind, as in Stanisław Lem's book *Solaris*, in which a spaceship hovers above the vast ocean of a liquid planet.[8] The astronauts on board the spaceship becoming increasingly susceptible to the oceans' ability to penetrate and unlock their subconscious thoughts. Taking over their rational minds and forming from their hijacked thoughts a new reality. A virtual reality of chimeras with which each of them must now interact and live. Tumbling pell-mell, these different realities crash into each other as the astronauts struggle to make sense of it all. To grasp something real when all before them seems to be mere mirrors. Such thinking took him back to another series of work by Smithson, *The Mirror Displacements*, in which rectangles of mirrors are clustered flat or slightly angled on the ground, often with earth piled into them to fix the angle. How these reflective mirror surfaces set up a strange discord between where they were placed and what could be seen in them, the sky. This displacement establishing a strange dislocation of place and time. Relating to this Smithson wrote, 'Much modern art is trapped in temporality, because it is unconscious of time as a "mental structure" or abstract support'.[9] Smithson's photographs documenting the works were accompanied by texts under the title of 'Incidents of Mirror – Travel in the Yucatan'. The text for each image described something of the location and circumstances as to where the specific work was placed. Sweeping in range they are also speculations on the nature of time and space, the peculiarities of place, and how place can become almost surreal when viewed as a displacement. Concerning the *Second Mirror Displacement*, Smithson wrote, 'Timelessness is found in the lapsed moments of perception, in the common pause that breaks apart in a sandstorm of pauses'.[10] To pause, the holding of time, the stepping out of time. To stop the clock sits at the core of human consciousness. A moment held apparently outside of time, which separates the mind from what it sees. He remembered one winter being stuck in eastern Siberia, snowed in, going nowhere. He walked to the outskirts of the city, stood on the shore and stared out at the frozen wasteland. Random blocks of ice stacked up haphazardly, the coastline taking on the appearance of a mass of chaotic tilting planes. He found himself looking for order, a sense, in what appeared to be a totally random fix. The frozen landscape made him think of the lava flows in Iceland, how in their molten state they rolled down to meet the sea, to then turn solid again as they met the icy water. Their forms buckling back on themselves like a reversed wave, as if seen from the other side. Ice and lava, states fixed and held in different time scales, folded by time into other meanings.

• • •

Robert Smithson's *Third Mirror Displacement* shows twelve mirrors placed slightly angled into the ground. Their right-hand edges are pushed into the earth, with more earth covering this portion of the mirrors to hold them in place. The mirrors occupy the lower part of the photograph, the top half revealing the landscape in such a way that it is hard to judge the scale. Situating the *Third Mirror Displacement*, Smithson wrote, 'The road went through butterfly swarms. Near Bolonclan de Rejan thousands of yellow, white and black swallowtail butterflies flow past the car in erratic, jerky flight patterns'.[11] This and the indeterminate scale depicted in the photograph made him think of the book *Roadside Picnic* by Boris and Arkady Strugatsky, subsequently adapted by them into a screenplay for Andrei Tarkovsky's film *Stalker*. The stalker must enter and cross the 'zone', a seemingly inconsequential wasteland of detritus and ruins. He must go beyond the parameters of normality and on entering the 'zone' engage in a series of highly ritualised actions, follow patterns of behaviour, which to all intents and purposes appear meaningless. However, if he is to negotiate the 'zone' then these must be followed. To stalk one's own thoughts, enter that strange territory of displacing one thought with another. Letting the resulting cascade flow and flow again. To be immersed in the fullness of it, the magnitude of it, the sea of consciousness, yet able to float, to feel one's place, not only physically, but also as thought, crystalline in its exactitude. Yet to try to hold such thoughts for more than a second is hard, knowing their brittleness could at any moment shatter into the greater chaos of things. To lend oneself to such wonderings seemed ultimately to be what it was all about, beyond the physical world, the mind's rectitude, beyond painting even. For painting's allure, its capacity to make seen, to hold the liquidity of paint on a surface, in fluxing and frozen moments, is all well and good, but what then? 'From sea to shining sea',[12] from the mind's fluid zone to the fixed physical plane that is the painting. Layer upon layer, painting's history is held in what has become the vertical canvas on the wall, yet all the while gravity seeks its seepage back to the horizontal, down to an unavoidable ground.

...

The sea raged. There were no rocks for it to release its anger upon, so instead it dug in and curled back into itself. Dragging the shoreline back into its depths. Again and again, it scoured the beach, the sound of sucked-in rolling pebbles blurring into the waves' incessant poundings. He had spent his whole childhood close to the sea. Felt daily the intense light reflected off the sea's surface, even on a dull day. Felt this light as part of himself. But the sea itself, he was never a part of, beyond the sound of its ebb and flow, which pulsed inside him becoming the rhythm of his own blood. The mass of the sea, its unending form, was always beyond him. Even when in the sea swimming, it was ungraspable, out of reach. Lying on his back, buoyed up by the salt water, floating high, apparently safe, he still needed to feel a thread back to the land. Like a dog on a lead, he had to know he was retrievable. He did not trust the sea. Its mood could change from being as calm and enticing as bath water, to a creature sucking hard at his heels as he stood at the water's edge. Without the thread back to the land he knew he would be lost, would be all too willing to be taken into that limitless fluid expanse.

...

Words floating. On the surface, and at depths, and oft-times quietly seeping away. At other times, they pooled, gathered, as if a shoal of fish, circling around themselves into an ever-tightening ball. To then rise to the surface as form, as meaning awaiting anchorage. Pooled, and now held, meaning spirals within itself, for in its stillness it holds its own violence, pulls to rupture the line by which it is tethered. Seeks release, the freedom to flow back into the greater stream of things.

...

SUBSTRATUM

Artesian Well at The Passaic Rolling Mill, Paterson

The following is the tabular account of the specimens found in this well, with the depths at which they were taken, in feet. The boring began in September 1879, and continued until November 1880.

Depth	Description of Materials
65 feet. . .	Red sandstone, fine
110 feet. . .	Red sandstone, coarse
182 feet. . .	Red sandstone and a little shale
400 feet. . .	Red sandstone, shaly
404 feet. . .	Shale
430 feet. . .	Red sandstone, fine-grained
540 feet. . .	Sandy shale, soft
565 feet. . .	Soft shale[13]

And so it continues in rough incremental measures to a depth of 2,100 feet, when foul water is detected, and the drilling abandoned. In these matter-of-fact geological statistics halfway into Book 3, Part III of *Paterson*, William Carlos Williams itemised the very land the town of Paterson is built upon. Going below the surface, he gives physical depth to the lives of the people who inhabit it. It is a recurring theme throughout the epic poem, holding deep time and horizontal time as an ever-fluxing continuum. The now of the past and the past that is now. Later in the poem he writes:

> The past above, the future below
> And the present pouring down, the roar,
> The roar of the present, ...

Above, below, their mutability, proximity to the present, the warp and weft of time that surfaces as the present. A time present, which unlike the waters of the Passaic, as Joseph Brodsky would remind us, flows horizontally.[14] Yet life's flow would seem a never-ending exchange between the horizonal and the vertical. A rising and falling ever susceptible to gravity's downward drift, for we are steeped in the slope of time. Its push and pull skews the vertical and the horizontal, constantly putting them under pressure. Yielding, they bend and slope towards the future. Light waves, sound waves; perhaps in the greater scheme of things there are time waves too. Accelerations and slowings down that pass through us moment to moment, as they rise and fall. Time is a displacement affecting everything.

Sedimentation, accretions, played an important role in the works of Robert Smithson. The excavation of geological strata placed against its own surface, set against the mind's own depth and width. What is above and below the surface allowing the spread of accreted time to form its own sense of mind and matter. In earthing his works, Smithson also aimed to ground his own thinking, so that even when in free fall, drifting, he could still sense its place in the greater strata of being. In his essay 'A Sedimentation of the Mind: Earth Project', he wrote, 'one's mind and the earth are in a constant state of erosion, mental rivers wear away abstract banks, brain waves undermine cliffs of thought, ideas decompose into stones of unknowing'.[15] For Smithson, this inevitable seepage rushed towards an entropic state, a condition of formlessness, which even in its randomness might still hold the possibility for future excavations, suggest other structures and meanings in its apparently arbitrary flux.

On the following page of Book 3, Part III, after drawing up his list of sediments of the artisan well, William Carlos Williams wrote:

> ... when the water had receded, most things had lost their
> form. They lean in the direction the current went. Mud
> covered them.[16]

Robert Smithson's *Partially Buried Woodshed* of 1970, again a work I know only from photographic documentation, shows a structure onto which the artist piled twenty cartloads of earth until the central beam cracked. In speaking about the project Smithson alluded to something analogous to a buried architecture or an inverted archaeology. It is a recurring theme in Smithson's oeuvre, the overlaying of one history over another, of material and context laying each other to then again replace the other. The boundary between history's stratification and material, context and material, idea and material, their hierarchies dissolving, melding, as process takes over. With process itself often being subsumed and historicised in this commingling. An earlier drawing by Smithson from 1966 entitled *A Heap of Language*, in which words are arranged in a triangular shape, like a stepped pyramid, finishing at the apex with the single work 'language', lays out this territory in its use of both language and form. As a concrete poem it pictorially reveals that strange inversion which takes place in stacking things. That which is put down first becoming bottom and last, and what was put down last becoming uppermost and first. The first and the last, their interchangeability, the dissolving of hierarchies to meld and mould anew.

'How to begin to find a shape – to begin to begin again, turning the inside out', William Carlos Williams wrote.[17] Turning any thickness away from itself until it can be seen, spread out as if its thickness were no more than that of a thin film. Yet looking itself has a thickness Maurice Merleau-Ponty reminded us,[18] the eye gives weight to form and depth to time. Time's thickness layering itself until dense and opaque, weighted with its own looking.

...

Memory slides with ease across the floor and settles. Finding form, it shapes itself until it appears to reach a state as concrete and real as any object the floor supports. Once vague, memory has become a part of living, occupying space and seeming to breathe the air around it. How, he wondered, did the mind learn to behave itself, make sense of the omnipresent twists and turns of the lived moment? Perhaps, he thought, we are but memories, not that ubiquitous notion of memory being a recalled past, but a deeper archaeology of memory which constitutes all that we have become and are. The habits of living, dressing, eating, following the hardwired routines of life, put the mind at a distance to the physical world around us. Creating a gulp and a gap between word, meaning and being.

...

Clutterbrook walked the beach daily. Meeting the incoming tide as it settled into a steady rhythm of lapping high onto the shore, to then turn on itself seawards again. This was when he found his stuff, driftwood, pieces of rope, the odd car tyre and endless pieces of faded plastic, scoured by the sea and sand as they made their way towards the beach. The bodies were just one of those things. Sometimes, at first, they did not even look like bodies and Clutterbrook had to rummage around a little to see what exactly it was. For him, finding one was an inconvenience. It meant he had to cut short his combing and set off back to the town early to go to the police station. They more or less knew every time he came in what was afoot. 'What is it this time?', was their usual reaction and whether they could get down the cliff close to where the body was or if they would have to trudge back along the beach with him to the spot. 'Don't the dead have any consideration', he would say to himself as he led the procession along the shoreline retracing his steps. As the police began their examination of the scene, Clutterbrook would stare out across the open sea. Tomorrow would be different he thought, something good, useful, would be waiting; the sea rarely disappointed. Over the course of his 60-odd years of walking daily on the beach, old man Clutterbrook had found five bodies. The following week the news was always on the front page in the local *Gazette*. Clutterbrook, a celebrity for a few days, accepted this with resignation rather than any sense of pride. People talked of course, rarely to him that is, rather among themselves as town gossip, about how weird it was that he had found another one. No doubt others had walked the beach that day before him, but had not noticed it, he must have some special powers or be jinxed. Over the following days interest and conjecture would wane, life would go back to normal and Clutterbrook could continue uninterrupted his daily pilgrimage along the shore.

• • •

Towards the end of *Paterson*, Book 1, William Carlos Williams wrote four simple words, 'My surface my skin'[19]: words that seem full of redolence for the painter. From the surface of the painting to the surface of one's self, from skin to skin, body to body, in the gap between all is held which is possible and might be. That which is excluded lapses into the folds of the past, becoming part of a history already gone. To stand in the moment is to accept that the moment cannot be shared; it is held out of reach. Can only be felt and made concrete knowing it is a selfish act of withdrawal. Always shy and fragile in its uncertainty, yet for a moment it can at times become as hard and concrete as the movement of air. Breathing in, breathing out, the air pulsates. In the gap between the mind's incessant roaming, the surface of oneself and the surface of the painting, a meaning finds form and begins to glow. And everything else stands firm, like a table or a chair, marking all too readily its place in the world.

Painting/Sculpture/Architecture

(2019)

One could say that architecture somehow sits at the juncture of sculpture and painting. On one level it houses just about all paintings – they need walls – and much of sculpture, which needs floors. Architecture is in essence the meeting of floor and wall. These two elements, together with a roof, give architecture its form and its limits. Of course, some would argue, as in the case of Louis Kahn,[1] that most buildings consisting of these three basic components, walls, floor and roof, are not architecture. Rather, they are simply buildings and do not rise above this status, while architecture is by definition of a more noble stature. But for the sake of argument let us for the time being call all buildings architecture. I prefer that term to buildings, as the word building somehow connotes more a place of human occupation, while architecture seems to embrace a greater sense of a wider cultural engagement. It is less preoccupied; it is before building in an abstract sense. In simple terms the inside and the outside of a building could be said to be its architecture. How these two things in coming together to find form define themselves. Perhaps here there is a parallel between the nature of sculpture and that of painting. Sculpture's presence in the world is primarily one of an outside. No matter how solid, dense or hollow, the form sculpture takes, the physical space it occupies, its presence is revealed via an exterior, its outer shell, while painting is perceived as being inside the surface that supports it. In that sense sculpture and painting are differing manifestations of the outside and inside, which together constitute a latent architecture. An architecture which is not and cannot be a building. Perhaps this is one reason why increasingly sculpture and painting have such an uncomfortable relationship with architecture. They bring into doubt architecture's capability to fully disclose both inside and outside as being fully authentically realised, questioning the limits as to the possibility of outside and inside finding unity as a single entity.

Piero della Francesca
(2019)

Coming home on the train from London I sit next to a fellow passenger reading the guide to the 'Charles I: King and Collector' exhibition at the Royal Academy, works from the Royal Collection. We start talking. He has just been to see the exhibition and so I ask him if there were any works he found particularly rewarding. 'The Henrietta Maria', he replies with enthusiasm. It takes me a moment or two to realise he is speaking about the portrait of Henrietta Maria by Anthony van Dyck. Except instead of referring to the artist he is identifying the painting by it subject matter, the person depicted. Talking further, I came to understand that for him the exhibition was a catalogue of historical characters, before it was an exhibition of works by artists. One could say this is another way of looking at paintings: instead of artist spotting, his interest was in subject spotting. Or to put it another way, if I look at the nuts and bolts of a model of car to see how it is put together, how it works, then his interest was in who was driven around in it. This difference is perhaps what distinguishes how the artist looks at artworks from how the art historian does. The historian cannot resist the temptation to tug at the collar of the character depicted, repeatedly asking, 'is it you ... is it really you?', sitting in that car.

Attempting to write about the work of Piero della Francesca is to venture slap bang into the hard core of painting. It is like walking into an immovable rock. It simply is not going to move. The figures depicted are somehow unapproachable, reducing any speculation as to who these characters might actually be so far away that they cannot be reached. For the models depicted are not present in the world in any normal sense, with no hint of the baggage of daily life. There is no flicker of emotion, of pleasure, surprise or threat. Always they are composed, resolute, indifferent to our gaze, ascribed a presence which takes them beyond 'specific meaning' and attributes them with the quality of dispassionate actors. Making of them abstractions in a theatre of quietude. Even in one of Piero della Francesca's more 'active' works, in terms of subject matter, such as the battle scene *The Victory of Heraclius*, part of the fresco cycle in S. Francesco, Arezzo, there is an overriding sense of stilled movement. The scene functions more as a tableau, is fixed, rather than being a representation of action. Indeed, the artist could be said to have wilfully taken as much action out of the scene as is possible. The films of Robert Bresson come to mind when I look at the 'characters' in Piero della Francesca's work. Bresson worked with non-actors, the characters in his films being props. In many ways no more charged with action or meaning than the doors they walked through or the floors they walked across. He referred to this quality of 'non acting' as that of simply being present.[1]

If at this juncture I appear to be deviating away from the works of Piero della Francesca, towards the methods underpinning the films of Bresson, then perhaps it is because I see so many parallels. And to find a way into the work of Piero della Francesca is not easy. His work has been overly scrutinised, over analysed, by art historians, yet to stand in front of one of his paintings is to see all of that cast aside as so much noise and to be left searching for one's own centre. When Bresson wrote in reference to his working methods, 'No actors (No directing of actors,) ... BEING (models) instead of SEEMING (actors)',[2] then perhaps we are touching upon something at the core of Piero della Francesca's work. The redundancy of meaning as being held in the narrative of what is depicted, to be replaced by the mute construct of a painting as painting. His works are perhaps one of the first conscious attempts by a painter to make a painting silent, post Byzantine, divested of the intrusive flotsam and jetsam of subject matter.

In Piero della Francesca's painting of the *Nativity*, in the National Gallery in London, part of the scene consists of five singers and musicians standing behind and slightly to the left of the infant Jesus. Two play instruments while the other three are singing. Yet not a single sound appears to be coming forth. It is as if the pitch they have reached is inaudible to the human ear, or so quiet it cannot be heard. We have no means of defining or describing the sound. Unusually for Piero della Francesca's work one of the singers looks directly out at the viewer, as if recognising someone may be looking back into the scene depicted. Usually in his works, even those figures presented full on are gazing slightly away from the viewer, as if oblivious to the fact that they are party to anything beyond their own reverie. This separation, of standing aloof, a strange state of being present but somehow absent applies equally to groups of ostensibly interconnected figures. It is as if we have just arrived at that moment in the conversation when nothing is being said. The characters depicted are as the figures in a Greek or Roman frieze. Held in a moment of self-internalisation, separate from what is around them. Adrian Stokes, in writing about looking at the paintings of Piero della Francesca in comparison to another painter in the collection in the National Gallery, observed, 'Compared with Piero della Francesca, Botticelli is as the sea to the land',[3] implying in other painters a restlessness, a restlessness which of course in the subsequent development of painting after Piero della Francesca won out as the modus operandi as to what painting might be. A theatre for action. Through Raphael, Tintoretto, Peter Paul Rubens, etc., painting after the fifteenth century built itself on the grand eloquence of operatic theatre, leading eventually in the eighteenth century to the over-abundance of the Baroque, and subsequently calming down again. Yet this difference of painting's temperament between hot and cool is still being played out today.

'Flatten my images (as if ironing them)', Bresson wrote.[4] There is in the work of Piero della Francesca a beguiling sense of articulated space that is somehow completely flattened out. His paintings are pictorially as flat as a pancake. This is curious given his active engagement in constructing perspectival space. Of course, fresco, a medium used in some of his works, has in itself a pronounced tendency to push visual space back to the surface. It flattens things out. However, this characteristic seems to be carried over into the paintings too. We are always aware that we are looking at a surface, a surface which contrary to what is being suggested by depictions is always hermetic. Our only way into and beyond this surface is through abstractions, by thinking our way into the painting, the paint surface being as inscrutable as the models depicted. Both defy access to meaning as being understood through incident or anecdote.

A block of stone out of which a figure is carved. It is obdurate, immovable, yet it must yield. Must allow exchange. Its weight tells us that it is rooted to the ground. Seeks out surety with that ground. Needs this emphatic contact in order to fully be itself. Weight necessitates a certain heft to retain its composure. The foot needs to be completely flat on the ground, otherwise it will become simply momentary inertia. A given mass, the figure must stand as if it has always been there. Such thoughts as yesterday or tomorrow must seem impertinent. The transitory has no place. The models in Piero della Francesca's works are as sculptures: thick limbed and solid, rooted to the ground. A bent knee or foot is always firmly anchored. There is no possibility for things to take off and fly. No, man must know his place and must soar on another level, out of his white luminescent blocks of semi-transparent marble.

To Begin
(2019)

To begin at the beginning, is that not the aim? Of course, it is both delusional and a conceit, impossible. The weight of painting's history is ever present, pressing down like a ton of memories and half glimpses of the past. But one has to try, at least for oneself. Try to jettison the seduction of overt referencing, trusting that going at it raw, more naively, one might be able to approximate something closer to the self. Either way, knowing or unknowing it is a can of worms.

Where to begin? In the first of a series of declarations from 1955, the painter Antoni Tàpies writes, 'From the Altamira caves to Picasso, and Velasquez in between, painting has always been an abstraction. In the face of the fanatics of Realism, I have reiterated that "reality" has never existed in painting, that it is only to be found in the head of the observer'.[1] If one thinks about it, nothing is less like an arrangement of apples and oranges on a tabletop than paint is on a flat surface. Paint always has a physical material reality. It is only when paint jumps beyond this materiality that with painting things start to get tricky. Then what is real? Perhaps in simple terms it is those things which for the artist feel solid in the world, which he is able to begin to know and give substance to.

In the first paragraph of a modest pamphlet titled *An Introduction to Metaphysics* from 1912, the French philosopher Henri Bergson distinguishes between two ways of knowing a thing.[2] The first being dependent upon the view at which we are placed, and the symbols by which we express ourselves. The second dependent neither on point of view nor any symbols. The first kind of knowing Bergson identifies as being relative; the second as having the possibility to attain the absolute. It is not hard to see which of the two the painter would prefer. After all, the absolute could be of itself pure substance, not simply a fictive representation. If this seems airy-fairy it is not. If viewed as an abstraction the absolute could be tantalisingly near.

Jukka Mäkelä: Talking Away the Night
(2022)

On the walls of one of the bedrooms are works by Kurt Kocherscheidt, Martin Disler and Jukka Mäkelä. All three have now left. Kocherscheidt died in 1992 aged 49, Disler at 47 in 1996 and Mäkelä in 2018 aged 68. All three were good friends of mine, with whom I enjoyed spending time. To the painter, such friendships are like fertiliser to a plant, encouraging strength and growth, life-affirming. I try to think back to conversations we had, to call forth moments shared. Memories, like water, flow out of full grasp, half-hinted as thoughts seep and meld into other times; thoughts becoming concrete only as feelings. Like Krapp in Samuel Beckett's one-act play, sitting at his desk playing old tapes to himself, the past echoes in and out of the present.[1] Prompting memories to surface, which then become fragile threads of thought, only to then sink back into memories again.

It is 1980. Jukka and his wife Marika Mäkelä are staying in London for six months. London is alive during this time, and we are young and hungry. We gravitate to Nigel Greenwood's Gallery near Sloane Square where I and the painter John Walker both exhibit. Walker is 'big' now, and both Jukka and Marika are keen on his work. Somehow, their being there and in London all seems to make sense. One late afternoon I cycle over to the garden flat in Wimbledon where they have based themselves. Sitting in the garden we talk ...

It is five in the morning, and we have been sitting on the terrace talking away the night. Our minds are tired, and the eyes are looking to find themselves again. As the light gently enters into the day, shapes begin to emerge and take on volume. The light is soft, slow to give itself; forms must first declare themselves unto themselves before they are revealed to us. There is a milky greyness to the light, colour is shy, and when it does declare its presence, shyness makes pale.

'And what of old man Giotto, Jukka ... what can you say to him as he tends his sheep under clear blue skies?'

'It has to be an overcast day', you say.

Is this to take away light's emphasis on form, the play of light against shadow and colours' insistent demand to be present? Perhaps one of the great distinguishing features between the northern painting tradition and that of the south is the differing quality of light. Mediterranean painting walks out into crisp, clear morning air, displaying a world of vistas; it is a world view that is both fully proportioned and apportioned. While in the north with its more diffused light, such clarity is clouded into the immediacy of atmospheres and moods. The painter must rather look inside himself, at a world interiorised physically and mentally, and landscape too becomes a psychic space.

When I look at your paintings, Jukka, I sense that like August Strindberg or Vilhelm Hammershøi you painted towards the night, for there will be less light, not more, and in this mellowing down there was the desire, perhaps the need, to shy away from the full glare of the day.

'And what of old man Munch, Jukka ... as he stalks his Nordic haunts?'

'I paint the elements and the mood of the landscape', you say.

A simple answer, unadorned, yet redolent with atmosphere. The history of painting in the second half of the twentieth century was a history of taking subject matter out of painting, messing it up and putting it back in again, or of losing content through means. Sometimes content confused means and at other times means confused content. Either way, this duality still ongoing can hijack painting. For a painter such as you Jukka, steeped in a specific sense of place, I suspect that with your feet firmly placed on your Finnish earth and snow, subject matter has always been in your blood and that the means would thus follow. I come to your paintings through my feet and my body. People are sensed after the first moment of seeing, to paraphrase John Steinbeck,[2] and it is the same with paintings; we feel our way into them. Our body senses meaning in paintings before the conscious mind takes hold. A thicket of lines, sometimes under the feet, like tangled branches, or directly before us, as if cracks in a wall of rock, always your paintings are in the here and now of where we stand. Distance is shrunk to close proximity, and texture becomes place. What is directly before us is brought to the fore, the texture of surface becoming the texture of substance, the two becoming one. The surface of the painting, its skin, is also inseparable from a body, the body that is the painting itself.

It is 1996. I am in Spain for the exhibition 'New Abstraction' where some of my works are included. Having been at the Museo Reina Sofía in Madrid, it is now in Barcelona. Jukka and his wife Pirkko have come over for the opening and to spend a couple of days in the city. What with one thing and another, we do not get much time to talk.

'And so, Jukka, as we have both been in the land of old man Goya, what of his impossible dog?'

That damned dog whose apprehensive one-eyed stare upwards with such foreboding into empty space takes the breath away. And what a space he stares into. Painters have spent the last 200 years filling that cavern of a space, no more than 2 sq. m of canvas. They have spent lifetimes spreading paint over metre after metre of canvas asking the same question: what should go into that pregnant space?

Artists, including painters, emphasise either culture or nature in their work. Of course, this is tricky. All artists work out of a specific culture and equally one way or another are 'of' nature.

However, when I look at your paintings, Jukka, I see your thrust is an urgent need to grasp and hold the nature of those things immediately around you, just as tightly as your desire to grasp the nature of the activity of painting itself. Your work has neither the detached cultural knowingness of Akseli Gallen-Kallela, nor the bittersweet anxiety of Helene Schjerfbeck. Instead, its immediacy risks the possibility of everything or nothing. It is predicated on what might be, not on what already is and the uncertainty this entails.

'The act that springs from the moment is what really counts', you say, reinforcing our understanding that the painting's authenticity is constantly at play. To jettison a knowingness in favour of the unknowing is in itself a risk, yet it is what the moment dictates.

'And what of old man Cézanne, Jukka ... that rough diamond who pruned the line and polished the eye?'

'When I use a line, I do not draw the boundary between two different surfaces ... Every line has the potential to shape up into something', you say.

In that sense, Jukka, perhaps in looking at your work we are in a theatre of beginnings. It is as if at times your mark-making harks back to a prehistory before 'picture' making came to the fore. There is something of this quality in, say, the paintings of Mark Tobey, Cy Twombly and Joan Mitchell, in which the ritualistic act of mark-making per se has to carry its own meaning. Articulation sits right at the edge of recognition and is always close to collapse, the dumb mark-making process having no default position to fall back on. Maurice Merleau-Ponty inferred looking has a thickness, suggesting that part of the job of being a painter is in nurturing such a thickness.[3] Hence, for the painter, the accumulative act of painting, of putting one mark next to another, building layer upon layer, repeated day by day, year by year, is an attempt to make real in the world another way of seeing. To make concrete another way of looking.

'And what of old man Halonen, Jukka ... and his dwelling place of white?'[4]

Was he to you, Jukka, like the billowing sailing ships, the galleons and schooners were for me, which were depicted in the nineteenth-century paintings that lined the walls of my local art museum and which I saw as a teenage boy? In whose lofting sails, as they sailed over oceans and seas, I could begin to wonder and dream. Did you see cathedrals of snow and ice in the mounds of white upon white, which old man Halonen was able to conjure up in his frozen world? Did his paintings give you the space to dream and marvel? Your paintings have always forsaken colour for tone and tight articulation for atmosphere; there is always the intimation that we are seeing through a glass palely.

'... when the first snow falls, and again ... the first ice, and what we see ...', you say.

The rhythm of winter's season, its coming and going, the natural palimpsest of the arrival of ice and snow. The covering and obliteration of what lies beneath to then subsequently thaw and melt to reveal again; a natural cycle, so close to the act of painting itself in its process of layering and taking away.

It is 2006 and I am in Helsinki visiting Jukka and Pirkko. We are in Jukka's studio looking at the new group of works. He is one of those painters who, when he works, the paintings pour out; the energy is palpable and I love it. The paintings crowd and lean haphazardly around the studio. Later in the evening, as I prepare to leave, Jukka gives me a small recent painting as a present from himself and Pirkko and also a box of large sticks of charcoal, the kind he draws with. Sitting in the taxi going back to the hotel, I think of the tall stacks of wooden branches I had seen on the roadsides in Morocco waiting to be slowly charred to make this simple drawing tool. And I wondered, Jukka, if there had ever been a time when you too had been in Morocco and seen these blackened mounds, negations, which in their reduction to carbon sticks hold the means to set one mark against another.

'And what of Old Man Time himself, Jukka ... where do we begin or end?'

Time's seepage, unlike water, has a horizontal flow: line follows line, line covers line. Time's warp and weft become the visual residue of experience enacted and stilled. For a painting has its own time, just as surely as it has a form and a content. Painting is greedy for time and, if allowed, will subsume the painter in its restless and relentless flow. This certainty with its uncertain end the painter feels more than knows.

'... uncertainty has, in fact, become a working method for me', you say.

Could it be any other way, I wonder? The painter goes to bed each night hoping that the next morning when he steps into the studio, he will see the painting anew, as if for the first time. As if for the first time, to be alive to this moment, the moment of painting becoming the moment of being. Then all things, time past, time present, time future, as T. S. Eliot would tell us, become one.[5]

Published in *Jukka Mäkelä*, exh. cat., Sara Hildén Art Museum, Tampere, Finland, 2023, pp. 43–7.

Notes on 'Against Architecture'
(2023)

Against – the double meaning of the word: adjoining, bringing one thing into contact with another and to stand in opposition to.

Architecture – the rub of architecture, from the hut to the high-rise. Airports, railway stations, public buildings, sites of passing through, their shell an umbrella for a lack of fixity.

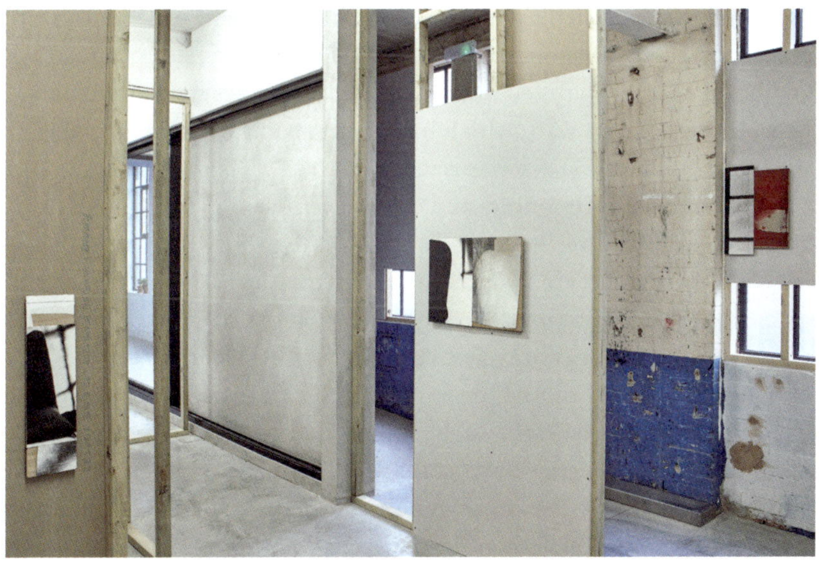

The eye is restless; the photograph taken full on, yet more often than not, first glimpsed out of the corner of the eye.

The gap between the painting and the photograph, belonging to neither, yet of both.

I make works on paper, studies, after I have finished the actual paintings. Just as the *Hartgrove Photographs* were made some years after I completed the *Hartgrove Paintings*. The 'Against Architecture' installation at the Arts University Bournemouth (AUB) was made six years after its first presentation at Matt's Gallery. I see the second iteration of the work at AUB as being in many ways a model. Just as an architect would make a model prior to the construction of the building itself. Except, following my usual practice, this procedure of making first the model and then the building has been reversed: the model came later.

A reinterpretation by definition is modified and simplified, becoming a model of that which it represents.

There is no master plan or floor plan for 'Against Architecture'. Its construction evolves wall by wall, panel by panel, in the process of being built.

Matt's Gallery, located on the ground floor of an old industrial warehouse, had one gallery entrance; one had to turn left to then enter a rectangular space with windows along one side. The walls of the space carried the random patches of paint, roughly filled-in cracks and holes and half-painted drainpipes left by the previous occupants. Except for one short wall, which had been specifically replastered for the installation, the space was rough and raw.

The three entry points and exits into the built structure of 'Against Architecture' led directly back to the gallery entrance.

At AUB there are four entry points into the gallery: the main gallery entrance, two further entry points via the passageway separating the main gallery from the lower gallery with doors at either end, with yet another entrance via the lower gallery. Only two walls meet as a closed right angle, otherwise the space extends into more general walkways. The installation 'Against Architecture' was built with multiple entry and exit points to reflect this, each 'façade' having a different feel. The gallery space is roughly square in plan and contains two large circular pillars as well as two narrower square-section pillars. Painted white, the space has something of a neutral feel to it reflecting its role at AUB to serve as a study gallery.

Conventional building materials, 3 x 2 inch (7.6 x 5 cm) stud-wall timber and sheets of 8 x 4 foot (240 x 120 cm) plasterboard, have been used in the construction of both installations. The working module for vertical open and closed sections in the Matt's Gallery construct was the height of the sheet of plasterboard, 240 cm, while for AUB, the working module became 198 cm, the standard height of a domestic doorway.

Matt's Gallery established a dialogue between the nature of the rough gallery space, the stud-wall construction and the pictorial language within the photo-painted panels. At AUB the structure of 'Against Architecture' functions more hermetically within itself, emphasising the notion of being modelled in a neutral space and establishing a conversation between the two differing languages of a supporting stud-wall construction and the photo-painted panels that are placed in it.

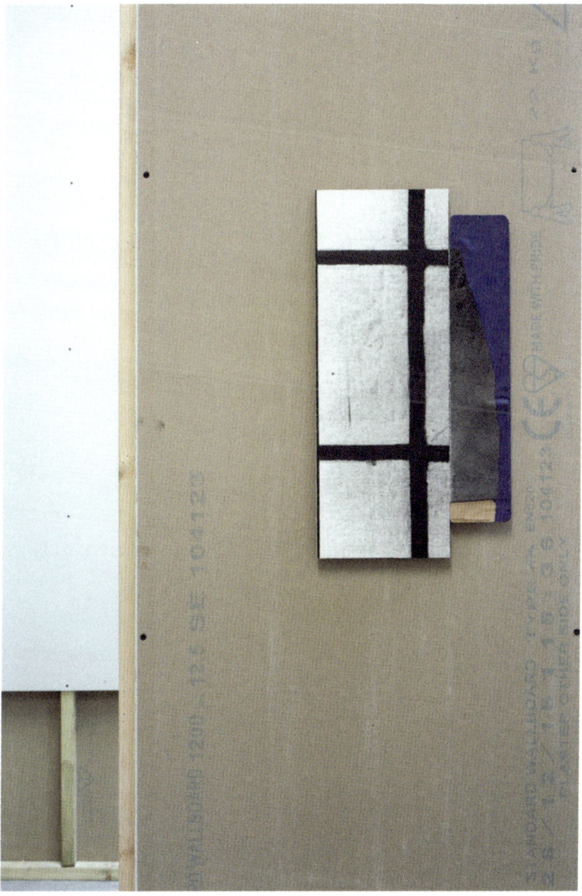

Published in Ian McKeever, *Against Architecture*, exh. cat., co-published by text + work, TheGallery, Arts University Bournemouth and Anomie Publishing, London, 2024, pp. 135–9.

Colour Chart
(2023)

Black
paled
black
thickened
black
on
black
on
black
to
light

Stain
of
black
white
on
white
cotton duck
warm
cooled
by
white

Cobalt blue
under
black
on
black
cobalt blue
exposed
on
cobalt blue
on
black

Black
thinned
to
faint
white
thickened
then
white
on
white

White
on
white
on
white
canvas
behind
in front
of
white

Centred
white
on
white
left
grey
under
white
on
white

Monet: In Search of Lost Time
(2024)

He ate books. Consumed books the way one eats sandwiches, knowing they are only a filler until something more substantial comes along. All 3,681 pages of the six volumes of Marcel Proust's *In Search of Lost Time*, wonderful with or without the madeleines. In reading it he was thrown back to the Heidegger conundrum: was the book's meaning held in the relentless turning of pages or was there in Proust's writing a harder kernel? A nugget to be gleaned. Did he read in search of lost time, of a feeling of loss, or a sense of something always being just out of his reach? As if clutching at straws, at empty air in the desperate hope it might yield something more. Reading purely for information's sake seemed useless, so many heads full of facts without knowing. Pleasure, was it reading for pleasure, the joy of one word following another? The narrator's obsession with the secret life and motives of Albertine? Her apparent duplicity turned into a state of mind inside the narrator's head, swirling backwards and forwards like a runaway roller coaster. Or earlier in the book Madame Swann, her beguiling inaccessibility, bitter and sweet? Do we read books in search of lost time he wondered, the desire, perhaps even the need, to sense the worth of what we have or have not done? For affirmation, and at times a release from who we are?

The inner world of the book, beyond bland storytelling, was the search for a thread, no matter how tenuous back to his own state of inner being. Shelf after shelf of words, millions, billions of them packed next to each other along the height and width of the walls. How many words had he read he thought, how many words had he spoken? Did he read, did he say a single word or phrase on any given day of worth? Or was it all a soothing enveloping blanket, an ever-increasing ballooning duvet of words smothering him with verbal comfort food? Looking at the walls of books he wondered what in essence each book could be boiled down to. Could he take from one of the shelves a book and crush it down to a cube no more than a few millimetres in size? At what point would its voice say, enough, you have got to the bottom line? Or would the words escape leaving nothing in the hand? He thought of that strange sensation of trying to read books on a Kindle, which, try as he may, he could never get into. How do you get 22 per cent into a book? He could neither feel the weight of the book, nor the sense of its unfolding from screenshot to screenshot. The backlit text felt dead, just word following word, and the strange reversal, the light physically behind the word instead of in its meaning. Word follows word, over time he had come to think that poetry was the best that words could do. Distilled to a few lines and left somehow open-ended, narrative as such dispensed with, poetry seemed to achieve this better than any other form. To read as if a poem, to think as if a poem, to speak as if a poem. What was it Wallace Stevens suggested, something to the effect that to speak about poetry critics turned to the language of painting, looked for meaning where there were no words.[1]

...

Divided time, cut up into chunks, manageable allotments, a plot for each state of being. He wondered how many selves he had. He envied those who seemed at ease with themselves, those who moved from one thing to the next with such apparent nonchalance. Only in recent years was he able to answer the telephone without first putting on his shoes. Even now to make a call he had to be standing, like the good Boy Scout prepared for whatever was coming down the line. Call it anxiety, he still found it hard to speak to someone when he could not see their face, to talk to a disembodied voice. In a letter received by William Carlos Williams and published as part of his poem cycle *Paterson* the correspondent writes, 'There are people – especially among women – who can only speak to one person. And I am one of those women'.[2] He could identify with these women. He did not know how to speak across the table, could never quite work out who he was speaking to. For him conversation held an intimacy; what was said was only for one other. Just as he never painted a painting with any notion of a public audience, always somewhere at the back of his mind there was someone for whom the painting was made. Even if that person was long gone and all he was holding onto was the lingering idea of who they were. He increasingly nurtured this intimacy, needed it to feel the justification to paint. Just as when in a museum standing in front of a painting, he desired to be alone. Speaking to another, or listening, sharing the experience, was an anathema to him, depriving him of the solitude and intimacy of looking. Eyes, over time he had come to think, shared the world reluctantly.

• • •

While standing in the queue for tickets outside the Musée de l'Orangerie on a crisp spring morning his eyes looked up to the first-floor windows. Through these he could see a series of dark rectangular shapes. They arranged themselves in sequence, two horizontal shapes followed by a third, in the same proportions but vertical, then the same sequence repeated again, and then a third time. He found these clean shapes, their proportions, the rhythmic sequence, almost hypnotic, as if they carried a secret sign.

Claude Monet's great cycle of paintings known as the *Grandes Décorations*, or the *Water Lilies*, at the Orangerie were installed in 1927. He began working on the cycle in about 1914, with numerous paintings being abandoned and destroyed along the way, and others completed yet left out of the final configuration. During this late period (he died in 1926), Monet battled with diminishing eyesight, while not far away from Giverny, Marcel Proust in his cork-lined apartment in Paris lay incapacitated by his acute asthma and neurasthenia. *In Search of Lost Time* was written between 1909 and 1922, the final year of his life. Of course, these superficial chronological connections, the contemporaneity of Proust and Monet, could be deemed just that, yet he could not but feel there was a deeper thread which linked the two. The expansiveness of *In Search of Lost Time* and the *Grandes Décorations*, both tightly rooted in the specifics of place, the narrator's rarefied aristocratic atmosphere of his haunts in Paris, Combray and Balbec, and the water lily pond in the garden at Giverny. In both the writer and the painter one could sense a standing still, a strange passivity, a waiting game for time to do its work. To let time, its fleeting yet relentless passage, flow by under the artist's gaze. Yet where the artist stood, the place, locale, can all too easily become confused with the gaze. 'The only true voyage ... would be not to visit strange lands but to possess other eyes, to see the universe through the eyes of another ...', Proust wrote.[3] This could equally be applied to Monet: the reverence of place that gave rise to the exalted status of Giverny, paradoxically allowed the artist to abandon place and replace it with another way of looking.

The passage of time across the surface of the painting, of page following page of the novel. He found it hard to take in the full 12-m-plus spread of a work such as *The Clouds*, which billowed across one of the long walls in the Orangerie. Instead, he had to break it up into parts, move through his own time from painting episode to painting episode, to then, as if almost reducing the painting to an idea, an ideal state, bring it back to being a whole. Always with time it seems we need to segment it, compartmentalise it, as if not trusting its essence as a continuum. The unfurling of disrupted time, its episodic nature, is ever-present in Proust's novel, as we go from sentence to sentence, episode to episode. Yet sitting behind these incidents is a wall that goes on and on, carrying the narrative by often inchoate degrees as if it were a minutely painted fresco, which as we go from detail to detail engulfs us in its sheer expansiveness.

The thought of a Japanese screen came to mind: its perfect proportions and flow from one panel to the next, the assured sense of completeness. Did Monet's interest in Japanese prints extend to screens too? Were they his model for the *Grandes Décorations*? He thought of Noguchi Shohin's double-sided screen, which on one side depicts in sumptuous gold and colour a gathering at the orchard pavilion of the emperor, and on the reverse side in delicate soft black and grey wash the arrival and nestling of geese among reeds, almost as if an afterthought. Looking at the contrast between the two sides, what struck him was that all paintings tend to have a reverse side too. Not just the side facing the wall when the painting is hung, but also somehow a facing out reverse side, the ghost of the painting, so to speak. The painting's inner life, which we as viewers cannot gain access to. This brought him back to the word: did it too hold a reverse side, a life that faced away from us? Was the act of reading an attempt on our part to gain access to a world that has turned its back on us? They say that true meaning is held in the white gaps between the words, in what is not said, or the still pauses between mark over mark on the painting's surface.

The eye's spread, its span of focus, wider than vertical, as if the vertical blinkers sight. His mind let itself flow horizontally between *In Search of Lost Time* and Monet's cycle of paintings. Both emphasised the spread of the horizontal, gave little credence to the vertical. Monet's thousand and one water lilies that peopled his paintings, Proust's thousand and one characters that adorned his novel, both seemed to oscillate between the meandering restless flow of time and the need to hold onto the moment as if their maker's life depended upon it. To give time fixity. Yet somehow always aware that time's relentless horizontal drift would sweep them ever further on. There could be no final ending as such; both projects embraced the cruel irony that at some point things would just stop.

Monet's late great project, the paintings of the *Grandes Décorations*, were 'in search of lost time'. If his earlier days of painting *en plein air* (outdoors) were over, a practice that he lauded as being his distinct contribution to painting, even when often the works were reworked after the event, then the late paintings, because of their size, were studio-based. A studio he had specifically built to accommodate the project. As such, as in Proust's *In Search of Lost Time*, he needed to call forth a whole history of looking, of editing, distilling and summing up. Monet could now paint what was needed as opposed to what was there. This freedom, one could call it a liberation, pushed his work and painting in its wider meaning somewhere else. Time was no longer fixed to the specifics of place, which was becoming an abstraction, nor to time as an exact moment. Instead, time became an accretion of times, one layered over the other, one panel of painting dissolving into the next. The desire for a moment of resolution evident in the earlier paintings gave way to a release into the fluidity of extended time. A time analogous to Proust's seeming infinity of time. Although Monet's contribution to painting can be seen formally as a dissolving of the image into the broader picture plane, establishing a democratisation of paint across the surface of the painting, the foregrounding of both paint and image, perhaps his greater contribution was in our understanding of painting and time. Time as being central to a painting's meaning.

If in his earlier *plein-air* paintings there was a quest for the exactitude of time, in the works around the project of the *Grandes*

Décorations such parcelling of painting into discrete chunks, small rectangles, gave way to an immersion in the open continuum of time as an ongoing project. Just as *In Search of Lost Time* tails off at the end, as such there is no grand ending, just a short, reflective, summing up, as if to say, well it seems I have to stop now. Had not Proust's time been cut short by illness and death no doubt another page would have been written, followed by another, then another. On the final page of *Time Regained*, the last volume of *In Search of Lost Time*, he writes, 'So, if I were given long enough to accomplish my work, I should not fail, even if the effect were to make them resemble monsters' (man that is).[4] He then alludes to the epochal nature of time, of man reflected in all mankind through time. The latter sections of *In Search of Lost Time* were published posthumously, with certain sections lacking any final corrections or revisions Proust may have wanted to make to the text before publication. The nature of his project, of lived time and memory's ebb and flow, could not by definition end other than by the collapse of time itself. Equally, with the large horizontal canvases that were still in Monet's studio at the time of his death, the 22 designated for the *Grandes Décorations* installation at the Orangerie and the 20 others remaining, one senses that if more time had allowed there would have been a 43rd and a 44th. The wider project was greater than the physical needs of the Orangerie. This simply gave the artist a framework to house the more abstract nature of the enterprise. It was the equivalent of Proust's book, a container, yet neither book nor the physical space of the Orangerie were big enough for either. Monet had repeatedly procrastinated over the removal of the paintings from his studio to the Orangerie. He never saw the work *in situ*. It was as if he could not face the idea of the paintings being taken off their stretchers and adhered to the walls, fixed for good, locked in time, perhaps knowing all too well that this would be less than the magnitude of his painting ambitions.

'Time, colourless and inapprehensible time, so that I was almost able to see it and touch it ...!', Proust wrote in one of his reflections that flow through *In Search of Lost Time*. On another occasion he observed, 'As there is a geometry to space, so there is a psychology in time'.[5] The difficulty of laying a geometry over the space that is landscape. All too easily it clouds into atmosphere. An atmosphere which like any atmosphere holds a latent psychology.

The distinct resonances time and space evoke which cohere as they transfer themselves to memory. If there is a geometry of space, is there also a geometry of memory? As page follows page of the novel and painted canvas follows painted canvas of the *Grandes Décorations*, both housed in their rectangles of the vertical and horizontal, does a geometry edge its way across the surface of what is gone? Do rhythms of atmospheres and psychological dimensions form themselves to gain a fleeting solidity? Form can have the quality of an idea, the idea of time, its form in the moment and in its magnitude. Proust in his epic novel spread out time as if time itself were a complex web of space. Monet's great cycle of late paintings took the space that is painting and turned it into the ceaseless flow and sweep of time.

Robert Rauschenberg and the Photograph
(2024)

Seemingly out of the blue I have been thinking again about Cy Twombly and Robert Smithson, specifically why I chose to write about them, viewing their works through the lens of the written word. There are two photographs, the first a black-and-white photograph taken by Robert Rauschenberg, which shows a young Twombly standing in profile, notebook in hand, next to a larger-than-life, even taller than the artist himself, classical stone sculpture of a hand with the index finger pointing directly up, as if it were a divine calling interrupting his horizontal gaze. The photograph was taken in 1962 when the two artists were travelling together in Italy. The second photograph in colour was taken by the artist Nancy Holt in 1969, depicting Rauschenberg and Smithson, both suntanned and wearing shorts, and pushing what appears to be a large clod of seagrass or the root of a tree across the beach at Captiva, Florida, where Rauschenberg then lived and worked.

In the mid-1970s I had a studio at Martello Street, Hackney, in the East End of London, in one of the artists' collective buildings set up by SPACE. The studio had no heating, and in the winter periods when it was too cold to work I would go to the local library, across the road from Hackney Town Hall. There I would read and sometimes write, and of course upon leaving also borrow a book. One of the books I took out was a monograph on the work of Rauschenberg, a rather bulky volume in an unusual horizontal format. On the cover, or it could have been the frontispiece, I cannot remember which exactly, was a photograph taken by Rauschenberg showing Twombly descending a broad set of stone steps. One can only presume that this was taken at around the same time in Rome as the photograph mentioned earlier. The black-and-white image depicts Twombly dressed in a shirt, sleeves rolled up, and denim jeans. He is cut off at the top of the photograph at mid-chest and the lower half of the image shows the sweep of the stone steps coming towards us. This photograph is one of a series of five, all in black and white and square in format, which as they chart Twombly's descent down the steps go from seeing just his legs from the knees down at the very top of the first image to the last photograph of a close-up shot of him cropped from just below the shoulders to above the knees occupying most of the picture space. But to come back to the monograph I borrowed from the library, for some reason I did not return it by the date it was due back and after the reminder letters ceased coming, I somehow felt that I had claimed it and that the book was now mine. A few years later, when I was living in Germany, the monograph came with me, as did a book of the writings by Smithson, which, just to be clear, I had bought. During that time, I also purchased a lavish publication of the drawings and works on paper of Twombly. At the end of my stay, both the Rauschenberg and the Twombly books went into storage there, where they have remained to this day, while the book of Smithson's writings I brought back to England, and I still have on the shelf.

Quite some years later, in 2017, I was standing in one of the rooms of the Rauschenberg retrospective exhibition at Tate Modern. As I looked across the room, I noticed a young woman standing in front of a painting, which, as I later learnt, was *Ace* from 1962. She was wearing a pale blue top, almost the same blue as in the painting, and hanging from her shoulder was a tan-coloured leather shoulder bag, again just like the orange colour in the painting. It felt as if by some strange serendipity she had inadvertently become an extension of the painting. Her presence there was neither jarring nor distracting; quite the opposite, it all seemed perfectly natural. I was so surprised by this fluke encounter, this seemingly casual coming together of art and life, that I reached for my phone and took a photograph, something I rarely ever do. This action on my part was even more unusual in that I never photograph people. There is something in the works of Rauschenberg that is unconditionally generous. It is as if there are no caveats: the boundaries between art and life somehow dissolve and the presence of a young woman dressed in a pale blue top with a tan leather shoulder bag can take a legitimate place next to the work. The works do not stand aloof.

Some rooms further on into the exhibition I came across a photographic installation that was unknown to me, and later, reading the extensive text in the catalogue, I found no reference to it, as if the work's inclusion was a late afterthought. It was a photographic slide projection using 35 mm black-and-white images arranged along one wall, always presenting a sequence of four. As the slides moved one to the right with the sequence progressing, through the introduction of a new slide on the left this simple shift of one image set up a curious dialogue. What I liked about this work was its directness, also the rawness that comes with slide projections. There was none of the artifice or hidden construction, sleight of hand, which often comes with photographic projections today. Such 35 mm slides tend to have a handmade feel to them, with the corners rounded and, in this case, where one image met another the black vertical line separating them had an ill-defined fuzziness, as if the images by the medium in which they were presented held onto the blurred boundaries between making and meaning. At times, through these seemingly disquieting faults that mirror the casual character of the photographs themselves, something takes hold, where their frayed edges meet our own vague limits and the pale blue top and orange-tan shoulder bag turn into the grey tones of a now seen past.

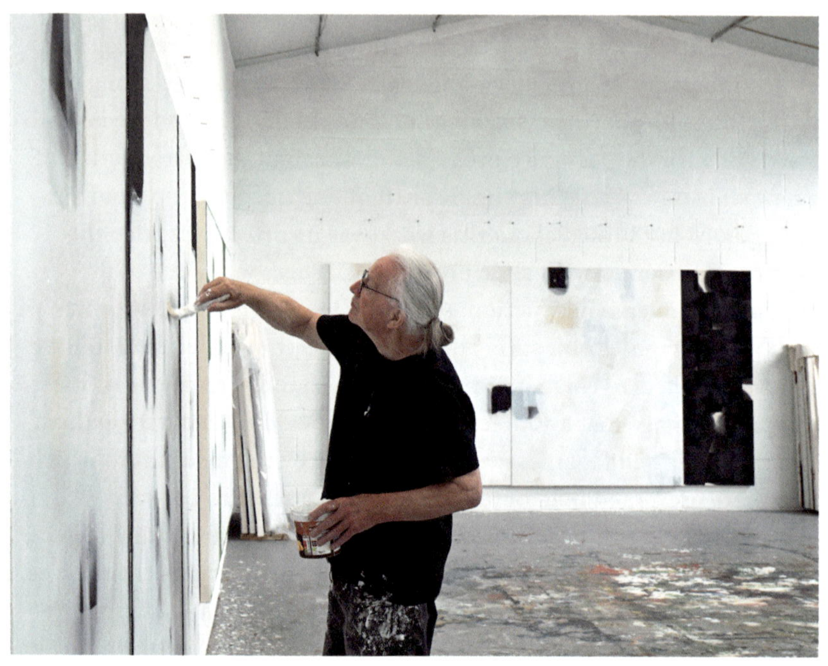

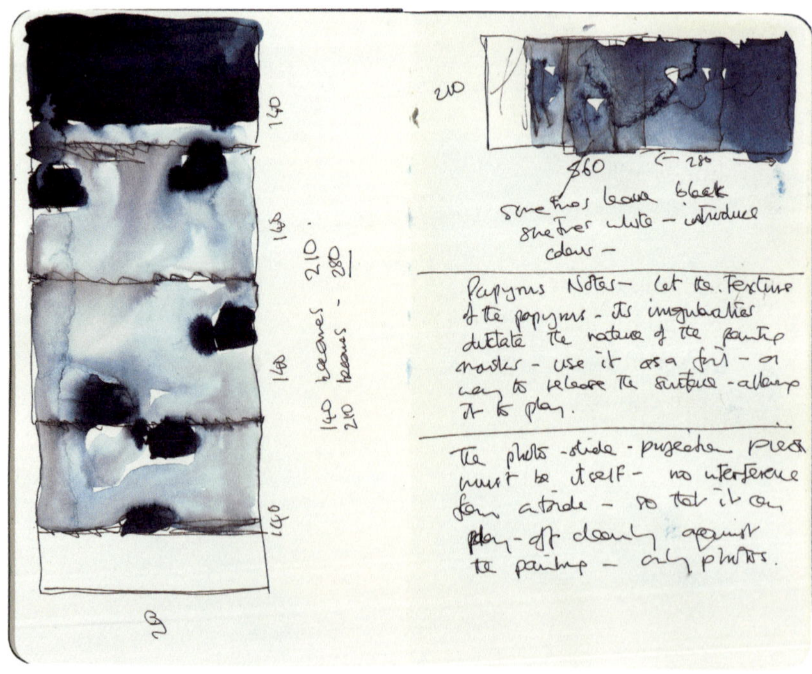
140
140
140
140
210
280
Papyrus Notes

... *And Now*
(2024)

The artist's proximity to his work, the nearness of it. Where the line of separation exists and how to chart that gap which lets us enter. It is usual to chart an artist's work through his life, the chronology becoming the works' meaning. Of cause it is a safe bet: A follows B, followed by C. By this system we arrive at a coherence that transfers from one artist to another. We could call it art history by comparison. To step outside of this, avoid a prescribing system of some sort, is difficult. Even the most esoteric writing requires a preordained model in which to then place extended thought, this then, more often than not, reverting to a shoehorning. Who now reads Bernard Berenson, Roberto Longhi or Adrian Stokes? It would seem the artist has relinquished, has had taken away from him, all capacity for the work to be seen outside of or beyond his biography. Thinking, writing about art, has become an exercise in rudimentary history, general knowledge and basic geography. There has ceased to be the critic or writer who understands that art is an abstraction, existing outside of the general state of things. Instead, the artist is now trapped in his biography. It matters little if he would have the wings to fly. The critic, the curator, will keep him tightly tethered to the ground, or held prisoner within a model of their choosing. Art has never been so easily assimilated into popular thought. One could say the artist has been flayed, his skin stretched out across the surface of our culture for all to see. And his body, the spirit inside him, well like the gods it has been superseded by the news and daily weather report, which, like the gods, we can choose to believe in or not.

Cy Twombly: Ezra Pound
(2024)

Apparently, Ezra Pound would give to visitors and those with whom he corresponded a reading list of authors he thought they may find of benefit. He advised William Carlos Williams to catch up on his theory by reading Aristotle's *Poetics*, Longinus' *On the Sublime* and the essays of Thomas de Quincey and W. B. Yeats. Coming to Pound's own magnum opus, *The Cantos*, one may well wish one had indeed read the suggested list, anything to help get an angle on such a sprawling text. Then again, perhaps not. There is a beauty in coming across a page of text where parts of it appear incomprehensible, at least to the layman. So that instead of reading one has to look and take pleasure in the placement of words on the page or, as is sometimes the case, words replaced by ideograms and even a sequence of music notation. The shift from reading to looking, in which another kind of poetry comes into play. The last seven lines of Canto LXXXVIII simply read:

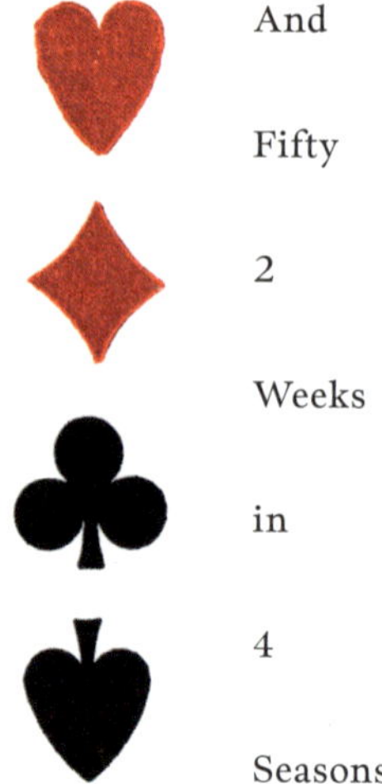

To the left of the sequence of words are the four symbols of the suits of a pack of playing cards. Starting at the top with the two reds, first hearts then diamonds, followed by the blacks, clubs and lastly spades.

The shift from words as letters to numbers set against a third language of coloured symbols. How easily the eye moves almost effortlessly between the three disparate forms. While on another level one senses in the back of one's mind the rupture these shifts entail, as each declares themselves as being distinct. It is as if for a moment Pound hijacks the gap between reading and looking, turning it into a play of forms that play for the sake of it. Concerning reading *The Cantos* Pound wrote, 'if the critic (reader) will read through them before stopping to wonder whether he or she is understanding them: I think he or she will find at the end that he or she has'.[1]

From one language to another. A work in three parts. The word BACCHUS in capital letters scrawled across the surface of three separate large sheets of paper in red crayon. As the word moves from one letter to the next it tails off and begins to drop off towards the bottom of each sheet. Above the word BACCHUS on each sheet is drawn again in red crayon the rough outline of a heart, each then filled in with brushed smudged paint, the colour moving from on the left sheet pink to deep red on the middle sheet to reddy-purple on the right. Underneath sheets two and three, going from left to right, is a separate smaller sheet. On the one under the central larger sheet is the image of a leaf of cavolo nero, its stem and veins intense, looking remarkably like the shape of a heart. Under the third large sheet is the image of a bunch of blue grapes. The 1981 triptych by Cy Twombly is entitled *Bacchus I, Bacchus II a and b, Bacchus III a and b.* As with all Twombly's works containing a written text, even those early works seemingly without, the word is never far away. His sense of a fastidious line, its rhythm and fall, articulates a language that we are drawn to read. Casual, at times seemingly almost absent-minded, the way one might scribble on a piece of paper as one speaks on the phone. In coming to his work there is something of the sensation of sitting down to breakfast to find that the previous occupant of the table has left a few drops of intense yellow soft-boiled egg on what is otherwise a pristine white tablecloth. This we might understand as a soiling, yet at the same time, intriguingly, a past rushes towards us of an event in which we had no part. Except instead of taking us back an hour, or maybe a few minutes in time to the previous anonymous table guest, Twombly's marks herald us back to a distant time we both know and do not know. The classics of Homer, the Greek and Roman gods Dionysus and Bacchus, are wedded to our own myths, loves and anguishes. Just as in our Western culture Christianity, no matter how vehemently we push it aside, still sits ghosting centre stage, nudging our collective psyche every once in a while. The enactment of the present moment is a repeat of the past; they are never far apart. Dionysian fertility runs all the way through to the soiling of the white tablecloth by the encrusted yellow droplets of a soft-boiled egg.

...

The surface of looking, the surface of reading. The text's flatness on the surface of the page and across the width of the canvas. The handwritten word, its rhythm and tilt as it moves towards becoming a signature. Shifting the word from what it sounds like to that which it looks like. The look that can creep into a page of poetry. Lines of text abandoned to the flow and rhythm of the look of words as one flows into the next. To see a page of a poem by Ezra Pound is different to seeing one by T. S. Eliot. How the words gather or disperse in the act of looking already holds a personality before words begin to flesh it out.

...

Two Americans who left their homeland and lived the major part of their artistic lives in Italy. Ezra Pound, after a few restless years in London and Paris, settled in Rapallo, northern Italy, in 1924. He only returned to America at the end of the Second World War after being extradited by his compatriots for the crime of treason, for his support of Benito Mussolini and rants against the Jews. Considered too insane to stand trial, he spent the next thirteen years in St Elizabeths Psychiatric Hospital, Washington, DC. After his release, he returned to Italy for the rest of his life. He died in Venice in 1972. Cy Twombly first visited Italy together with Robert Rauschenberg in 1952. He returned in 1957 to then settle and work in Rome, occasionally making extended trips back to the USA. He died in Rome in 2011.

It is known that Twombly attended a public reading by Pound at the 1969 Spoleto Festival. Apparently, the painter held the poet in high esteem, no doubt fostered by their mutual love of the classics. There is no record of them either meeting or speaking, however.

Putting this aside for a moment, let us abandon the known facts and venture that such a meeting did take place, perhaps the occasion being one of Miss Rudge's soirées at her house in Venice where Pound ensconced himself in his later years. And venturing still further in our imaginings that Pound, now an old man who seemingly took pleasure in silence for the sake of it, was roused momentarily out of his mute state by the prospect of meeting a younger American who had painted works entitled *Hyperion (to Keats)* or *Veil of Orpheus*. Twombly, feeling the need of a break from the heat and pollution of Rome having travelled to the home of Giovanni Bellini and Titian and being at a loss, finding himself at Miss Rudge's door. Of course, there is no record of this hypothetical conversation between the two great men and so if we are to conjecture further we must seek out, as would the overzealous amateur detective, clues wherever we can find them. Pound with his mercurial capacity to range over apparently infinite territory had been good friends with the sculptor Henri Gaudier-Brzeska and had visited Constantin Brâncuși during his time in Paris. Indeed, he had written on both artists. When in full flow his mind could vault shifts of discipline with the ease of an athlete. Perhaps things began with him referring to something Brâncuși had said to him, 'All my things date back fifteen years. Every day I can begin something new but finish it ...?'. This then leading to a discussion of the bittersweet taste of the yearning for and the putting off of the moment of completion of a work of art which stalks the creative process. The striving for the ideals of the Greeks and Romans, never met, always pierced by reality like the heal of Achilles, neither god nor demigod, simply mortal man.

Or perhaps the conversation never reached such lofty heights and instead reverted to the niceties of when and where; after all, Americans are fond of the where. The where of Hailey, Idaho and Lexington, Virginia. As if the vast subcontinent that is America has to be pinned down to the specifics of place, to a geography of the known, accessible to all. Within this precise placement of who lives where, there is neither ambiguity nor doubt, just the fact of place. A literalness that seeps through the American psyche even as it roams the vastness of the mindscape of E. E. Cummings, Marianne Moore and William Carlos Williams.

...

If we are to entertain the idea that poet and painter sat down one early evening on the terrace of Miss Rudge's house and mused over the thought of where, then perhaps it was in their adopted homeland of Italy that they sought the place. Indeed, could this connecting thread have been Rimini and perhaps even more specifically the Tempio Malatestiano with its fresco depicting Sigismondo Malatesta paying homage to St Sigismund by Piero della Francesca, which provided the link? It is known Pound spent time at the library in Rimini, and also just a stone's throw down the road in Cesana at the library there, researching the life of Sigismondo. In an article published in 1936 for an issue of *The Delphian Quarterly* he wrote, 'My research into the life of Sigismondo Malatesta took me to Cesana'.[2] Within the 116 cantos, plus fragments, which Pound wrote during his lifetime, there are four cantos known collectively as the Malatesta Cantos, nos VIII–XI, which introduce us to Sigismondo Malatesta, and chronicle his life and the building of the Tempio. Canto IX begins with the following four lines.

> One year floods rose,
> One year they fought in the storms,
> One year hail fell, breaking the trees and walls,
> Down here in the marsh they trapped him in one year.

With a little help from *A Companion to the Cantos*,[3] I can begin to understand these lines as referring to the flooding of Rimini in 1440 and the subsequent years of bad weather as Sigismondo fought his local feuds for land and power in the name of the Medicis and the Pope. Much of *The Cantos* eludes me, is way over the head of any rudimentary understanding of Italian Renaissance history I may have. Even so, there is pleasure in the reading as what might be termed a poetic flow takes place, connecting Sigismondo's trials and tribulations and the fraught building of the Tempio. One is tempted to try to picture the man for oneself, or understand something of him in the portrait in the fresco, as he kneels in profile and devotion before the exalted saint. Later, in Canto XI, Pound writes:

And he wrote to young Piero
Send me a couple of hunting dogs.

I would like to think this refers to the two hunting dogs that lie alert like Egyptian sculptures to the right of Sigismondo in the fresco. The one a sooty grey-black facing into the picture; the other in muted white facing out. However, Pound's interest in visiting the Tempio seemed more to do with the idealisation of a Renaissance man pitting his wits against friend and foe, a man of action rather than the serene depiction of the man Piero della Francesca gave us. The temple was built by Sigismondo as a shrine to his beloved Isotta, intended to be worthy of the gods, ornated with pagan sculptures in their honour. The trials and tribulations of acquiring the marble to build it mirrored Sigismondo's own fortunes and subsequent downfall, leaving him in the end sitting desolate between four roofless walls, with the glaring void of the open skies above.

In Twombly's case, perhaps one needs not to be so concrete as building and man. In his paintings there is little to connect him to the early Italians, the world of piety running through Fra Angelico, Masaccio or Piero della Francesca. Little intimation of Christian iconography. Instead, Twombly's world aligns with Italian painting when it embraces the swagger and bravura of the great myths, of Classical Greece and Rome. When painting becomes action, the bull is taken by the horns and man presumes, indeed conspires, to challenge the gods. Titian, Tintoretto, painting becoming peopled with the grandeur of heroic endeavour. I seem to remember, though, when asked as to his painting antecedents Twombly cited not the Italians but the seventeenth-century French painter steeped in the Classical world, Nicholas Poussin. Apollo and Daphne, Venus and Adonis, the triumph of Pan, Poussin entwined his often densely populated Classical themes across the canvas as if a restless frieze, a narrative curiously fixed and frantic at the same time. Similarly, Twombly's stilted words move as they make their way across the surface of the canvas, from the haptic to meaning. With Poussin, bodies become a language of action, feet and heels pushing in from the edges compressing a corporeal mass that jerks and twists to find, if only for a moment, a fleeting statis. This is, of course, to do with content and the nature of painting a painting, so if we are to take the plunge and suggest Twombly stood with arms folded before Piero della Francesca's fresco, then perhaps our approach, like that of the crab, needs to be sideways. A more glancing look than head on. It is possible the light in the fresco may have drawn Twombly to seek it out, turning as it does mere wall into a luminous plane. How paint sitting on such a hard surface appears aerated, somehow denying the wall its solidity and mass. Twombly's own paintings with their customary restrained palette, set against larger passages of white or off-white, through which ideas and air circulate, hold in them a similar play of loft and weight.

To paint directly on a wall, even without the technique being fresco, is not easy. The wall unlike a stretched-up canvas on a frame is unyielding, desirous to pull back to the surface as quickly as it can. From what I understand, Twombly painted many of his works with the canvas stapled directly to the wall. Often very large pieces of canvas. This way, scoring into the canvas or spreading paint, often with the fingers, would not run into the usual problem of the canvas sagging and catching the stretcher crossbars, indenting a crease into the painting surface. This would also allow the painting to find its own edges in the making rather than this being pre-imposed by a wooden frame. For the painting, like the lines of a poem, to gather and disperse unhindered by a preconceived structure. There is a monumental painting by Twombly entitled *Say Goodbye, Catullus, to the Shores of Asia Minor*, consisting of three abutted panels: a long central panel with vertical panels either side. The work's total size is 4 m by nearly 16 m long. Painted over 22 years, the passages of script and marks across its surface, punctuated by large areas of near white, echo the turning of pages as a text is being written, as it goes from one completed page to the next blank white page awaiting what is to follow.

...

The surface upon which a word sits. The word handwritten and in printed form. How this simple change of form inflects the word's character, how we understand the meaning of the word. The one individuated by the manual act of writing, the other somehow more abstract, still locked in, as if waiting for another word to push it towards its own singular personality. Waiting to be aligned in a thought process that nudges it out of its abstract void and gives it colour and voice. The poet needs this juxtaposition of word following word to lift them out of their lethargic rest, to make them begin to breathe and come alive in the world. The handwritten words 'Vengeance of Achilles', as they scratch their way across the surface of the canvas in red crayon, get smaller and fainter as they go, holding meaning as if a wound. Words held in check by the weight of their inscription. Words nurtured into form on the canvas and words released from the mind in the turning of the page.

Knowing as we do the two men never met, and that our imaginings concerning such a meeting and the conversation which ensued are indeed imaginings, we can of course allow our speculations to wonder unimpeded. It is known Pound was a keen tennis player, even in his years in the 'bughouse' as he referred to St Elizabeths Psychiatric Hospital. Whenever the weather was suitable and an opponent could be found, he was to be seen out on the court in the grounds, sometimes playing as many as five or six sets. If my memory serves me correctly, I remember reading somewhere that T. S. Eliot played a few sets with him on one of his visits there. Twombly, in his off-white creamy chinos as there was a mild chill in the air while sitting out on the terrace, has thrown his white V-neck pullover across his shoulders. This sight of the younger man in fine fettle looking sporty may well have taken Pound back to his days on the tennis court, lifting him out of his quietude and eliciting what became a toing and froing, of game followed by game as verbal utterances and riposte played themselves out. As things loosened up leading to the occasional surprise lob or smash over the net. Indeed, we can conjecture their verbal exchange metaphorically speaking reaching the pitch of chips and drops followed by powered volleys from one baseline to the other as the match played itself out. A game of relative youth, Twombly was about 40 at this time, set against the wily cunning of the older man.

But then again, perhaps Twombly preferred not to engage, his mind already awash with circumstance, and although he admired Pound's poetry, felt no desire to get to know the man. To most Americans Pound was off limits, a traitor, his anti-Semitic tirades against the Jews inexcusable. Having served out his twelve years in the mental institution in Washington, he was now back in Italy very much a man living in exile. So, we could envisage after a formal introduction by Miss Rudge, the customary handshake, instead of banter the two men settled back into a state of seeming indifference. Something of a damp squib, so to speak, necessitating the indomitable Olga Rudge pick up her violin and entertain the intimate assembly of guests. She was an accomplished concert performer, and had no doubt somewhere in her repertoire works by Antonio Vivaldi and these would have been part of her impromptu recital. Miss Rudge had performed works by the composer on several occasions, and she had spent time digging out long-neglected scores in order that they might find the light of sound. On one of her sorties, she had found 309 Vivaldi concerti lying silent in the National Library in Turin, and even unearthed an oratorio on a visit to the Fitzwilliam Museum in Cambridge. So, there they are, poet and painter, each slipping into their own inner world of silent thought as the refrains from *The Four Seasons* wafted through the early evening air.

The one, Pound sliding backwards into what might be described as a meditation on the past. A rethinking of times and time as expressed in one of *The Cantos*, 'And / Fifty / 2 / Weeks / in / 4 / Seasons'. The intertwining of the prosaic normality of life, duration summed up in a week, set against the elemental cycle of the four seasons. As if life oscillated by some supranatural force between the banality of the moment and the primal mystery of its becoming. Framing itself in the moment, a moment so fleeting we can pass it by unnoticed, mistaking it for yet another instance of what is already known and relegating it to the realm of mere incident. While all the time it is attempting to surface, to call forth its newness, its uniqueness, set against the normality of what has already gone, all too easily sucked into a past which, once there, lingers only as a shadow. That first found momentum which brought it into our consciousness, not screaming as an aberration of profound revelation, as a shift from state of being to state of exaltation, but as a whisper, a hair falling from the shoulder towards the floor, only in an instance catching the light as if a dust mote, pointing away from the past into nothing more than the moment now. In the final fragment of *The Cantos*,

Canto CXX, first published in the third edition in 1972,[4] the year Pound died, he wrote:

> I have tried to write Paradise
> Do not move
> Let the wind speak
> That is paradise.
> Let the Gods forgive what I
> Have made
> Let those I love try to forgive
> What I have made.

While Miss Rudge plays, Rome burns. Twombly leaning back in his chair is lost in thought. Not of Nero, but about to begin the long and often time-consuming process of gently fanning the spark of a reluctant, but nevertheless insistent, idea as it begins to ignite and catch flame. Bringing it up from the dark depths of the subconscious into the air from which it will feed and gain substance. Not as a whale fully formed surfacing for air, but rather as a silent bubble of thought, which as it gestates and thickens gathers not only a volume but also a volition. Slowly forming itself over time, maybe over a decade or even more, into a form, a form which as it moves from vapour to substance begins to cast the veil of its shadow across the surface as paint on canvas.

The Four Seasons, Vivaldi's most well-known work, its rhythm and moods transforming themselves from the sound of time to the hard reality of being seen before the eye. Twombly entitled his second set of the four seasons painted between 1993 and 1995 *Quattro Stagioni*, sliding them out of the elemental seasonal orbit of mood into the realm of Italian cultural reference, replacing nature with culture, back towards the accompanying sonnets of Vivaldi and the word. His *Quattro Stagioni* is a painting in four parts, a cycle. Twombly had used this multi-part sequencing of paintings on several previous occasions: one need only think of his monumental group *Fifty Days at Iliam*, a work in ten parts, painted between 1977 and 1979. The telling, or perhaps better said, reflections on incidents in Homer's *Iliad*. However, there is a difference between the loose narrative of a sequence and that of a closed cycle, which by its nature calls forth a specific duration and sense of repetition. The melancholy associated with and felt in the repeating of time becoming times, holding as it does the past as being imminently present. One senses this even in Barnett Newman's cycle of paintings *The Stations of the Cross*, of the fall and rise, of despair, resurrection and redemption, that somehow the fourteen canvases hold tight to them, as if a need, the desire to be repeated, to be enacted again and again. Twombly, in reducing back to the hard reality of the four seasons, harnessed not the pathos of a god, but the gap between the mind of culture and a body that is the actuality of being. The blunt reality of season following season, to then repeat itself. For all our flights of fancy we are stuck in the world of life's cycle, glued to the rhythm of season following season and year following year.

And ...
(2024)

... and although Robert Bresson stilled the film, it continues to be part of the tradition of the moving image. Remains a part of cinema, or as Bresson would say, cinematography. I remember seeing a documentary about the making of *The Turin Horse*, the film by Béla Tarr, and realised that the wind and the rains which raged through the film, giving it its bleakness, unrelenting harshness, were all made by wind machines and hose pipes of carefully sprayed water. I had been watching artifice and its capacity to conjure up the mood and atmosphere projected in the film. I believed the waggon driver and his daughter truly were living and experiencing the desolation and poverty depicted, and that it was real. To place a work of art, be it a film or a painting, at such a pitch is rare. Emotions now come cheap in the arts and great claims are made for works that are second-rate, even mediocre. Reviews speak about how someone really 'nailed it', or that they are a genius. Such vapid use of language becomes as meaningless as the attribution to which it is given. The gap between the act of performing and the prosaicness of life is lost in the suffusion of cheap bankrupt compliments, which like the act itself have not the distance to understand art as separate from our daily lives but would rather they become one and the same. This fosters a melding that in the process allows the denizens of taste, or the mere spectator, to also feel they are a part of it because they too are touching the same moment of significance in the normality of daily life.

We have stopped giving art distance, the distance to stand outside of our own lives, to claim its own territory as being sovereign unto itself, to be art. In this sense, art is no longer art; it has become just more life, blurred into the vicarious world of reality TV and Instagram. A book on the shelf, two hours with a film, two minutes before a painting, any separation art now has shrunk to the cosy distance between a cappuccino and a cliché. Our knowingness in all its knowing has left art bereft of a place of sanctuary. Like life, it has become nomadic, an incident without moorings. A crack in a concrete floor, which is not a crack, yet does not have the guile to hide its clumsy making. A car with a textile draped over it, the gesture already made by another artist in another country some years before ignored, presented as exotic.

If we give art distance now, it is by turning it first and foremost into a monetary value, by taking it beyond our means, something only for the super-rich. Regressing us back to the medieval and Renaissance times, when the wealth of a doge, a bishop, the Church, the Crown, placed art high above us, out of reach to the ordinary person. A time when the artist was at the behest of a patron, locked into a system which, unless he or she had the glorious resilience of a Francisco Goya, the distance to step back from the piggy-faced and pudgy-handed aristocrats and paint friends or family, meant that they became the handservant of wealth's needs. Studios churning out painting after painting; ah, the value we now give to such artists as Piero della Francesca or Johannes Vermeer because there are so few known works by them. It is legitimate to ask, what now is the value of art in its making? What does its popularisation, and by definition dilution, bring to us? Does it make us better human beings, the incessant striving for novelty, even if more often than not such apparent newness is simply a riff on the past? Increasingly a recent past, as if history itself has lost its own capacity to remember. Memory too shrunk to the now. The artist foregrounding the self as being of itself the significance and legitimacy of art. The 'I' of making, the 'I' of positioning, the 'I' that is me (me, me), walking straight through the door to meet not the eye of you, but the 'I' of you. Art has become a mutual gratification system, my 'I' meets your 'I'. And the eyes, well the eyes have got lazy, too easily distracted by the next flick of a finger, the twitch of a button, to care. All the eye now wants is to see its own reflection, a mirror image of the self in all its glorious panoply of significance. And what is left after we have become mere decoration, ornamented and resplendent in the infinite reflections of the self in our halls of mirrors? What then?

Tell me now, what graces your walls in homage to what things could be? And not in looking back at that which it is now already too late to receive. And where sits the Fisher King, turned dotterel? Is he out on open waters, his eye impaled to the surface, his sideways glance lost in the glare? And T. S. Eliot's *The Waste Land*, which has become our wasteland, the garbage we heap and prise into micro mechanisms, as if attempting to stuff the molecules we are made from with the abundance of our enterprise, of that which we have become. And still more to come, as we are emptied hollow as fast as we can feed. And what nurtures us, the bridge between the plastic of our lives and the ever more rigid inflexibility of our minds? And in the end is that all there will be, our once fluid heads ossified with micro particles which have stiffened in both form and content, regularly inspected and checked to see that all is in order and correct? And we, we have become the image we made of ourselves, inseparable from the looking and being looked at. And art ... what of art? Who will have the courage to clear the walls and begin ... yes, begin?

Bonnard's Touch
(2024–25)

Gerlinde, her presence and absence, the cloth on the kitchen table arranged diagonally so that its four corners hang one on each side over the edge forming neat triangles, leaving the four rounded corners of the wooden table exposed, warm against the creamy white of the linen cloth. The white duvet folded down, one could say almost rolled towards the foot of the bed, lofted as if it were the white crest of a wave coming in to meet the shore, symmetrical in its highs and lows. The quality a space and an object are imbued with when taken into care, whereby their neutrality is shifted into what might best be understood as that of an embrace. The ache of an absent touch, which holds its place until an interruption takes it out of its repose. To make an object relax into a space instead of being an indifference. To bring about this could be said to be a talent that holds within it a settling, a stilling which could be seen as an unspoken pact between object and hand, allowing for a new beginning.

Marthe, her presence never far away. I first saw her seemingly without embarrassment in the bath, her head leaning back into the bathtub's curve, her body outstretched, arms by her side, legs crossed and slightly floating in the water. I cannot remember how many times I saw her on that day in 1996. I know, it was three times in the bath, and even when she stepped out of it and left the room her presence somehow lingered in a warm afterglow that could change colour from one moment to the next. For upon seeing her one moment she would be bathed in blue, or perhaps better said blues, only for a few moments later for me to find her wrapped in a luminescence of ethereal pinks and yellows. Marthe's absence in itself seemed to leave the light in the room different, other than it was before. It was as if her fleeting withdrawal imbued the space she left behind with an aura, an atmosphere tingling with particles of light.

It was many years later that Marthe and I crossed paths again. In the time between that first encounter and now, much had happened and to be quite honest my memory of her was vague. She had become just one of the thousands of experiences and images that had occupied my gaze. Of course, I recognised her immediately, once again in the bath or going about her ablutions as if she had not a care in the world. It was as if I had seen her only yesterday, yet I sensed a difference to our first encounter, for it was as if her body, her corporality, had given way to something more vague, something which I could not quite put my finger on, but which engendered a strange sense of aloofness, a distance. She had become more a memory I was recalling from the past than an actual presence, this combined with the feeling that she herself was not quite with me, distracted by something, her attention elsewhere. She was there but not there, if you can understand my meaning.

Thinking back to that time I could again sense her presence in the room as I had on our first encounter, the placement of the pink tablecloth with red stripes that somehow filled my eye, or the bowl of fruit which I could not help but feel her hand had earlier in the day arranged. As I went from room to room her presence continued to linger on. The chair, the crockery on the table, the bottle, all seemed to hold her as if her touch alone were itself a presence. It was only when I stepped out of the French windows into the garden that I sensed she was no longer there. Although the garden was in full bloom, blossom and flowers saturated with the light of the summer's warmth, it seemed to me the garden with its multiplicity of textures and tones, its almost chaotic arrangement of fragmentary forms, did not hold the structures and surfaces her presence required. It was not her world. It could not reciprocate her gentle touch, and although Monsieur Bonnard had discreetly kept his distance in my engagement with Marthe, he too was somehow adrift out there, unsure of what he was giving structure to and to what the flowing caress of his brush was directed towards. And so it was that I found myself being drawn back into the house to ponder on what had now become more an idea of Marthe as a feeling than any sense that I might see her again in the flesh. This absent presence I now sensed of her was not only held in the furnishings and objects in the room, but also as a special kind of light, a light that took the finite nature of colour and turned it on its head, seemingly to make one colour flow into the next without jarring or distress, the colours sliding into each other as on a bed of pure light. I wondered if in my losing Marthe's physical being had I by chance transposed her into light, turned the now increasingly distant memory of her in the bath into a body of light allowing her to be seen, to live on in another way?

Over the ensuing years again the memory of Marthe faded, yet the light I had on that second encounter with her remained, for I found myself now not looking at paintings for their subject matter or formal concerns but rather for their sense of light. To what extent they held a light and how that was emanating from within beyond ideas of subject matter, and that paintings were in and of themselves rectangles and receptacles for light itself. I collected these differing lights as one might collect stamps or postcards, except instead of there being a physical object they were as feelings and thoughts. Often fragile in their comings and goings, sometimes even fleeting, yet never what one might call itinerant or transitory, always with a little coaxing they could be evoked, pulled back to the centre of my looking. Indeed, at one point I thought that if ever I were to make an exhibition of historical paintings, it would not be of this or that subject matter. Instead, it would be of paintings as manifestations of light, from the solidity of Piero della Francesca's omnipresent light to that of the dust motes circulating on the air in the gathering of a fading light in the paintings of Vilhelm Hammershøi. Making a room not of paintings as we tend to understand them but as volumes of light, some being crystalline and pure while others more nuanced in their gentle inflection. A room which held the mystery of light as if it were a long-lost sepulchre. I imagined that even in apparent total darkness the light from these paintings would find a way out, that their emanations would imbue the space with their differing lights, light which only the mind's eye could see.

My third encounter with Marthe, again, as on the two previous occasions, caught me off-guard, for although I had seen her fully revealed on our first meeting attending to her ablutions, and then later going from room to room taking in her absent aura, it occurred to me that I had never really seen her face. She always appeared to be avoiding my gaze, her head tilted downwards as she towelled herself or turned sideways concerned with other matters, oblivious to one's attention. To see her face, I found myself turning to a photograph. She was standing next to Pierre Bonnard, wearing a bulky striped fur coat, her hat pulled down to just above her eyes, head in profile. She was looking up at the much taller Bonnard, neither seemed to be speaking, caught in that moment between words. Seeing this small black-and-white image I found myself thinking the photograph did not so much hold a memory, one which aligned with my thoughts and imaginings of Marthe's presence, but rather it housed a moment at a market in Vernon and as such its fixity stood outside of my realm of speculation. In another photograph Marthe is facing out towards me, she is sitting on a balcony, a table in front of her and a dog on her lap. Again, her hat is pulled down close to her eyes and because of the angle of the light her eyes are in shadow. Only the line of her nose and the shape of her mouth to indicate that indeed it might be her, yet even so I cannot say I have seen this woman before, much less that I know her. Trapped as she is in black and white, distant to the feel and the shape of the light, I found myself lost, bereft of a point of contact.

What surprised me on this last visit to see Marthe was the directness of Monsieur Bonnard himself. If previously he had always managed to avoid my gaze, left my looking to itself, now however he stared back at me. There was in his look a suggestion of intrusion, as if to say some things are best not known, left at a discreet distance, and that perhaps my desire to lift the veil would all too easily break the spell which held me. The request for this unspoken pact was not so much held in his expression as in his hands, which not quite touching each other were held up to shoulder height. They did not push me away, or hold me off in any direct way, but in their semi-clenched form suggested a closing off, a separation from inside and out. Framed in the mirror, Monsieur Bonnard's head turned slightly to his left, one sensed in this silent gesture, in this reverse image, the desire to hold his world and that of Marthe beyond an intrusive gaze of looking, whereby the intimacy of their exchange remained removed from mine and the scrutiny of others. Search as I may on that day for Marthe's face I could not find her and came to accept Bonnard's unspoken request, for in his generosity he had not closed the door to her, as one could still sense her presence in the luminescent yellow panelling reflected in the mirror behind him. Its living glow bathed him in colour and light as he had bathed her in a homage of pure colour, which in its clarity had turned the unspoken into a world of pure light.

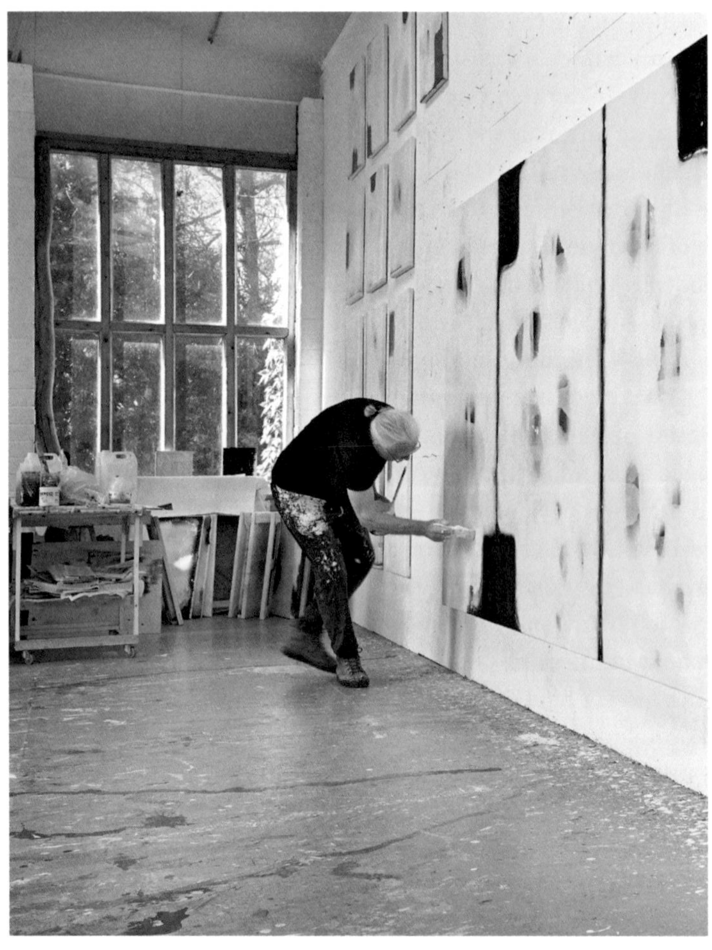

The Mirror and the Sea
(2025)

The mirror and the sea, the photograph and the painting. The title is of course taken from W. H. Auden's prose poem *The Sea and the Mirror.*[1] However, it is no more than a borrowing. I did not set out to comment on Auden's work; it was simply the registering of those words, the sea, the mirror, which brought to mind the play between the flow of life and the moment of its comprehension.

One might phrase it differently and instead encapsulate it in the photograph, the moment of its taking and the flow of time across the painting's surface. Equally, for me the two words, sea and mirror, are replete with associations of my childhood. The constant presence of the sea and the light from the town lighthouse, its beam mirrored out into the night sky across the open expanse of the North Sea.

It never fails to astound me how specific words can hold and unlock deep subconscious murmurings within oneself, evoking thoughts and associations that ricochet off one another, gathering volition and a density so counter to the norms of daily life. As if the body and the senses shrink as one goes through life, while the mind expands ever more into realms of generosity, gathering momentum, which spreads out as it progresses in its wanderings to compensate for the body's retreat.

Perhaps, the photograph's insistent mirroring of life's moments is an attempt to pull it back to a reflection of the body, to affirm where one stands, our place in the world. And, the sea like the mind, upon which the body floats its antithesis, which has no beginning and no end, only the endless ebb and flow of what has been and what might be.

I remember the light and I feel the pulse, how memories, not of incidents but of feelings, cohere between the rhythm of the sea and the light's mirroring. Its brilliance bounced off that endless watery expanse, suspended in the air, becoming almost graspable in its solidity. The point at which what seemed real and tangible in the world somehow fades, loses its form, to be replaced by something more crystalline, its shape never defined as would be an object, nevertheless acquiring a kind of solidity. What shape is a thought, what shape is a memory, mirrored as light on the sea of one's being?

It is late summer 1965, and I am nearly nineteen years old. I am taking the bus from the small seaside town of Withernsea, where I have spent my childhood, to Hull, a journey of about 20 miles. I am going to meet a man, a man I have never met before. That man is my father. A few days earlier, in a brief telephone conversation, from the local call box to a number given to me by my mother, I had arranged to meet him at a pub just a short walk from the central bus station. I arrived early and took up a stool at the far end of the long bar. The place was almost empty except for a few solitary souls sitting at the odd table. Minutes later a man walked through the door, a person I did not know, but then again, he somehow looked familiar to me and I sensed this man was my father As he walked along the bar towards me, I could see that he had the same way of moving I had, something in the rhythm of his gait, and although his build was heavier than mine, I saw myself in his body and in his roundish face. I felt in this first moment that I was looking at a mirror image of myself but older, how I may come to be in middle age. This sudden apparition of my older self in its unexpectedness startled me and as my father pulled up a stool and placed his hands on the bar, I was momentarily lost, adrift in the distance between myself and this reflection now sitting beside me. We talked for an hour or so, not of anything significant. I learnt little about him, his past and his absence from mine and my sisters' lives. I sensed the door that separated us was firmly closed and could not be opened. We left together, shook hands on the pavement and went our separate ways. I never saw my father again. That strange and disturbing encounter, in a soulless pub in a nondescript part of Hull, was the only time I ever saw him.

Except then again, was that really so? When we were children, a weekend treat would be to go to the local cinema. One of the films I saw in my teens that has stayed with me was the war drama *The Cruel Sea* made in 1953, directed by Charles Frend and starring Jack Hawkins and Donald Sinden. The film chronicles the trials and tribulation of the officers and crew aboard the HMS *Compass Rose*, a corvette escort vessel accompanying a convoy of cargo ships as they make their way across the Atlantic, the objective, largely in vain, to deter and counter the attacks of German U-boats. The story is gripping, however what really held me was the sea itself, its portrayal. From the very start of the film, with its titles and credits, displayed in large lettering across the screen, set against the sea's restless movement pictured behind, its swelling and falling, tilting and turning as it heaved against an ever-moving horizon line, I was transfixed. It was as if the sea were alive, a living, breathing organism, its presence more powerful and real than any single human being.

In talking with my mother after I had met my father, she for the first time began to open up and speak about the man. Our somewhat awkward conversation revealed few details to help me understand this absent past and I sensed in her reticence there was a resignation and a need for letting be. So, I left it there. However, what struck me was something my mother did say about my father being in the Navy in the war and afterwards continuing to serve for some more years. During this time, he had been co-opted from the Navy as an extra to flesh out the crew of HMS *Compass Rose* for the filming of *The Cruel Sea*. And in this role, he had made a brief appearance on-screen, standing at the top of a steep metal staircase, looking down, blowing a whistle, uttering a few words to then, just as suddenly as he had appeared, vanish off-screen.

So, I have two senses, or perhaps it is better put as two images, of the man I never knew and who was my father. The first what might be called the feel of someone, the distinct bodily presence in the world that sits within everyone as if it were a signature. What we might call the rub of their being. This I used to feel more strongly with the passing years as I stared into the mirror each morning, sensing my look becoming increasingly blurred into his look. Yet strangely, as I passed through middle age, this mirror image faded into something resembling more of an abstraction, becoming not the feel of a human presence but more a state of mind, one that gave another way of seeing. The second image I have of my father, which although I did not know it then was when I first saw him, is of that short sequence of black-and-white cellulose frames when he appeared fleetingly in *The Cruel Sea*. Over time, however, this projection of light, never more than a passing glance, has changed too, at least in my mind's eye, into a single fixed black-and-white photograph of a young sailor unknown to me, looking as if he had not a care in the world.

The phrase 'to take a photograph', implicit within it, no matter how seemingly innocent, holds a sense that something illicit is taking place. 'May I', 'could I possibly' or any one of a hundred phrases are used to seek approval, to navigate the distance between the look and the lens, during which a strange reversal occurs, and request gives way to a favour bestowed, as if the photograph were a gift, a privilege, not the taking but the granting. No wonder some cultures have believed this seduction, the taking of their photograph, to be the stealing of their souls. The loss of something of themselves which, although perhaps tacitly given, nevertheless holds a lingering sense of regret. A semblance of themselves is fixed in time. Unlike the mirror image which can be turned away from or revisited in the now, the photographic image does not change. It is like a flattened Dorian Grey, everything around it is in flux, ageing, while it remains the same, tenaciously holding onto the moment of its taking. The photograph yearns, when looked at, not to be returned to the moment of its taking but to be released into the here and now, when eyes meet eyes, so its captured soul can be given back and once more life is rendered complete.

…

If a painting could weep would a tear roll down the cheek of Doge Loredan's face as he looks out of his immaculate painted surface now in front of me, or does a tear fill my eye as I gaze into a past that reaches out towards me.[2] Does the uncertainty of where I stand at this moment solicit a response which leads me back to the all too human. How to distance the eye so that if only for a moment things can be seen not as a mirror but as a sea. The mask of semblance be replaced by the unadorned look of a Paul Valery or a Rilke, who stood exposed in anticipation of the space before him 'as though space were slowly thinking thoughts for him'.[3]

…

Standing on the shore looking out towards the slate grey horizon where the sea met the sky and separation dissolved, he imagined the sea as a manifestation of the infinite, something immeasurable, beyond the norms of accountability. As such, its mystery beguiled him, one could say even bewitched him. It was there, emphatically so and pressing, concrete even in its mass and solemnity. At the same time somehow not there, in its ungraspable form, held off as though more the equivalent of a feeling, which nevertheless in its fullness pulsed with the moment. Yet in its lack of definable edges eluded hard definition, as if it were no more than a sound. Perhaps, he thought, the sea was a sound, a clear yet at the same time vague presence the epicentre of which echoed out indefinitely. Its form, not form as we have come to understand it, not a shape as such which could be clumsily described by words as they seeped out of a conscious mind. Instead, he wondered if the sea was not a mirror, not the form of a thought, but an equivalent of the mind itself, in all its totality and unfathomable mystery. This suggestion brought him full circle to where he stood on the shore all those years before as a teenage boy, who could only comprehend the magnitude of the sea as being something other, outside of himself, a mystery too large and foreboding to be understood. Now, however, he could hold in the moment both the past and the present in a sea of time, as it expanded out of the leaden sky that compressed any notion of height, taking out the vertical, and transforming space into a pure horizontal stretching out as far and as wide as the eye could see. Then further still into a space that could only be imagined, turning time into times.

He tried to think of distance, its abstract nature, of a time beyond his own, of a past that could still somehow bring separation closer. The fickleness of distance, its elasticity set against its hard actuality. A hair's width between one thing and another, which equally could seem oceans apart, like a long-forgotten memory that could rush into his consciousness as if it were a living, breathing part of him. A time past and the time present melding into each other to become something that lay hidden deep within him, which, once exposed, began to take on a form, one could say almost a body, the surface of which was mirrored back towards him revealing the patterning of its warp and weft as it moved in and out of focus. He thought of the times embodied in a painting, laid layer over layer, times that are remembered and times that are still to be, all folded into the now, turning the surface into a veil of being, which flipped back and forth between the past and the present at the blink of an eye. There, but then again not there, never fully consolidated; instead, remaining only ever an intimation of a ghosting form.

As he continued to look out across the dull sea's surface towards where it met the ill-defined greyness of the sky an almost imperceptible line appeared. At first, he thought it was just his eyes playing tricks on him, attempting to make a clear distinction between sea and sky, but as he continued to look the line became more pronounced until it was a line of light. Although no wider than a narrow crack, in its intensity it made clear the separation of above and below. Slowly the line of light grew wider losing none of its precision, then spilled out across the surface of the sea transforming it into a plane of light, and with this change of light his thoughts too were lightened, the weight of the past momentarily lifted, and he could think anew. The first thought was always bigger than the last, he mused to himself; things shrank the more they were dwelt upon, their embellishment in its refining and defining took away the rough edges that allowed a thought to stay out in the open, to have what might be called an ambiguity of meaning. Pinned down the mind shrank. The holes in it vital to its full life became congested, just as the air around him needed holes to prevent a consistent density from becoming stifling. Of course, he could not see the holes in the air, but he knew they were there, could feel how the air around him sometimes yielded and at other times offered a resistance. How even the air's weight seemed to vary, lighter in the mornings then becoming denser as the day progressed. Then, during the night the air was cleansed, so by the morning both the holes in the air and in his own mind too were refreshed, becoming once again open and fluid. He was fascinated by how the mind, or perhaps it was more his own mind, related to the world. Not in conscious thought but more to do with how it sat in his head, somehow untouchable, unseen. He could not literally give it a good poke to check if was still there; instead, it was as if it had its own secret way of living, of existing inside him. The only way of getting even the slightest inkling of its nature was to let it seep out into the world with all the uncertainties this entailed. Most of the time he felt like Jorge Luis Borges who while half of himself nonchalantly strolled through the streets of Buenos Aires, the other half remained closeted in the confines of himself as a writer, unable to release itself from the burden of his prose.[4] Except for him as a painter it was painting that exposed the divide, its capacity to be both mirror and sea, to reflect back, grab him by the scruff of the neck and haul him up against himself, or else cast him adrift, divesting him of his too-knowing self to leave him floating as flotsam upon the restless surface of the canvas plane and the uncertain world it veiled.

He felt that the shape of his own consciousness did not so much mirror as echo the sound of the sea, and that though it had both a surface and a depth and its measurement was conditional upon where he was in relation to what was around him, this surety was only ever provisional. Standing on the shore, the sea inside him meeting the sea beyond induced both a sense of elation and a curiously comforting ache, like the sensation of pressing a wound to feel that the pain is real. Was this he wondered the closest he ever got to seeing his own mind, to experiencing it as something external to himself. It was for good reason sailors referred to the sea as 'she', the mother from which all consciousness had been birthed. As the sky continued to open up and the light caressed the sea's surface it ceased being dense and opaque, lost its smouldering malevolence to give way to a glistening presence offering another side of itself. One in which another temperament reached out to meet him. For now, the sea's depths surfaced and offered in its fullness an acknowledgement of fraternity, of a connection as deep and as wide as the outer limits of his mind could reach.

As he walked back along the shore towards the town, he remembered something he had read about Fra Angelico's stone epitaph, on which were inscribed in Latin the words, 'The glory, the mirror, the ornament of painters…'.[5] The distance between an experience, its reflection and its understanding. How he wondered did the painter navigate this sea, its tides and eddies, its ceaseless rhythm that seemed to belie any negotiable form. How did the ornaments of painting, which once fixed become decoration, find a way to return to the sea, to the full glory of what might be as opposed to the limits of what was? How did the painting deny the mirror its surface, cast itself adrift never to look back? He longed for the sea's surface mirroring as it did, to dissolve, to abandon its attachment to the horizontal and once released to engulf everything, the ensuing flood, its deluge, to sweep the mirror and its ornaments aside, leaving not less but more. A more so big, voluminous and formless that it left nothing out, was everywhere and everything, and in the moment of experiencing it there would be nothing other than to be, to be in an inviolate completeness. Could this, he asked himself, not be an ending but the beginning, the primordial state from which consciousness began and from which all would grow, such that in this new beginning there would be held the possibility of a self as crystalline and as pure as the first thought that had entered human consciousness.

Halfway up the concrete steps to the promenade he turned and looked back once more out towards the sea, its now glistening surface, luminous with light, so intense he had to screw up his eyes to take it in. He found this light to be how he imagined pure light to truly be, omnipresent, without even the slightest intimation of intruding form. The light's brilliance had a physical presence that he could only understand as an earthly manifestation and affirmation of the divine. His earlier thought of Fra Angelico returned, how the paintings of the Beato Angelico held a light that transcended the mundanity of the physical properties of life to replace them with a clear intensity. How the warmth of Italy infused the light, mellowed it without a loss, which the painter then tempered, modelled until it formed a warm glow, which circled back on itself enclosing the painting in a realm of pure light. As he sat down on the steps and took off his shoes, shaking out the loose sand, he looked one last time towards the sea. The light did not hold the Italian painter's warmth of place and conviction; instead, it was as if it were the fundamental stuff of light itself, its untouched, raw primordial state. When again would he see, feel, this light? Could he hold onto it even if only as an ideal? Did he have the strength to carry it away with him, or would it slowly seep back to the sea? Climbing the last of the steps he set off along the promenade towards the town centre, his mind still awash in thought.

It was early evening before he could take the bus to the city to then catch the train south. The light was already fading as he sat in a front seat on the top deck and looked out across the flat open landscape, its expansiveness even after all these years still surprising him. The same sensation he had felt as a child when staring up at the sky, his neck arched back as far as it would go, with nothing between himself and the billowing clouds above. How strange the world was he thought. Now of course there really was nothing to separate it all from the surface of his skin, no hint of indifference that allowed at least the suggestion of a divide. The only way he could describe it was to say that the world around him was pressingly palpable. At times an almost paralysing membrane analogous to the butterfly's cocoon, which girded him in, and like the butterfly he had to wait for the sheath to peel away so that he could feel a moment of release. Make his way out into the world as if he were no more than a pair of disembodied wings, caressed by the air's warmth. Everything which existed in the world he sensed was all that could be imagined by the mind, the birds, the worm, the blind mole, the whale's echoing cry, wind and rain, moods of the sea, states of being which sat within him, as if his mind in its multiplicity was no more than a mirror. As the warmth and the rhythm of the bus slowly took hold of him, he began to doze off. In this half-conscious state, as his mind drifted untethered, he remembered the sea's rage and its seduction, he remembered the light's vagaries and its solidities, and he remembered the mirror.

Notes

Early Days (1977), pp. 9–10

1. In the talk Greenberg expounded on his formalist position emphasising formal purity, colour, form, etc., in abstract painting. This he placed against the more subjective Expressionism associated with 'Primitivism'.

Field and Flow, the Drawing and the Photograph (1979), pp. 11–14

1. See Maurice Merleau-Ponty, *Sense and Non-Sense*, Hubert L. Dreyfus and Patricia Allen Dreyfus (trans.), Evanston, IL, 1981, p. 15.
2. Daniel Buren, *Five Texts*, New York and London, 1973, p. 24.
3. *David Smith*, Garnett McCoy (ed.), Documentary Monographs in Modern Art, London, 1973, p. 80.
4. *The Writings of Robert Smithson*, Nancy Holt (ed.), New York, 1979, p. 208.
5. In his extensive writings Mondrian used a dialectic form to outline his position. This he visually expressed in his paintings by the interplay between the horizontal and vertical. See *The New Art – The New Life: The Collected Writings of Piet Mondrian*, Harry Holtzman and Martin S. James (ed. and trans.), London, 1987.
6. Marcel Duchamp, *Salt Seller: The Writings of Marcel Duchamp*, Michel Sanouillet and Elmer Peterson (eds), Oxford, 1973, p. 33.
7. Jorge Luis Borges (1946), in *A Universal History of Infamy*, Norman Thomas di Giovanni (trans.), Harmondsworth, 1973, p. 131.

Night Flak (1981), pp. 15–16

1. Novalis, *Hymns to the Night and Other Selected Writings*, Indianapolis, IN, 1960, pp. 3–15.

Swedish Lapland (1986), pp. 20–3

1. John Ruskin, *Modern Painters*, Volume 4, London, 1904, p. 59.

Grønland (1988), pp. 24–7

1. Michel Foucault, *The Archaeology of Knowledge*, A. M. Sheridan Smith (trans.), London and New York, 1972.
2. *Qilakitsormiut 1400-kkunneersut*, Nuuk and Copenhagen, 1985.

Marianne North, Olana, Hudson, New York (1995), pp. 40–3

1. Marianne North, *A Vision of Eden: The Life and Work of Marianne North*, Royal Botanic Gardens, Kew, London, 1980, p. 119.
2. E. M. Cioran, *On the Heights of Despair*, Ilinca Zarifopol-Johnston (trans.), London, 1995, p. 60.
3. Simone Weil, *Gravity and Grace*, Emma Craufurd (trans.), London and New York, 1972, p. 136.

Northeast Siberia (1995), pp. 44–9

1. Kolyma is a region of eastern Siberia where many of Joseph Stalin's labour camps were located. In his book *The Gulag Archipelago* the Russian novelist Aleksandr Solzhenitsyn refers extensively to this area.

Thoughts on Emil Nolde (1995), pp. 51–5

1. The 'blue flower' became one of the key symbols of the Romantic movement in the late eighteenth and early nineteenth centuries, representing the yearnings of the poet's soul. Novalis used this image as a recurring theme in his fragmentary novel *Heinrich*

von Ofterdingen, written in 1880. Novalis, *Henry von Ofterdingen: A Novel*, Palmer Hilty (trans.), Long Grove, IL, 1990.
2. Eduardo Galeano, *Genesis*, Memory of Fire series, Volume 1, New York, 1987, p. 144.

Thinking about Georgia O'Keeffe **(2002)**, pp. 61–7
1. William Carlos Williams, *Selected Essays*, New York, 1969, p. 14.
2. *Georgia O'Keeffe: Some Memories of Drawing*, Doris Bry (ed.), Albuquerque, NM, 1988, n.p.
3. E. M. Cioran, *Tears and Saints*, Ilinca Zarifopol-Johnston (trans.), Chicago, IL, 1995, p. 101.
4. See William Blake, *Jerusalem: The Emanation of the Giant Albion*, Morton D. Paley (ed.), Blake's Illuminated Books, Volume 1, London, 1998.
5. Simone Weil, *Gravity and Grace*, Emma Craufurd (trans.), London and New York, 1972, p. 1.
6. Bob Dylan, quote from 'Idiot Wind', *Blood on the Tracks* album, Columbia Records, 1975.

For Kehnet Nielsen – In Praise of Painting **(2002)**, pp. 68–71
1. Kehnet Nielson in conversation with Ian McKeever, November 2001.
2. *Clyfford Still*, exh. cat., San Francisco Museum of Modern Art, 1976, p. 123.
3. *Yves Klein, 1928–1962: A Retrospective*, exh. cat., Institute for the Arts, Rice University, Houston, 1982.
4. *Kehnet Nielsen, Maleri*, Paul Erik Tojner (ed.), exh. cat., Forlaget Ekely, Copenhagen, 1997, pp. 122–3.

Talking Painting **(2004)**, pp. 73–74
1. Milan Kundera, *Testament Betrayed, An Essay in Nine Parts*, Linda Asher (trans.), London, 1995, p. 208.

Light **(2004)**, pp. 75–82
1. Quote from a letter from Vincent van Gogh to his brother Theo van Gogh, Letter number 673 (Van Gogh Museum Edition), dated 3 September 1888, written from Arles, France.
2. Robert Grosseteste, *On Light* (*De Luce*), Clare C. Riedl (trans.), Milwaukee, WI, 1942.
3. *Louis Kahn: Essential Texts*, Robert Twombly (ed.), New York and London, 2003, p. 229.
4. The reference broadly refers to Burroughs' writings concerning the camera and the desire to imprison.
5. Ludwig Wittgenstein, *Remarks on Colour*, G. E. M. Anscombe (ed.), Linda L. McAlister and Margarete Schättle (trans.), Oxford, 1990, Part III, pp. 172–229.
6. Gunnar Ekelöf, *Selected Poems*, W. H. Auden and Lief Sjöberg (trans.), Harmondsworth, 1971, p. 122.
7. Rolf E. Stenersen, *Edvard Munch: Close-up of a Genius*, Reidar Dittmann (ed. and trans.), Oslo, 1994, p. 70.
8. Paul Auster, *Mr Vertigo*, London, 1994.
9. Rudolf Steiner, *Colour: Twelve Lectures by Rudolf Steiner*, Joan Thompson (ed.), John Salter and Pauline Wehrle (trans.), London, 1992, p. 102.
10. Quote from a letter from Virginia Woolf to Roger Fry, dated 27 May 1927. See *The Letters of Virginia Woolf, Volume III (1923–1928)*, Nigel Nicolson and Joanne Trautmann (eds), Nashville, TN, 1980, p. 385.
11. Ezra Pound, *Section: Rock-Drill 85–95, De Los Cantares*, London, 1995, p. 70.

Black **(2004)**, pp. 83–4
1. Rainer Maria Rilke, *Letters on Cézanne*, Joel Agee (trans.), London, 1991.
2. *The Collected Writings of Robert Motherwell* (Documents of Twentieth-Century Art), Stephanie Terenzio (ed.), New York and Oxford, 1992.

Kurt Kocherscheidt: Between the Wall and the Floor (2004), pp. 85–90

1. Max Kozloff, *Renderings: Critical Essays on a Century of Modern Art*, London, 1968, p. 175.
2. *David Smith*, Garnett McCoy (ed.), Documentary Monographs in Modern Art, London, 1973, p. 46.
3. Mario Merz, *I Want to Write a Book Right Now*, Beatrice Merz (ed.), Florence, 1989, p. 134.
4. Rainer Maria Rilke, *Rodin and Other Prose Pieces*, G. Craig Houston (trans.), Quartet Encounters, London, Melbourne and New York, 1986, p. 74.
5. *David Smith*, Garnett McCoy (ed.), Documentary Monographs in Modern Art, London, 1973, p. 82.

Painting and Countenance (2005), pp. 95–9

1. Paul Evdokimov, *The Art of the Icon: A Theology of Beauty*, Fr. Steven Bigham (trans.), Pasadena, CA, 1996, p. 226.
2. Mario Luzi, *Earthly and Heavenly Journey of Simone Martini*, Luigi Bonaffini (trans.), Copenhagen and Los Angeles, 2003, p. 267.
3. Rainer Maria Rilke, *Letters on Cézanne*, Joel Agee (trans.), London, 1991.
4. Paul Evdokimov, *The Art of the Icon: A Theology of Beauty*, Fr. Steven Bigham (trans.), Pasadena, CA, 1996, p. 244.
5. *Barnett Newman: Selected Writings and Interviews*, John P. O'Neill (ed.), New York, 1990.
6. Henry James, *The Wings of the Dove*, London, 2003, p. 20.

Morocco (2010), pp. 108–13

1. Jean Genet, in *What Remains of a Rembrandt Torn into Four Equal Pieces and Flushed Down the Toilet*, New York, 1988, n.p.
2. Juan Goytisolo, *Marks of Identity*, Gregory Rabassa (trans.), London, 1988, p. 52.
3. Inger Christensen, *Butterfly Valley: A Requiem*, Susanna Nied (trans.), New York, 2004, p. 76.
4. Juan Goytisolo, *Marks of Identity*, Gregory Rabassa (trans.), London, 1988, p. 225.

Notes II (2010), pp. 115–18

1. Joseph Brodsky, *Watermark: An Essay on Venice*, London, 1997.
2. Paul Bowles, *The Spider's House*, London, 2009, p. 399.

Kurt Kocherscheidt: The Sense of an Ending (2013), pp. 119–24

1. Virginia Woolf, *Mrs Dalloway*, Oxford, 2008, p. 126.
2. Sue Prideaux, *Edvard Munch: Behind The Scream*, New Haven and London, 2007.
3. 1 Corinthians 13: 12.
4. *Joseph Roth, A Life in Letters*, Michael Hofmann (ed. and trans.), London, 2012, p. 142.

Painting on the Threshold, Richard Diebenkorn (2015), pp. 125–9

1. Grace Hartigan, in *The Outwardness of Art: Selected Writings of Adrian Stokes*, Thomas Evans (ed.), London, 2020, p. 425.
2. Roberto Longhi, *Piero della Francesca*, David Tabbat (trans.), Riverdale-on-Hudson, NY, 2002, p. 36.
3. *Richard Diebenkorn, The Ocean Park Series*, exh. cat., Orange County Museum of Art, Newport Beach, CA, 2012, p. 22.
4. Willem de Kooning, *Collected Writings*, Madras and New York, 1988, p. 64.
5. *Georgia O'Keeffe: Some Memories of Drawing*, Doris Bry (ed.), Albuquerque, NM, 1988, n.p.
6. Frederick van der Meer, *Early Christian Art*, Peter Brown and Friedl Brown (trans.), London, 1967, p. 96.
7. Adrian Stokes, *Three Essays on the Painting of Our Time*, London, 1961; reprinted in

The Outwardness of Art: Selected Writings of Adrian Stokes, Thomas Evans (ed.), London, 2020, p. 439.

Visiting Joan Mitchell **(2017)**, pp. 138–43

1. Siri Hustvedt, 'Joan Mitchell: Remembering in Color', in *Mysteries of the Rectangle: Essays on Painting*, New York, 2005, pp. 136–47.

Eye to Eye: Reflections on the Self-portrait and Helene Schjerfbeck **(2018)**, pp. 147–52

1. Philippe Ricord was a prominent nineteenth-century French physician and surgeon. Emilie Bickerton, 'Photomania. *The Great Nadar: The Man Behind the Camera* by Adam Begley', *London Review of Books*, 40, no. 22, London, 22 November 2018.
2. Bernard Berenson, *Piero della Francesca, or The Ineloquent in Art*, London, 1954, p. 7.

Robert Smithson: **Paterson (2019)**, pp. 153–67

1. Michel Foucault, *The Archaeology of Knowledge*, Abingdon, 2002.
2. *Clyfford Still*, John P. O'Neill (ed.), exh. cat., The Metropolitan Museum of Art, New York, 1979, p. 29.
3. William Blake, *Selected Poems*, Penguin Popular Classics, London, 1996, p. 171.
4. William Carlos Williams, *Paterson*, New York, 1992.
5. William Carlos Williams, 'Preface', *Paterson*, Book 1, New York, 1992, p. 7.
6. William Carlos Williams, *Paterson*, Book 1, New York, 1992. The quote by the author appears on the rear cover of the book.
7. J. G. Ballard, 'The Terminal Beach', in *The Terminal Beach*, Harmondsworth, 1974, pp. 136–57.
8. Stanisław Lem, *Solaris*, Joanna Kilmartin and Steve Cox (trans.), London, 1970.
9. *The Writings of Robert Smithson*, Nancy Holt (ed.), New York, 1979, p. 71.
10. Ibid., p. 96.
11. Ibid.
12. The quote is taken from the song 'Jack Straw' by Bob Weir and Robert Hunter on the album *Europe '72* by the Grateful Dead, Warner Bros, Los Angeles, 1972. The original line was written in 1893 by Katharine Lee Bates in the poem 'America the Beautiful'.
13. William Carlos Williams, *Paterson*, Book 3, Part III, New York, 1992, p. 139.
14. Joseph Brodsky, *Watermark: An Essay on Venice*, London, 1997.
15. *The Writings of Robert Smithson*, Nancy Holt (ed.), New York, 1979, p. 82.
16. William Carlos Williams, *Paterson*, Book 3, Part III, New York, 1992, p. 140.
17. Ibid.
18. Maurice Merleau-Ponty, *The Visible and the Invisible*, Claude Lefort (ed.), Alphonso Lingis (trans.), Evanston, IL, 1968.
19. William Carlos Williams, *Paterson*, Book 1, New York, 1992, p. 31.

Painting/Sculpture/Architecture **(2019)**, p. 168

1. *Louis Kahn: Essential Texts*, Robert Twombly (ed.), New York and London, 2003.

Piero della Francesca **(2019)**, pp. 169–72

1. Robert Bresson, *Notes on the Cinematographer*, Jonathan Griffin (trans.), Quartet Encounters, London, Melbourne and New York, 1975, p. 4.
2. Ibid.
3. Adrian Stokes, *The Image in Form: Selected Writings of Adrian Stokes*, Richard Wollheim (ed.), London, 1972, p. 139.
4. Robert Bresson, *Notes on the Cinematographer*, Jonathan Griffin (trans.), Quartet Encounters, London, Melbourne and New York, 1975, p. 11.

To Begin (2019), p. 173

1. Antoni Tàpies, *Selected Essays*, Antoni Kerrigan Barcelona (trans.), Eindhoven, 1986, p. 15.
2. Henri Bergson, *An Introduction to Metaphysics*, T. E. Hulme (trans.), New York, 1949; reprinted Indianapolis, IN, 1999, p. 21.

Jukka Mäkelä: Talking Away the Night (2022), pp. 174–8

1. Samuel Beckett, *Krapp's Last Tape* (1958), London, 1998.
2. John Steinbeck wrote 'people are felt rather than seen after the first few moments'. The quote appears in *East of Eden*, Penguin Modern Classics, London, 2000, p. 53.
3. Maurice Merleau-Ponty, *The Visible and the Invisible*, Claude Lefort (ed.), Alphonso Lingis (trans.), Evanston, IL, 1968, p. 135.
4. Pekka Halonen (1865–1933) was a Finnish painter in the national Romantic style, particularly known for his winter landscapes in which the landscape blanketed in snow appears reduced to simple silhouetted forms.
5. T. S. Eliot, 'Four Quartets', in *Collected Poems, 1909–1962*, London, 2002, p. 177.

Monet: In Search of Lost Time (2024), pp. 184–90

1. Wallace Stevens, *Opus Posthumous*, New York, 1957, p. 186.
2. William Carlos Williams, *Paterson*, Book 1, New York, 1992, p. 64.
3. Marcel Proust, *In Search of Lost Time*, Volume V: *The Captive. The Fugitive*, C. K. Scott Moncrieff and Terence Kilmartin (trans.), D. J. Enright (revised by), London, 2000, p. 291.
4. Marcel Proust, *In Search of Lost Time*, Volume VI: *Time Regained*, Andreas Mayor and Terence Kilmartin (trans.), D. J. Enright (revised by), London, 2000, p. 451.
5. Ibid., pp. 429–30.

Cy Twombly: Ezra Pound (2024), pp. 196–206

1. Ezra Pound, *Section: Rock-Drill 85–95, De Los Cantares*, London, 1995. The quote appears on the rear inside flap of the book.
2. Noel Stock, *The Life of Ezra Pound*, Harmondsworth, 1974, p. 317.
3. Carroll F. Terrell, *A Companion to the Cantos of Ezra Pound*, Orono, ME, Berkeley, LA and London, 1993, Canto IX 8/33. 9/34, p. 42.
4. Ezra Pound, *The Cantos of Ezra Pound*, New York, 1972, Canto CXX, p. 803.

The Mirror and the Sea (2025), pp. 215–23

1. W. H. Auden, *For the Time Being*, London, 1945, pp. 7–60.
2. Giovanni Bellini, *Doge Leonardo Loredan*, *c*. 1501/02, National Gallery, London, NG189.
3. Rainer Maria Rilke, *Uncollected Poems*, Edward Snow (trans.), New York, 1997, p. 35.
4. Jorge Luis Borges, *Dreamtigers*, Mildred Boyer and Harold Moorland (trans.), Austin, TX, 1968, p. 51.
5. John Pope-Hennessy, *Fra Angelico*, Florence, 1981, p. 4.

List of Illustrations

All works illustrated are by Ian McKeever unless otherwise stated.

Page 130, above: *Hours of Darkness. Hours of Light*, 2012–14. Acrylic and oil on canvas on wood, 45 x 33 cm

Page 130, below: installation view of 'Ian McKeever, Hours of Darkness. Hours of Light', Kunst-Station Sankt Peter, Cologne

Page 144, above: Ian McKeever at his exhibition 'Ian McKeever, Henge Paintings', Gallery Susanne Ottesen, Copenhagen, 2022

Page 144, below: *Studio Notebook*, 2020. Ballpoint pen and watercolour

Page 153: Ian McKeever in the Alpujarra, Andalusia, Spain, 2012

Page 179: installation view of 'Ian McKeever, Against Architecture', Matt's Gallery, London, 2017

Page 181: installation view of 'Ian McKeever, Against Architecture', TheGallery, Arts University Bournemouth, 2023

Page 194, above: Ian McKeever in the studio, Hartgrove, 2025. Photograph Anne Purkiss

Page 194, below: *Studio Notebook*, 2024. Ballpoint pen and watercolour on paper

Page 196: Ezra Pound, *Section: Rock-Drill. 85–95 de los cantares*, Faber and Faber, London, 1995, p. 49

Page 214: Ian McKeever in the studio, Hartgrove, 2025

Photographic Acknowledgements

Jonathan Bassett: pages 20, 22, 25–7, 33, 48, 56, 94 below, 110–11, 144 below, 179, 194 below

Waldo Bien: page 30

Stephan Brendgen: page 130 below

Gerlinde Gabriel: page 153

Werner J. Hannappel: page 114

Stine Heger: page 144 above

Caspar McKeever: pages 72, 130 above

Eliza Naden: page 181

Barry Phipps: page 114 above

Prudence Cuming Associates, London: page 101

Anne Purkiss: front and back cover, pages 8, 194 above, 214

Eileen Tweedy, London: page 84

Unknown photographer, Bridgeman Images: page 40

Timo Valjakka: page 94 above

Edward Woodman: page 42

Kurt Zein: page 123

Copyright Acknowledgements

Acknowledgements

I would like to thank Andrew Dempsey for his invaluable help and advice in reading my writings when the idea of a publication was first mooted, and for suggesting how a selection might best be structured. I would also like to thank Josepha Sanna for transcribing several of the early texts; Peter Sawbridge, Carola Krueger and Florence Dassonville at the Royal Academy for having embraced the project and followed it through with such enthusiasm and commitment; Linda Schofield for her considered editing of the manuscript; Coco McKeever-Ziff for helping to track down numerous older references; and Patrick Morrissey for his thoughtful layout and design. I would also like to express my gratitude to Gerlinde Gabriel, who, over many morning coffees, listened to or read the fruits of my late-night sessions at the kitchen table. I.M.